D0773255

Ten Arab

FILMMAKERS

Ten Arab
FILMMAKERS

Political Dissent and Social Critique

Edited by
Josef Gugler

INDIANA UNIVERSITY PRESS
BLOOMINGTON AND INDIANAPOLIS

This book is a publication of

Indiana University Press

Office of Scholarly Publishing

Herman B Wells Library 350

1320 East 10th Street

Bloomington, Indiana 47405 USA

iupress.indiana.edu

Manufactured in the United States of America

Library of Congress Cataloging-in-Publication Data

Ten Arab filmmakers : political dissent and social critique / edited by Josef Gugler.

    pages cm

  Includes bibliographical references and index.

  Includes filmography.

    ISBN 978-0-253-01644-7 (cloth : alk. paper) — ISBN 978-0-253-01652-2 (pbk. : alk. paper) — ISBN 978-0-253-01658-4 (ebook) 1. Motion pictures—Arab countries—History and criticism. 2. Motion picture producers and directors—Arab countries. 3. Motion pictures—Political aspects—Arab countries. 4. Motion pictures—Social aspects—Arab countries. I. Gugler, Josef, editor.

  PN1993.5.A65T48 2015

  791.430917'4927—dc23

2014044165

1 2 3 4 5   20 19 18 17 16 15

To directors who confront new challenges as they pursue just causes.

I consider myself a filmmaker who must be engaged . . . I'm happy to speak about the situation in my country, but at the same time I would point out that I'm not a politician. The responsibilities of someone who makes a film under these conditions are not the same as those of a European or North American director.

—*Merzak Allouache*

CONTENTS

PREFACE

Ten Arab Filmmakers completes a journey I embarked on a decade ago. As we were inundated by television and cinema presenting Western perspectives on the Middle East after 9/11, I sought to bring to my students voices and images from the region. Eventually I edited *Film in the Middle East and North Africa: Creative Dissidence* (2011), which presented the nine principal national cinemas of the region and featured eighteen films. The present volume complements it by focusing on distinguished Arab directors.

I thank the nine contributors from three continents who agreed to join our venture, who responded to my critical comments, endured my unending suggestions, and experienced unfortunate delays in the completion of the manuscript. I appreciate the critical comments and advice I received along the way.

We are indebted to the directors who made themselves available to us, provided us with copies of films not yet in distribution, and furnished illustrations. We benefited from the comments of two anonymous reviewers. Our book was enriched by the individuals and institutions, acknowledged in the credits, who provided illustrations.

My special thanks to Walter Armbrust and Nadia Yaqub for their excellent advice. Lynne Goodstein offered crucial support. Gordon Daigle, Maha Darawsha, and Ingrid Gugler assisted in various ways. But for the expertise and devotion of Alex Bothell, many illustrations would be in worse shape; others would have been abandoned altogether as unsuitable for printing.

I cherish the support my wife and our daughters gave me in spite of my sins of neglect and distraction while I was working on this project.

Doctors Without Borders have done remarkable work in Arab countries under difficult circumstances, and they have helped to bring the plight of people living amid war to the attention of the world; all royalties will support their work.

Josef Gugler

NOTE ON TRANSLITERATION

We strove for consistency in transliterations, except that we have adhered to
the transliterations of the names of characters used in the English subtitles of
films and to the transliterations of the names of directors and actors used in
the anglophone world by distribution companies. Arabic transliterations follow
American University in Cairo Press guidelines.

Ten Arab

FILMMAKERS

Introduction

AUTEUR DIRECTORS, POLITICAL DISSENT, AND CULTURAL CRITIQUE

Josef Gugler

This volume brings together specially commissioned essays on ten leading directors of the Arab world. They have produced many of the region's most renowned films, gaining recognition at major international festivals, and yet, except for Youssef Chahine, none has received major critical attention to date. They have supported the aspirations of the oppressed in some or all of their films. All have articulated political protest, most have denounced the deeply entrenched patriarchal culture, and several have taken positions in the cultural conflict that pits fundamentalist movements against moderate Islam. The chapters, by leading scholars in Arab film and media studies, combine accounts of the filmmakers' lives and works with in-depth analyses of their most important films. This collection is designed to complement *Film in the Middle East and North Africa* (Gugler 2011) and offers an up-to-date overview of much of the best of Arab cinema.[1]

Film producers in the Arab world face formidable competition from powerful producers in the United States and India who are firmly established in the region. The Arab-language film market in turn is dominated by the privately financed Egyptian film industry. Its production dwarfs film production in the other Arab countries: from its origins in the 1920s to 2008 it produced over three thousand films, while all the other Arab countries together produced less than a thousand.[2] The relative size of its production, its formulaic productions for a mass market, and its star system earned it the nickname Hollywood on the Nile. These characteristics invite comparison with Bollywood as well. The three industries produce for large populations sharing the same language. Egypt's population numbers more than twice that of any other Arab country, and Egypt's film industry has been able to export to other Arab countries. While films from other Arab countries face a veritable language barrier because their local vernaculars are not readily understood across the Arab world, Egyptian music stars have spread the Egyptian vernacular throughout the Arab world for generations, and Egyptian films have come to be readily understood everywhere. Exports to the affluent Gulf countries, much of it for private viewing, have seen major expansion since the 1980s.

AUTEUR DIRECTORS IN POOR COUNTRIES

Outside the commercial cinema of Egypt, most directors find themselves in extremely difficult circumstances. Commonly they develop their own scripts; they embark on what are usually protracted searches for funding; they try to avoid censorship and, when that fails, engage in difficult negotiations with censors; they proceed on minuscule budgets; they take on multiple production roles, recruit actors (oftentimes amateurs they search out and train), and assemble crews; they edit; they struggle to get their films distributed. They are truly filmmakers. If they face multiple constraints, they also exert much more control over their productions than directors of high-budget films. Commonly they establish their own production companies to co-produce their films. Theirs is a *cinéma d'auteur,* and it comes at a price—usually they manage to make only one or two films a decade. The notable exception is Youssef Chahine, who produced about forty films over his distinguished career.

Training opportunities for the older generation of filmmakers featured here were limited. Mohamed Chouikh, Elia Suleiman, and Jocelyne Saab did not have the benefit of film studies. They pursued varied paths. Chouikh started out in theater, then took on leading roles in cinema. Within a few years he went on to directing in the nascent Algerian film industry. Suleiman spent his twenties in New York with its rich cinematic offerings. He eventually produced his first documentary jointly with Jayce Salloum, a Lebanese-Canadian who had pursued film studies in the United States and had filmed in the Occupied Territories. Saab moved from journalism into documentaries. When civil war broke out in Lebanon, she devoted most of her documentaries to the war and eventually shot her first feature film while the war was raging. Daoud Abd El-Sayed and Yousry Nasrallah studied film in Cairo, then worked as assistant directors to Chahine and others before embarking on their own films.

The other directors studied abroad. They went to France, Belgium, and the United States. The experience of Syrian directors is remarkable. Most trained in "socialist" Europe, at a time when much of the intelligentsia was alienated from the regimes in Eastern Europe. On their return they became civil servants of the National Film Organization and proceeded to critique Syria's "socialist" regime more or less openly in their films. Nabil Maleh trained in Czechoslovakia but did not join the National Film Organization.

Rather few women directors managed to establish themselves in the Arab world, and the œuvre of those who did remained limited. Distinguished directors such as Moufida Tlatli and Farida Benlyazid moved into directing rather late in their lives, after a career writing the scripts of some of the finest Arab films. The contrast is striking with Iran, where the emergence of women directors under the clerical regime has been spectacular. The prominent role they have taken may be seen as a response to the clerical regime's assault on the position of women. Recent films by women directors suggest that Arab women will follow their example.

The academic literature has served Arab women directors relatively well. Rebecca Hillauer (2005) played a pioneering role with an exhaustive survey of Arab women filmmakers that is enriched by her interviews with many of them. Florence Martin (2011) followed with a major study of women directors in the Maghreb which, along with Lebanon, is the home of most of the established Arab women directors.

Several of the directors featured here went into exile overseas. Suleiman, at age seventeen, left his native Nazareth to flee the wrath of the Israeli authorities and eventually established himself in France. Michel Khleifi, also born and raised in Nazareth, stayed on in Belgium after his studies there. Saab eventually fled the violence of Lebanon's civil war and went to France. Merzak Allouache similarly fled the violence in Algeria in the early 1990s and stayed in France until 2004. Maleh left for the United States and Europe in 1980 as the political pressure was increasing, returned in 1993 when offered the opportunity to realize the script of *The Extras* he had developed in exile, then fled to Dubai in September 2011.[3]

A number of directors filmed beyond their home country. Saab started out with documentaries across the Middle East and North Africa. More recently she went to Egypt to shoot her feature film *Dunia*. Allouache, once exiled, alternated between films set in the immigrant community in France and films set in Algeria. Exiles Khleifi and Maleh filmed in Europe, exile Suleiman in the United States and Cuba. Chahine directed two films in Lebanon in the 1960s. He shot in Syria and Lebanon to recreate the splendors of twelfth century Andalusia for *Destiny*. He returned to the United States, where he had trained, for his autobiographical *Alexandria... New York*. Ayouch interrupted his focus on pressing issues in Morocco with *Whatever Lola Wants*, lighter fare set in New York and Cairo. He went on to shoot a feature-length documentary, *My Land*, in Israel and Lebanon. Nasrallah's *The City* is set in Paris as well as Cairo.

Many directors film for advertising or teach in film schools to make a living. Nearly all outside Egypt's commercial cinema are heavily dependent on subsidies to make their films. Governments have played an important part in funding national cinemas and encouraging the production of quality films, and the fortunes of national cinemas have waxed and waned with such support. Government funding entailed a measure of control that went beyond the ubiquitous censorship. Nevertheless most directors have pursued their critical agendas, even if some had to remain less than explicit.

Foreign government agencies, television networks, and foundations have provided the other major support for the production of quality films. Western Europe, and especially France, has been the principal source of such support. Palestinian cinema came into its own with funding that came largely from Western Europe but also included support from Israeli sources for Israeli citizens (Gertz and Khleifi 2011, 189). Support from the Gulf countries used to be negligible, but that has changed dramatically of late. In 2007, the Dubai International Film Festival launched its Film Market, sponsoring Arab directors to meet with key Arab and international film professionals. Since 2010, the Abu Dhabi Film Festival, the Doha Film Institute, and the Dubai International Film Festival have offered substantial financial support ranging from film development to production and post-production.

Foreign funding presents constraints of its own. Some constraints are explicit. Saab was compelled to use French rather than Arabic in part of the dialogue in two of her films because the French agency that provided support required the use of French so as to promote *la francophonie*. Foreign sources are diverse, and the principal constraint is implicit. Competition for foreign support is severe, and directors know that some topics are more likely to find favor than others. Such is the case of denunciations of the oppression of women.

International film festivals also exert a powerful influence on directors. As Cameron Bailey, co-director of the Toronto International Film Festival, has observed: "Festivals have multiplied and spread to become the single most important arbiter of taste in cinema—more important than scholars, or critics, more important even than film schools" (quoted in Ruoff 2009, iv). Awards bestowed on films, directors, or collaborators, give visibility to films and open up new opportunities for distribution. This is especially important for Arab films, which are by and large ignored abroad. Festival prizes bring prestige to directors, to national cinemas, and to Arab cinema in general. They enhance directors' access to domestic and foreign funding. Directors are also likely to find themselves in a stronger position vis-à-vis censors. Official selection for a festival or award brings recognition to films and their directors even if they do not receive a single award. And it entails an invitation for the director, who is likely to get media exposure and will be in a position to develop contacts with distributors, funding agencies, and fellow directors. Directorial strategies affect the prospects of films being selected and being judged favorably—by juries dominated by and large by directors and critics from the West. But long delays in production make it difficult for directors to catch up with changing fashions in themes and styles.

The three Egyptian directors featured here provide striking contrasts. Already well established in Egypt, Youssef Chahine managed by the mid-1980s to secure a strong foothold in France, where he received funds for every single film he directed henceforth. Despite his reputation, most of these later films have had only mediocre success in Egypt. Next-generation director Nasrallah started out with foreign funding. A prize from the French Cultural Center in Cairo for his screenplay allowed him to complete his first film. His subsequent films were co-produced by the prestigious Franco-German public television channel Arte, but had only limited distribution in Egypt. That changed when Nasrallah, now well established as a director, was able to secure Egyptian funding for *Scheherazade, Tell Me a Story,* which became a popular success at home. Abd El-Sayed, for his part, committed himself to produce within the framework of the Egyptian film industry so as to reach local audiences. He compromised on form at times to meet popular tastes. Still, he found it difficult to find local producers for his films, which invariably denounced the failings of Egypt's regime and critiqued patriarchy. He managed to produce rather few films over a lifetime by Egyptian standards, and only *A Citizen, a Detective, and a Thief* is readily available to viewers not conversant with Arabic.

Chahine eventually managed to establish a major production company, Misr International Films, that produced or co-produced the films of other directors as well. More recently Ayouch established Ali n' Productions, which secured about €3.3 million to create Film Industry and produce thirty television films. He helped train a number of directors, screenwriters, and editors to produce the films.

Auteur directors commonly work with amateur actors. Most are constrained by small budgets. Some have complained that professional actors do not readily adapt to their requirements. In Egypt, Abd El-Sayed found it difficult to persuade star actors to work with a director outside the mainstream such as him. Elsewhere film production is limited and offers little support for professional actors. Some actors have been recruited from the theater to film, but their adaption to the different demands of cinema oftentimes has proved difficult. The transition from television to film is easier, and expanding TV production is establishing a significant pool of professional actors in many countries.

Arab auteur cinema is quite conventional in style, by and large, irrespective of when and where directors trained. They may be seen to make their films readily accessible to their home audience. Most of the exceptions involve the use of daydreams and fantasy. Only recently have some directors ventured further—for example, Allouache in *Normal!,* Nasrallah in *The Aquarium,* and Saab in *What's Going On?*

Mohamed Chouikh stands apart. Guy Austin (chapter 8) emphasizes the importance of imagery, rather than dialogue, in conveying meaning in Chouikh's work. Images serve as symbols and suggest allegories in his films. Similar aesthetic choices have been made by a few other Arab directors, such as Nacer Khemir in Tunisia and Oussama Mohammad in Syria. In political terms such aesthetic choices are double-edged. They have allowed directors to escape censorship, but the political import of their films may remain hidden to large parts of their local audiences who, unaccustomed to this aesthetic, are unable to decode symbols and allegories.

Austin highlights a related aspect of Chouikh's aesthetic and suggests that it reflects the legacy of the ornamental in Arab art. He notes that the use of repeated patterns evokes the centrality in Arab art of the ornament rather than the figure. Analyzing the representation of space in *The Desert Ark,* he characterizes it as "quasi-ornamental." Austin also notes a formal difference between Western and Arab cinema that has major implications for the interpretation of Arab films. Left-to-right camera movement in Western cinema conveys forward movement. That notion is evoked by panning from right to left in Arab culture, since it is the direction of reading and writing in Arabic. Nacer Khemir has gone beyond stylistic choices, distinguishing himself by employing the rich artistic heritage of the Arab world, especially Islamic miniatures. He has drawn on the enormous variety of the colors of these miniatures and their non-spatial qualities, while using them as models for sets, costumes, and even the narration (Shafik 2007, 53–55).

Most directors outside the commercial cinema of Egypt may be characterized as artists critically engaged in society and politics. Like most intellectuals in the Arab world, they are opposed to authoritarian regimes, denounce Western interference in the region, oppose fundamentalist movements, and seek to improve the position of women. They have articulated political dissent and cultural critique in some if not all of their films, giving image and voice to people oppressed by authoritarian regimes, to people suffering the consequences of Western policies, to people enduring the onslaught of resurgent religious movements that persecute those who do not share their beliefs, to people struggling to overcome patriarchal traditions. Theirs is a *cinéma engagé*.

POLITICAL DISSENT

Prior to the Arab Spring, regimes ruled throughout the Arab world. The type and severity of restrictions imposed on filmmakers varied across countries and over time. Censorship was the rule. It commonly involved three stages: scripts had to be approved, production authorized, distribution allowed. Public funding involved restrictions of its own. Nevertheless, films critical of political regimes were produced throughout the Arab world. Syria, ruled by one of the most repressive regimes, presented an extreme case. Until the turn of the century, films could be produced only under government auspices. Most directors were employees of the National Film Organization, which commissioned, approved, and funded all film production from 1969 until a few years into the new millennium. Yet Syrian cinema was renowned for the critical stance its directors took time and again vis-à-vis the government. While the regime severely restricted the distribution of their films, pirated copies circulated widely. Perhaps the finest example was Mohammad's *Stars in Broad Daylight* (*Nujum al-nahar,* 1988). The attacks on the regime were coded, as is usual in such films, and many allusions to the regime remained opaque to foreign viewers, but they were readily apparent to the Syrian public.[4] Maleh ventured further than others in expressing his critique of the regime, and of patriarchal traditions, quite openly in *The Extras*. Some commentators were dismissive of the political significance of such criticism, but Lisa Wedeen (1999, 89) gave the artists opposing the Syrian regime a measure of agency: "Artistic transgressions are the site of *politics,* of the dynamic interplay between the regime's exercise of power and people's experiences of and reactions to it."

Wedeen's comment applies elsewhere in the Arab world. Some films stand out for the impact they are likely to have had on public consciousness. *Chaos,* Chahine's last film, directed jointly with Khaled Youssef, concludes with an uprising against the corrupt police officer who has terrorized the neighborhood. A vision of Egypt's corrupt and oppressive regime being similarly toppled, as was to happen in 2011, must have come readily to many viewers' minds. In Tunisia, Nouri Bouzid features an intellectual imprisoned and tortured for his political activities in *Golden Horseshoes (Safa 'ih min dhahab / Les sabots en or,* 1989)—he himself had been imprisoned for five years and tortured on his return from film studies in Belgium. Nabil Ayouch's *Mektoub* confronted Moroccans afresh with a scandal involving a high-ranking police officer. The "Trial of the Century" had been short and coverage limited to the printed press, where the case had quickly disappeared once the officer had been sentenced to death. The film's commercial and critical success suggests that Ayouch succeeded in returning the scandal, and its social, political, and cultural implications, to public view. With *Horses of God* Ayouch reminded his viewers of the shantytown conditions that bred the suicide bombers of the 2003 attacks in Casablanca.

Where there is no film production, regimes have no need to censor it. Such has been the case of the Gulf countries. Nearly all these countries have ample resources that could support a major film industry. And they present a promising market—for decades they were the principal foreign market for the Egyptian film industry. Very few films have been produced in the region so far, but even Saudi Arabia is changing. In 2012, Saudi director Haifaa al-Mansour wrote and directed *Wadjda* (2012), the first ever feature film to be entirely shot in Saudi Arabia, co-produced in the Kingdom.

Attacks on authoritarian rulers have usually implied a critique of Western governments that supported them. But the Palestinian conflict overshadows all other issues in the troubled relationship of the Arab world and the West. The pan-Arab reach of this conflict is illustrated by the *The Dupes (al-Makhdu'un,* 1972), the disturbing allegory of the abandonment of Palestinians by Arab regimes. Based on a celebrated novella by Palestinian Ghassan Kanafani, the film was written and directed by distinguished Egyptian Tawfik Saleh and produced by Syria's National Film Organization.[5] Khleifi and Suleiman both devoted their œuvre to telling stories of Palestinians living through tragedy and conflict.

Hany Abu-Assad in *Omar* (2013) conveys how many Palestinians in the Occupied Territories have become easy prey to be recruited as informants, given the conditions of Israeli military rule. Palestinian society has become permeated by a climate of distrust in consequence. The Palestinian conflict has affected neighboring Lebanon profoundly. Saab shot a number of documentaries and her first feature film during the civil war. After the war a large number of films addressed the experience in various ways (Khatib 2008).

If Western governments pursue policies inimical to the interests of most Arabs, or acquiesce in such policies, such policies are oftentimes widely denounced in the West, especially so in the case of Palestine. There can be little doubt that Palestinian films contribute to mobilizing public opinion. Most of the films of Khleifi and Suleiman are distributed in the West, unlike many of the other directors featured here. Denes (2014) lists eleven ongoing film festivals dedicated to Palestine, all but three of them established since 2007. Most of the festivals take place in Western Europe and North America, with others held in Australia, Malaysia, and South Africa.

International film festivals are one forum where the rejection of Western policies has been effectively projected. Mohamed Lakhdar-Hamina's *Chronicle of the Years of Embers* (*Chronique des années de braise / Waqaae' 'seneen al-jamer,* 1975), on the bitter experience of Algerians under French colonial rule, is the only Arab film to ever receive the world's most prestigious award, the Palme d'Or at Cannes. It was a slap in the face for the festival's hosts. The Golden Globe Best Foreign Film award for Hany Abu-Assad's *Paradise Now* (*al-Janna al-an,* 2005), with its sympathetic portrayal of two Palestinians preparing for a suicide attack in Israel, promoted an alternative to the dominant Western discourse of uncomprehending outrage.

CULTURAL CRITIQUE

Islam predominates across the Arab world. The ranks of Christian and Jewish minorities have shrunk as the Palestinian conflict resounded across the entire region. Coptic films have been produced in Egypt, but their distribution has been restricted to churches by law (Shafik, unpublished). Censorship commonly prohibits any material that might be deemed disrespectful of Islam, but most regimes are happy enough to have fundamentalists denounced. At the same time, in a country such as Egypt the influence of Islamists grew to the extent that, well before the 2011 revolution that brought them to power briefly, actresses and actors became loath to take on "immoral" roles, some abandoning acting altogether.

Chahine confronted fundamentalism with *Destiny,* arguably his finest film. The epic, set in the late twelfth century in the splendor of Córdoba, the capital of what was then Muslim Andalusia, recalls the achievements of Islamic civilization and its scientific and philosophical contributions to the rise of the West. It centers on the life and teachings of the renowned Muslim philosopher Averroës, a.k.a. Ibn Rushd, who was influential in Jewish and Christian thought and played a major role in classical scholarship reaching Western Christianity. *Destiny* shows a humanist Averroës confronting the fundamentalists of the day with the affirmation "No one can claim to know the whole truth." Chahine complements the philosopher's teachings with his own philosophy of *joie de vivre* in a thoroughly entertaining story of the sage and his merry friends confronting life-denying fundamentalists (Gugler 2011c).

Quite a number of directors responded to the violence of Islamist movements in Egypt and Algeria with summary denunciations or outright ridicule. A few presented more differentiated pictures. Mohamed Chouikh, in *Hamlet of Women,* gives voice to the grievances that made a young Algerian villager join the insurgents, and he shows Algerian villagers who fight off the insurgents—and fear the government. Atef Hetata, in *Closed Doors* (*al-Abwab al-moghlaka,* 1999), shows how a poor Egyptian youth comes to define himself as an Islamist. Unlike other directors, Hetata goes on to give voice to a radical Islamist leader.[6]

Nabil Ayouch, in *Horses of God,* tells the story of desperately poor Moroccan youths who find their home in the Islamist underground and are eventually recruited to carry out the May 2003 bombings in Casablanca, all the while learning of the rewards awaiting them in Paradise. Hany Abu-Assad's *Paradise Now* draws a different portrait of two Palestinian suicide bombers. They are well-integrated young men, long committed to giving their lives for the cause if called upon, one of them apparently secular in orientation. Contrary to its title, the film focuses on the experiences of these men living under Israeli occupation, and the final preparations for their mission emphasize its nationalist character rather than any religious dimension.[7]

Critiques of gender relations have been a recurrent theme in Arab cinema. Most recently they have found expression in the first-ever Saudi film, *Wadjda,* the story of a girl and her mother breaking free from patriarchal norms. Some films depict women as victims. Other films show strong women, but they usually remain largely confined within the family context. Most of the women in Nasrallah's *Scheherazade* fight back. Their stories are told by the host of a popular TV talk show who ends up telling her own story, covered in bruises, after a falling out with her husband. Mohamed Chouikh, in *Hamlet of Women,* presents women who take control of their village when the men are compelled to go away, leaving only the elders behind. Eventually the men return, but gender relations have changed.

Nadia El Fani moved beyond the critique of gender relations in *Bedwin Hacker* (2002). Her protagonist is a cosmopolitan woman for whom men are marginal as she pursues her political goals in Tunisia.[8] The protagonist of Farida Benlyazid's *A Door to the Sky* (*Bab al-sama' maftouh*, 1988) also finds independence, but in an altogether different way. Returning from France to Morocco, she discovers her Muslim cultural and spiritual heritage, Sufism in particular, and turns the family house into a shelter and spiritual center for women.[9]

Female virginity is a central element in patriarchal control, and quite a number of films have denounced the severe punishment inflicted on women who lose their virginity outside marriage. Female circumcision, however, more accurately genital mutilation (FGM), is rarely addressed, even though it is the rule in Egypt and is practiced elsewhere in the Arab world, and beyond, since well before the advent of Islam. Saab touched on FGM in *A Suspended Life* and more recently made it a central theme in *Dunia*. The Lebanese director set *Dunia* in Egypt, an obvious choice, given that FGM is near universal there. Saab had to overcome an initial rejection of the scenario by the Egyptian censorship board and faced harsh criticism from sections of the press.

The taboo subject of homosexuality was brought out into the open by Nouri Bouzid with the story of the abusive relationship between a carpenter and his apprentices in *Man of Ashes* (*Rih essed / L'Homme de cendres*, 1986).[10]

THE CHANGING POLITICAL CONTEXT

When the Arab Spring erupted, some directors managed to respond quickly. The Tunisian revolution erupted while Nouri Bouzid was shooting *Hidden Beauties* (*Millefeuille*, 2013), which contrasted Tunisian attitudes toward women wearing the veil, and he resituated the film in the context of the revolution. Nasrallah's *After the Battle* tells of the encounter of a young middle-class woman activist and one of the horse riders who charged the demonstrators in Cairo's Tahrir Square and who, like other riders, had been pulled off his horse and beaten. The distinguished Syrian director Mohammad Malas told of people drawn into the civil war in *Ladder to Damascus* (*Sullam ila Dimashq*, 2013).

Political issues and cultural issues are intertwined, and the Arab Spring is reshaping them and their relationship. Islamic movements have come to the fore. In Tunisia and Egypt the first-ever free elections brought to power

Islamic movements that had been suppressed by the repressive regimes, even if Egypt's elected government was soon overthrown in a military coup. They were recognized for the persecution they suffered and valued for providing the social services the corrupt regimes failed to deliver; their rejection of the West resonated with a public that resented Western countries that had propped up the authoritarian regimes and provided support for Israel.

Much of the cultural critique in Arab films used to be of little concern to the authoritarian regimes; sometimes it fit their political agenda. The Islamic movements, however, are committed, in varying degrees, to the very cultural values filmmakers have denounced. Patriarchal traditions in particular are at issue. In the past, committed filmmakers occasionally had to face the hostile reactions of Islamic movements whose cultural stance they critiqued. Now that these movements wield effective power, whether in government or in opposition, these values have become a salient issue in political conflicts across the region. It had taken courage, ingenuity, and perseverance for filmmakers to give image and voice to dissent from authoritarian regimes. Now filmmakers critical of the values the newly empowered Islamic movements promote face fresh challenges.

NOTES

1. This introduction draws on the chapters in this volume. I am indebted to Dalia Said Mostafa and Jonathan Smolin for helpful comments on an earlier version. Roy Armes's *New Voices in Arab Cinema* complements this volume's focus on established directors. It was published too late to be consulted by the contributors or myself.

2. For statistics on film production in Arab countries, see Gugler 2011b, 4.

3. Full details of films by the directors featured in this volume are provided in the respective chapters.

4. On *Stars in Broad Daylight*, see Salti 2007.

5. On *The Dupes*, see Yaqub 2011b.

6. On *Closed Doors*, see Gugler and Jensen 2011.

7. On *Paradise Now*, see Yaqub 2011a.

8. On *Bedwin Hacker*, see Gugler 2011a; for a different perspective, see Lang 2014, 191–222.

9. On *A Door to the Sky*, see Martin 2007.

10. On *Man of Ashes*, see Lang 2014, 40–66.

REFERENCES

Armes, Roy. 2015. *New Voices in Arab Cinema*. Bloomington: Indiana University Press.

Denes, Nick. 2014. "An Overburdened 'Brand'? Reflections on a Decade with the London Palestine Film Festival." In *Film Festivals and the Middle East,* edited by Dina Iordanova and Stefanie Van de Peer. *Film Festival Yearbook* 6, 251–268. St. Andrews: St. Andrews Film Studies.

Gertz, Nurith, and George Khleifi. 2011. "A Chronicle of Palestinian Cinema." In *Film in the Middle East and North Africa: Creative Dissidence,* edited by Josef Gugler, 187–197.

Gugler, Josef. 2011a. "*Bedwin Hacker:* A Hacker Challenges Western Domination of the Global Media." In *Film in the Middle East and North Africa: Creative Dissidence,* edited by Josef Gugler, 284–293.

———. 2011b. "Creative Responses to Conflict." In *Film in the Middle East and North Africa: Creative Dissidence,* edited by Josef Gugler, 1–36.

———. 2011c. "Destiny: Liberal and Fundamentalist Islam Clash amid the Splendor of Twelfth-Century Andalusia." In *Film in the Middle East and North Africa: Creative Dissidence,* edited by Josef Gugler, 252–260.

Gugler, Josef, ed. 2011. *Film in the Middle East and North Africa: Creative Dissidence.* Austin: University of Texas Press; Cairo: University of Cairo Press.

Gugler, Josef, and Kim Jensen. 2011. "Closed Doors: The Attractions of Fundamentalism." In *Film in the Middle East and North Africa: Creative Dissidence,* edited by Josef Gugler, 259–270.

Hillauer, Rebecca. 2005. *Encyclopedia of Arab Women Filmmakers.* Cairo: American University in Cairo Press.

Khatib, Lina. 2008. *Lebanese Cinema: Imagining the Civil War and Beyond.* London: I. B. Tauris.

Lang, Robert. 2014. *New Tunisian Cinema: Allegories of Resistance.* New York: Columbia University Press.

Martin, Florence. 2007. "Bab al-sama maftouh / A Door to the Sky." In *The Cinema of North Africa and the Middle East,* edited by Gönül Dönmez-Colin, 122–132. London: Wallflower Press.

———. 2011. *Veils and Screens: Maghrebi Women's Cinema.* Bloomington: Indiana University Press.

Ruoff, Jeffrey, ed. 2009. *Coming Soon to a Festival Near You: Programming Film Festivals.* St. Andrews: St. Andrews Film Studies.

Salti, Rasha. 2007. "Nujum Al-Nahar / Stars in Broad Day Light." In *The Cinema of North Africa and the Middle East,* edited by Gönül Dönmez-Colin, 100–110. London: Wallflower Press.

Shafik, Viola. 2007. *Arab Cinema: History and Cultural Identity.* Rev. ed. Cairo: American University in Cairo Press.

———. Unpublished. "Popular Egyptian Cinema: Industry and Society." In *African Cinemas: A Continental Approach,* edited by Josef Gugler and Kenneth Harrow (unpublished).

Wedeen, Lisa. 1999. *Ambiguities of Domination: Politics, Rhetoric, and Symbols in Contemporary Syria.* Chicago: University of Chicago Press.

Yaqub, Nadia. 2011a. "*Paradise Now:* Narrating a Failed Politics." In *Film in the Middle East and North Africa: Creative Dissidence,* edited by Josef Gugler, 218–227.

———. 2011b. "*The Dupes:* Three Generations Uprooted from Palestine and Betrayed." In *Film in the Middle East and North Africa: Creative Dissidence,* edited by Josef Gugler, 113–124.

Nabil Maleh at the Dubai International Film Festival 2006.

1

Nabil Maleh

SYRIA'S LEOPARD
(SYRIA)

Christa Salamandra

The anti-regime uprising that began in Syria in 2011 lends a particular poignancy and urgency to a discussion of filmmaker Nabil Maleh's life and work. The eminent director epitomizes the figure of the artist-activist, the socially committed and politically engaged cultural producer. Over decades of production and across genres, his work has challenged artistic, cultural, and political regimes. Maleh often cites a defining moment of childhood resistance: the seven-year-old Nabil confronted a soldier who tried to keep him off a public park swing so that military officers' children could have free rein. In return for his defiance, the boy received a slap which, as Maleh puts it, echoed throughout his life.[1]

Aesthetics and ethics merged early in the director's life. Born in 1936, the son of a high ranking army physician, and eldest of four siblings in an elite Damascene family, Maleh credits his mother for shaping his artistic and political sensibilities. Samiha al-Ghazi, an educated woman from a family of high-ranking nationalist activists and politicians, encouraged her son's creative pursuits from an early age and instilled an enduring resistance to authority. At nine Maleh attended his first political protest, for the Palestinian cause; at fourteen he had a poem about Vietnam published in a Beirut newspaper. Soon afterward he became a political cartoonist and columnist for the Syrian daily *Alif Baa,* writing of the 1950s tumult: multiple coups d'état in Syria, the Suez Canal Crisis, and the

Baghdad Pact. Upon completing secondary school Maleh worked as a substitute teacher in Syria's rural northeast, experiencing firsthand "a world of barefoot children, unjust labor, and the wasted future of generations."

Returning to Damascus and enrolling in law school, Maleh harbored an interest in science and a passion for writing and painting. By chance, at a party, he met the Czech cultural attaché, who encouraged him to follow his dream of studying physics in Prague. With no funding available, the seventeen-year-old sold one of his paintings to UNWRA (the United Nations Relief and Works Agency), earning enough for his first few months in Czechoslovakia. There he became the communist country's first student from a Western country, as Czechs considered Syria at the time. To support himself he worked as a journalist, host, translator, and editor for Prague Arabic Radio. An odd job as a film extra proved an epiphany, and Maleh transferred from nuclear physics to the Prague Film School, joining a cohort that included Jiri Menzel and Milos Forman. While still in Czechoslovakia, his criticism of the Nasser regime controlling Syria under the United Arab Republic (1958–1961) attracted attention from the Syrian intelligence services and earned him a reputation as a dissident that has remained a source of hardship and inspiration.

Returning to Syria upon graduation in 1964 as the country's first European film school graduate, Maleh made experimental shorts and continued to paint, holding his first art exhibitions. The state's newly established National Film Organization invited him to direct *Crown of Thorns,* a forty-five-minute experimental docudrama. Maleh next wrote a screenplay based on Syrian author Haydar Haydar's novel *The Leopard (al-Fahd),* a fictional depiction of Abu 'Ali al-Shahin, legendary rebel of the 1940s. Maleh cast newcomer Adib Qaddura, a waiter he discovered on location after failing to find a professional actor able to embody the fabled Robin Hood figure. A week before shooting was scheduled to begin, the Ministry of Interior revoked permission, arguing that the film glorified a thug. In 1971 *The Leopard* was given official clearance, and this evocation of rural resistance became the NFO's first Syrian feature-length film.[2]

Released in 1972, *The Leopard* captivated Arab audiences and introduced Syrian cinema to the global stage. The film is set in 1946, as the French Mandate forces scaled back their presence, and local feudal landlords, *aghas,* took their place as oppressors. *The Leopard* opens with, and periodically returns to, a close-up of the protagonist's scowling face set against a raging sea. A haunting voice-over recites poetry, drawing on folk ballad forms, composed for the film by acclaimed Syrian writer Mamduh 'Adwan. Suhayl 'Arafa's drum-heavy score adds an element of menace. In the second scene, shot in silhouette, Abu 'Ali's wife, Shafiqa, asks why he has acquired a gun, now that the French have gone. Abu 'Ali avoids the question, but the answer quickly emerges: Syrian landlords, backed by soldiers, demand more tribute than the peasants can afford after a bad harvest. The hero resists, is arrested and beaten, but escapes to the hills, staging guerilla attacks against the new forces of tyranny. Comrades from his days fighting the French try to join him, but Abu 'Ali turns them away. This is his fight alone.

The soldiers attempt to coerce the rebel's surrender by harassing the villagers and stealing their food. After a gruesome military raid kills Abu 'Ali's nephew, the hero's sister cries for her brother's blood. His rebellion has led to this fierce retaliation. Shafiqa visits Abu 'Ali in hiding, and assures him of the villagers' support, despite the agha's brutality. Their passionate reunion against a craggy backdrop marks Arab cinema's first partial nude scene, as the camera caresses the length of unclothed actress Ighra' ("Seduction," née Nihad 'Ala al-Din) underneath the amorous rebel. Shafiqa later joins her husband in defending his position against a well-armed platoon. As Cécile Boëx notes, this depiction of female resistance subverts commercial cinema conventions, as Shafiqa is no longer merely an object of male desire, but a rifle-bearing rebel for a collective cause (2011, 135).

The peasants' conditions worsen, and 'Abd al-Rahim "the One-Armed" is murdered for feeding his fugitive friend. Outraged, a group of village men join Abu 'Ali's battle, and this time he does not refuse. They raid a group of soldiers dining on the agha's meat, steal their weapons, and set fire to the warlord's warehouse. Shafiqa and her son 'Ali are arrested in an attempt to lure the rebel out of hiding, but he surprises the guards and stages a rescue. He returns to his posse and tries to move them to safety, but they have grown battle-worn and are captured by the agha's soldiers, then released. Abu 'Ali is again alone. He takes brief refuge with a village elder, who questions Abu 'Ali's endeavor, arguing that violent tactics have created a bloody cycle of vengeance. "I couldn't keep quiet," Abu 'Ali argues. "But your gun didn't speak well for you," the sage counters, noting that the soldiers, poor men trying to feed their families, are themselves oppressed.

Abu 'Ali's exploits become legend, as peasants exchange tales of his deeds. The rebel hijacks a bus but steals only from the agha's cronies. "Is there no law in this country?" cries one of his victims. "If there was law, would I be here?" Abu 'Ali retorts. A former comrade complains that the rebel started out wanting a revolution but knew nothing more than how to kill soldiers, and has ended up suspicious of all around him. The peasants accuse Abu 'Ali of fighting an unwinnable battle, bringing the village to ruin. They exchange blows. Yet the villagers continue to evade the authorities' demands for the hero's whereabouts.

In the end, a weary Abu 'Ali is betrayed by his uncle, whom the rebel strangles before the arresting soldiers can pull him away. The hero is tied up and dragged through the village, then shackled in a web of chains and beaten. The seaside refrain shot widens to reveal the rebel's manacle-bound figure walking along the shore to the gallows, where the villagers, along with the agha and his henchmen, wait in glum silence. As Abu 'Ali hangs, an aerial shot scans the countryside, and a hazy silhouette of revolting peasants emerges on the horizon.

Maleh identifies with his protagonist, a lone and often lonely rebel fighting for true independence, "motivated by dignity, self-esteem and the will to go to the limit, carrying his own cross with no regret." He draws a parallel between Abu 'Ali's battle and the Palestinian resistance struggle. *The Leopard,* he argues, illustrates "the contradictory relationship between the external world and the internal world, the individual 'no' and the collective 'no.' In the film, my hero loses the battle against backwardness, stupidity, the absence of collective conscience, the fragmentation of the social order, individual opportunism and shortsighted selfishness" (Salti 2006, 89).

The Leopard represents Nabil's first sustained effort to explore, through narrative example, what has gone wrong in, and continues to plague, Syrians' revolutionary endeavors. Politics enhances rather than overwhelms the film's form. In telling Abu 'Ali's story, as in his other efforts, Maleh strives for a new cinematic language, and claims no affiliation to schools of cinematic style: "I've never felt that there is a school that I can follow, but rather try to find my own methods. Sometimes I'm successful; but an unfolding of what we don't know about ourselves seems to me more important than following a cinematic movement . . . there are no forms to be resurrected, only forms to be created and discovered. I avoided pre-established schools and tendencies."

Yet *The Leopard* employs techniques of neorealism, including the theme of poverty and oppression, the use of non-professional actors, location filming, and black-and-white film. The film arguably set the stylistic tone for the following decades of Syrian visual cultural production. *The Leopard* reflects what I have termed—in the context of television drama—a "dark aesthetic" that has become the hallmark of a distinctive Syrian visual style (Salamandra 2012, unpublished manuscript). Syrian artists like Maleh manipulate a limited autonomy to produce a visual language of critique for both creators and audiences. The current uprising's dissident cultural producers draw, wittingly or not, on a gloomy aesthetic introduced in *The Leopard.*

Lovingly framed shots of the countryside and its traditional stone houses reflect careful attention to authenticity of décor and clothing. Maleh sees the film as part cultural documentation, a form of salvage anthropology, tracing what remained of "the real environment of the countryside." Scenes of rural harvest show everyday practice under the soldiers' threatening watch. Maleh describes the motivation behind his realist techniques:

> The harsh environment demanded harsh solutions. I hated and still hate pretension. Color, for me at that time, felt like a false bleeding over the originality of things, characters and emotions. With *The Leopard,* I scouted for locations and people. The authenticity of both [in Syria's coastal region] amazed me and corresponded exactly to my conception of the film. I even rejected makeup. I told everyone that the sunrays were the best makeup artist. Working with people from those villages who had never been to a cinema brought me an ecstatic joy.

The film's rich local authenticity stops at language; dialogue is delivered in generic Syrian idiom. This, Maleh argues, reflects the political ethos of its era; films of the 1980s and television dramas of the 1990s onward employ local dialects—with their attendant sectarian and regional associations—often to controversial effect (Salamandra 1998, 2004). Yet the late 1970s still carried the hope of Arab unity: "I didn't give particular attention to the dialect, because for me *The Leopard* was a pan-Syrian or even a pan-Arab symbol. At that time, the dialect of the Syrian coast didn't have the same political or social connotations that it does today. I didn't predict the apparent transition from a dialect to a position."[3]

The Leopard was awarded the Locarno International Film Festival's Special Leopard Prize in 1972. One of but a handful of Arab filmmakers to have achieved this level of European recognition, Maleh served on the festival's jury the following year. The film also enjoyed unusual local success. In the paradox-ridden Syrian film industry, most productions financed by the NFO are either banned from or simply fail to achieve distribution within country (Salti 2006). Yet the film screened in cinemas throughout Syria, despite its implicit message: foreign colonialism is dead, but oppression lives on. It occupies a privileged place in the collective memory of Syria's artistic community, inspiring generations of Syrian media makers. Cherif Kiwan, a member of the Abu Naddara collective of dissident filmmakers, cites *Ighra*''s love scene as formative: "Seeing the body of a woman on film was my first feeling of freedom, of having crossed boundaries. It influenced me more than anything directly political."[4]

The film is remembered beyond the Middle East. In 2005, South Korea's Pusan International Film Festival chose *The Leopard* as one of the "immortal masterpieces of Asian cinema," although the NFO refused them a copy (Hatahet 2011). This forms but one of numerous instances revealing the state's ambivalence toward Maleh in particular, and art in general. The Assad regime's relationship with artists of both elite and popular forms involves an ongoing process of compromise, cooptation, and constraint.[5]

Maleh embodies the Syrian cinema paradox: despite receiving NFO financing, the filmmaker is often treated as a dissident, a distinction he bears with honor. State funding has enabled him to forgo foreign sources, permitting, he believes, a greater local authenticity. A militant independent, Maleh is proudly among the few Syrian filmmakers to avoid serving as NFO employees. Yet his films are perhaps those most widely viewed within Syria. As Walter Armbrust has shown, Arab "art house" films produced for the international festival circuit offer didacticism in the guise of authenticity, giving foreign viewers culture and history lessons unnecessary for Arab audiences. Commercial Arab films, on the other hand, often employ implicit, ironic, intertextual references that render them much more reflective of their environment (Armbrust 2000). Unusually for an Arab film, *The Leopard,* like Maleh's other major work, *The Extras,* is both internationally acclaimed and locally popular. Screened in more than twenty Syrian theaters for over three months, the work established its creator's formidable reputation in the Arab world and beyond.

Despite sporadic interference from the state representatives who, as Maleh puts it "acted more like *mukhabarat* (intelligence) agents than owners and administrators of cultural projects," the 1970s proved a fruitful decade for a nascent Syrian industry. Cinema clubs in Damascus and Aleppo introduced filmmakers and intellectual audiences to global film classics, and helped forge a field of cultural production. In 1972, Damascus held its first annual international film festival, promoting an alternative Arab cinema. During this time Maleh produced numerous experimental shorts, including the ninety-second *Napalm,* linking the Vietnam War to the Israeli Occupation (Ginsberg and Lippard, 2010, 265), and *Rocks (Sakhr)* exposing the perilous labor conditions of Syrian quarry workers (ArteEast 2006). He also directed *Labor (al-Makhad)* the first third of *Men under the Sun,* a triptych exploring the Palestinian situation released in 1970. His privately financed spoof, *Jealous James Bond,* brought Durayd Lahham's comical television character to the big screen in 1974. *Mr. Progressive (al-Sayyid al-Taqaddumi)* of 1975 follows an investigative journalist's attempts to expose middle-class corruption. For its negative portrayal of a regime figure the film was banned in Syria.

By the end of the 1970s, Syria faced rising tensions, with militant challenges from Islamists, culminating in the brutal suppression of the Hama uprising in 1982. The Ba'thist state consolidated its control of creative expression. Maleh "collided with a cultural environment ossified in false slogans of progress," but continued working. The year 1979 saw the release of his second masterpiece, *Fragments* (*Baqaya Suwar*), a realist treatment of the autobiographical novel by Hanna Mina, acclaimed chronicler of social life in rural Syria.[6] Maleh was attracted to Mina's richly drawn characters and feel for his rural environment, one evoking a "fragile human existence and search for life with dignity." Shot in color and set at the end of the 1920s, the film recounts the hard-drinking Abu Salim's struggle to reclaim his wife's land—usurped by a Turk—and his foiled efforts to sustain his impoverished family. *The Leopard*'s Adib Qaddura returns as Abu Salim, a grounded sailor reduced to odd jobs in a coastal village. He regales his neighbors with tales of seafaring exploits—"Oh Egypt, the women!"—and botches the menial work he is offered. Life on land suits him poorly; he turns to smuggling but is hijacked. His wife, Umm Salim (actress and theater director Naila al-Atrash), forages for food and begs from neighbors, including the beautiful widow (Samar Sami) with whom her husband is having an affair. Hunger sets in; the couple's three children are forbidden to eat until the afternoon shade hits a certain rock.

The family moves to the mountains, where Umm Salim's Uncle Barhum finds Abu Salim work with a village leader (*mukhtar*), a pernickety miser who washes his own clothes. But the seaman quickly tires of working the land and peddling proves equality disastrous. The couple's eldest daughter, barely a teen, is forced to join the mukhtar's household as a servant to help support her family. Sericulture promises salvation; joyous scenes show villagers coddling silkworms on mulberry leaves. But India floods the international textile market with cheaper synthetics. The family's debt to the mukhtar, who controls the village food supply, grows, and a younger daughter is sent to work in the house of an agha in the plains near the Turkish border. The family joins her after Uncle Barhum has the eldest daughter released from the mukhtar's service.

The village is in turmoil, after the ahga's warehouse is robbed. No one seems to know, or care, about Abu Salim's promised job and housing. Instead the family witnesses a confrontation between the lord's men and the cowering villagers. The fearless Zanuba (a triumphant Muna Wassif), named for Syria's ancient warrior queen, strides in with a bitter laugh, accusing the village mukhtar of stealing the grain on the agha's behalf. "You're a dog," she taunts, "wag your tail for the agha and he'll give you a bone." Abu Salim approaches the lord but is rebuffed. 'Abdu, a soldier supporting the agha, recognizes his cousin Abu Salim and finds the seaman a job guarding the lord's warehouse. He is given a rifle, earning the suspicion of his new neighbors, except for the marginal Zanuba, who befriends the family. She takes the hungry son Salim on lengthy journeys to the local version of a soup kitchen, and bathes the little boy's infected eyes in the sea.

'Abdu tries to attack Zanuba, but Abu Salim protects her. Tensions between the two men emerge over the soldier's attitude toward the peasants, who, he argues, "don't come out to work unless threatened with a rifle." They escalate after the hungry farmers are accused of stealing the agha's food, and the cousins find themselves on opposing sides of a battle between villagers and soldiers. The sharecroppers gather to storm the warehouse, to "take what's rightfully ours," the soldiers try to stop them, and an exchange of gunfire ensues. Outraged, the sailor kills his cousin. Zanuba, laughing wildly, sets fire to the lord's warehouse, and is shot off the roof. A wounded Abu Salim delivers the film's final line in earshot of his terrified son: "A wasted life."

The film plays on shifts of weakness and power. Though a secondary character, it is the tall, strong, justice-seeking Barhum, rather than Abu Salim, who embodies the heroic masculine ideal. Zanuba emasculates villagers and soldiers alike with her aggression. The film widens the novel's intimate domestic landscape to emphasize themes of domination and oppression. Maleh transforms Mina's Abu Salim—a dissolute, womanizing drunkard—into a thwarted but dignified romantic: "Honestly, I didn't like the idea of an alcoholic. Abu Salim had something noble and honest about him, and sought dignified existence. I could not let that go. I didn't like the experience of the author, so I opted for what I love in people: that hardship and poverty create nobility."

Despite the film's success, Maleh's relationship with the Syrian authorities deteriorated after *Fragments,* which the director sees as the end of an era in his professional life. A pivotal incident occurred on his birthday in September 1981. As the filmmaker drove by the Foreign Ministry, a guard signaled him to pull over and let an official car pass. The director stopped, but apparently not quickly enough, for the guard beat him on the head with a rifle butt. Maleh passed out and woke in a police station to the voice of an officer apologizing. He decided to leave Syria and traveled to the United States on a Fulbright Grant, despite his longstanding hostility to the country's foreign policy. Maleh found a warm, enthusiastic reception in various academic settings. A University of Texas at Austin screening of his *Napalm,* a film critical of America's involvement in Vietnam, concluded with a standing ovation. He taught film production at Austin and UCLA, but, longing to direct, he joined a Libyan production company in Geneva, in a Switzerland he found culturally cold and creatively sterile,

Abu 'Ali frees his wife and his son from prison in *The Leopard.*

Nada and Salim in *The Extras.*

"a world of banks and businessmen." For seven months afterward the director and his family toured Europe, finally settling in Greece, where they remained for a decade; here he produced films for Libyan television, including *Chronicle of a Dream,* a Marxist-inspired reverie on human progress imagining an eventual utopia of freedom. It was during his Greek sojourn that Maleh wrote the script for his next major work, *The Extras (al-Kumbars)*.

Maleh originally envisioned *The Extras* as an Egyptian production, featuring that country's stars Nur al-Sharif and Yousra. But on a visit to Damascus he called on the then NFO director, Marwan Haddad, who offered him funding to film in Syria. With Syrian actors Bassam Kusa and Samar Sami in the lead roles, shooting began in Damascus in 1992 on what was to become the best known of Maleh's films outside his native land. It is also Syrian cinema's foremost object of scholarly attention.[7]

Released in 1993, *The Extras* reflects the social and political concerns long central to Maleh's work. The film depicts the struggles of a law student and gas station attendant, Salim, and his widowed seamstress girlfriend, Nada, to forge a romantic relationship amid layers of oppression and censure. The couple has had no privacy during their eight-month courtship. The young protagonist, an aspiring actor with a stammer, borrows his friend 'Adil's apartment for a tryst. The entire film, save opening and closing, takes place between the drab abode's claustrophobic walls, a setting symbolic of the Syrian and perhaps the Arab condition. Establishing shots signal the lead characters' dreary existence: Salim polishing cars and rehearsing bit parts for a theater director who forgets the extra's name; Nada at her factory sewing machine, and sharing a humble courtyard house with her brother's family.

On the day of the tryst, 'Adil lingers; he will leave to meet his future in-laws—he is poised to marry well—but frets over his friend's assignation. A suited stranger knocks on the door and barges over the threshold, asking polite but insistent questions about the next door neighbor. Salim imagines pummeling this *mukhabarat* agent, who suggests he has met the hopeful actor before. The menacing figure leaves, and 'Adil dismisses the incident as none of their business, but both men are unnerved.

Alone and waiting, Salim tidies the bed and imagines the agent cavorting with wiggling lovers beneath the sheets. A peddler knocks, but protests when Salim offers money without taking her goods: "I'm not a beggar." Nada arrives, late and flustered, worried her brother has spotted her and that the neighbors she has passed on the stairs sense her visit's illicit purpose. Salim urges her to consider the apartment a "free space," disconnected from the outside world. A siren punctuates the absurd suggestion.

Salim's fantasies of making love to Nada interrupt their awkward conversation. When they finally embrace, a toppled glass shatters Nada's abandon. She asks to leave the apartment, terrified of being discovered. Salim proposes exchanging marriage vows instead, so they no longer need fear. The strains of a neighbor's plaintive 'oud filter through the thin walls.[8] Salim talks of acting and delivers a few lines from his latest production, in which he plays seven different roles but is given no mention in the program. Nada has never been to the theater; Salim stages a mock production for her, draping curtains and bedclothes around the living room. He gives her the part of an oppressive ruler who sends his rebellious subjects to prison. Nada objects to the injustice, but Salim tells her they have no choice but to play the roles as written; he would never countenance the insult if it happened in real life. He then performs two of his other parts: a prison guard and an intelligence agent, figures that rulers "can't survive without." Nada dislikes these new characters; she prefers his extra roles which, though minor, are decent people. Salim argues he must accept such parts in order to succeed. Every Syrian, Maleh implies, faces a similar dilemma.

'Adil's fiancée, a crass parvenu from Aleppo, barges in looking for a missing shoe. She teases the couple, but sympathizes—if only they had the money to marry, as she and 'Adil do. She leaves them alone, and they laugh their way to the bed, which promptly collapses. To fix it they climb under the grid of the iron frame, and Nada notes the mesh's resemblance to the prison bars behind which so many of their compatriots languish. A distant bell, like that of a bicycle, interrupts another embrace. Nada prepares to leave, and the suited agent returns—this time with two thuggish sidekicks—asking about the neighbor's frequent visitor. Then the brutes drag the blind 'oud player, pleading for help, into the apartment. Salim tries to intervene, but one of the thugs knocks him to the ground, and the musician is taken away. The extra cannot act; terror renders him mute, even to Nada's entreaties. She leaves the apartment, breaking down only when out of Salim's earshot, and furtively exits the building. Salim follows in the next shot, lingering despondently at the gate before walking in the opposite direction. The camera crawls up the mammoth apartment block, and out over the concrete cityscape.

The Extras is Maleh's—and perhaps Syrian cinema's—most explicit condemnation of the Ba'thist police state. The film's critique extends beyond the political elite; its skillful linkage of sexual and political impotence and repression indicts Arab society and patriarchy (Wedeen 1999, 116; Gugler 2011, 129–130). Salim's vocation is telling. An obligation to act against one's own beliefs and desires implicates all Syrians in a simulated courtship of the regime, one Lisa Wedeen has illustrated in numerous social and cultural contexts (1999). Nada laments that she and Salim are forced to behave like a pair of thieves, stealing time alone. Even at this, she notes, they are unsuccessful. Syria, Maleh implies, offers its citizens nothing but bit parts which they must often perform reluctantly and in secret. Many of these roles involve collusion and cooptation.

The film reached global audiences, earning Samar Sami and Bassam Kusa top acting awards at the Arab Cinema Biennial in Paris and winning Maleh best director at the Cairo International Film Festival (Gugler 2011, 131). It also won the Silver Award at the Rimini International Film Festival in 1995. *The Extras* was first screened in Syria as a Friday morning side event—rather than a competitor—of the Damascus International Film Festival in 1995. Maleh recalls this as the happiest of day of his life, one that "broke the ice of a long exile." An official from the latter festival, on a visit to Damascus, embarrassed the Syrian authorities into releasing *The Extras* in Syria, where the film triumphed. Audiences packed the six government owned al-Kindi theaters during its four-month run (Wedeen 1999, 116).

While the 1990s saw a slight improvement in the conditions of artistic production, the hope that political liberalization would accompany the economic opening were dashed early in the decade. When journalists asked Maleh to assess the state of Arab cinema, he would reply: "It's the state of the Arab world generally: a block governed by the law of inertia, run by thieves, beneficiaries, clans, and those with agendas. Opposing it are scattered, individual creators who possess neither money, power nor weapons, but who embody the national project."

With his production company Ebla—named for a Bronze Age fount of Syrian civilization—the director produced several documentaries for foreign markets, including *A Bedouin Day* (1994), which was narrated in English and distributed in Europe by a British company. Yet Maleh's commitment to Syria and its audiences remained constant, and is reflected in his television work. Uniquely among Syrian filmmakers, he has directed several miniseries, *musalsalat,* for the country's TV drama industry, among the Arab world's most prominent.[9] Works such as *Situations* and *Top Secret* won awards at the Cairo Radio and Television Festival. After conducting extensive research, Maleh wrote the screenplay *Asmahan.* This television biopic of the Syrian-born singer and star of the Egyptian screen was directed by the renowned Tunisian Shawqi Majiri in 2008 and aired on various Arabic satellite channels.

The new millennium ushered in an increased margin of freedom as thirty-six-year-old, British-educated Bashar al-Assad took the reins of the regime after his father's death in 2000. Cultural producers joined many other Syrians in anticipating the dissolution of the police state and the emergence of participatory politics. Maleh spearheaded the formation of the Committees for the Revival of Civil Society, which met at the director's Damascus home. The organization formed one of the most prominent new "forums" (*muntadiyat*) in what became known as the Damascus Spring, the brief flowering of reformist discussion and debate that marked the new president's first months in office. Maleh, the group's appointed spokesperson, joined other prominent intellectuals to air concerns over the country's increasing poverty, corruption, and militarization and the growing influence of puritanical Salafi Islam. They signed a series of declarations calling for the same democratizing reforms that opposition groups of 2011 would demand, such as the repeal of the four-decade-old emergency law. Less than a year later, a new series of repressive measures, including mass arrests, laid bare what dissidents see as the apparent liberalization's true aim: to identify and silence the opposition. The NFO's new director, according to Maleh, quickly sidelined him, along with the country's other leading filmmakers—Omar Amiralay, Oussama Mohammad, and Mohammad Malas—as a dissident. The other members of this cohort received foreign support; Maleh faced a financial dry spell. He borrowed money for a television film, and *Najla's Love Affairs* (*Gharamiyat Najla*) became the first Arabic-language film shot in digital format. Broadcast on Syrian Television, this work explores the upending of life in a Syrian village during the hosting of a television drama crew.

Continuing to write, he produced a screenplay, a political thriller about a fictional escaped Iraqi official hiding in Lebanon. A work Maleh considers his "dream film," *The Hunt Feast* (in English) tells the tale of a corrupt officer's escape from Baghdad on the eve of the American invasion. The villain, a high-ranking torturer for Saddam Hussein who has doubled as a CIA agent, takes a stash of stolen cash to the Lebanese mountains, where he poses as a lone hunter. After murdering the other Iraqi exiles who follow him in pursuit of the money, he encounters a group of tourists who, in a final twist, are revealed as his former victims plotting to bring him to justice. The hunter becomes the hunted. For Maleh, the film posits a scenario where the victim judges his tormentor. *The Hunt Feast* was shot in 2005 as a Syrian-British joint venture, but it remains locked in a legal battle between producers.

The following year the Dubai International Film Festival honored Maleh (other honorees included American director Oliver Stone and Bollywood star Shah Rukh Khan), for his outstanding contribution to cinema. He then received a commission from the Syrian Commission for Family Affairs and produced sixteen documentaries and fifty-two "spots." Intended for Syrian television, most were promptly banned. Noteworthy among them is the three-part *The Road to Damascus* (*'A Sham 'A Sham*). This filmic journey across Syria uncannily presages the current uprising, visiting areas of hardship and deprivation that would, a few years later, erupt in groundswells of anti-regime protest. Maleh frames his road trip with the idiomatic opening to Arabic folk tales, "Once upon a time" (*Kan ya ma kan ayyam zaman*), to tell the all-too-real story of a failed nation. He drives past Syria's "forgotten cities," monumental ancient ruins, drawing a parallel with the contemporary devastation that forces so many citizens to abandon beloved towns and villages and seek a better life in the capital. The documentary crew travels against this human wave. Spoken in a patchwork of dialects, Syrians' laments are much the same: unemployment, exploitation, pollution, corruption. Most take the state to task, but a singular voice suggests a neoliberal individualism, or internalized regime rhetoric: "Isn't it enough, all the pressure they face from the outside," a young mother of many children asks, "why should I blame the government for my mistakes?" A singer laments in the background: "Every one of us has a story in his heart." Cinema provides a barometer: a village once had three movie houses, all have closed. Scenes of provincial poverty, and peoples' dreams of leaving it, are answered with those of migrants scraping an existence in the dilapidated informal settlements circling Damascus. Although it never reached Syrian audiences, *The Road to Damascus* celebrated its international premiere at the Dox Box Global Day in Malmö, Sweden, in March 2012 and was subsequently screened in various academic and nonprofit settings in Europe and the United States.

The film's masterful blending of imagery and storytelling, its weaving of the personal with the political, reflect its creator's enduring commitment to exposing an uncomfortable truth. Arab regimes, and other governments, would have done well to heed *The Road to Damascus*'s powerful message. When most of his colleagues pointed to a growing collective apathy, Maleh is one of the few Arab intellectuals to predict, four years in advance, the massive grassroots uprising sweeping the region since 2010: "I believe that something—an explosion—will happen, because it is not possible for human beings to accept these living conditions for much longer. At least these have been the lessons of history. A light will emerge from beneath the clutter, the pollution . . . I know there are many like me in the Arab world. We draw our strength merely by virtue of knowing that we are out there, alive" (Maleh 2006, 94).

This "explosion" occurred in 2011; its outcome remains uncertain. What began as a peaceful, largely secular movement of the sort Maleh had envisioned has evolved into a civil war with sectarian dimensions. Yet even if the anti-authoritarian protestors lose their battle against exploitation and oppression, they will, like Maleh's many protagonists, be "victorious on a moral and human register" (Salti 2006: 89).

NOTES

1. Unless otherwise noted, biographical details and quotations are drawn from personal correspondence with the author, June 22 and September 7, 2011.
2. The Yugoslav Poçko Poçkovic (Boshko Vochinich) directed the NFO's first feature, *The Lorry Driver (Sa'iq al-Shahina)*, in 1967.
3. Maleh here refers to the association of coastal dialects with the 'Alawi-dominated regime, and a growing sectarianism and regionalism in Syria more generally. Syria's Arab nationalists long held the use of dialect in literature, and the teaching of the colloquial to foreigners, as divisive practices. See Salamandra 2004 on the intersection of social, political, and religious distinctions in Syria.
4. Cherif Kiwan, interview with the author, 13 February 2012.
5. For various interpretations of the Assad regime's treatment of artists, see Boëx 2011, cooke 2007, Della Ratta 2012, Joubin 2013; Wedeen 1999, 2013; Salamandra 2011a, forthcoming.
6. Translated into English as *Fragments of Memory: The Story of a Syrian Family* (2004), the story draws on Minna's impoverished childhood. American readers will note the novel's striking similarity to Frank McCourt's *Angela's Ashes* (1996).
7. See, for instance, cooke 2007, 102–106; Gugler 2011; Wedeen 1999, 116–117.
8. An *'oud* is an Arab stringed instrument similar to a lute.
9. For more on Syrian television drama, see Salamandra 1998, 2011a, 2011b, 2012, 2013a, 2013b, forthcoming.

FILMOGRAPHY OF NABIL MALEH

Crown of Thorns / La couronne d'épines / Iklil al-shawk. 1969. 45 minutes.
Napalm. 1970. 90 seconds.
Labor / L'accouchement / al-Makhad, part one of *Men under the Sun / Des hommes sous le soleil / Rijal taht al-shams*. 1970. 45 minutes.
The Leopard / Le léopard / al-Fahd. 1972. 115 minutes.
Jealous James Bond / James Bond le jaloux / Ghawar James Bond. 1974. 105 minutes.
Mr. Progressive / Le Progressiste / al-Sayyid al-taqaddumi. 1975. 110 minutes.
Rocks / Les rocs / Sakhr. 1977. 16 minutes.
Fragments / Fragments d'images / Baqaya suwar. 1980. 130 minutes. Documentary.
A Bedouin Day / Une journée bédouin. 1981. Revision released 1992. 45 minutes. Documentary.
Chronicle of a Dream / Histoire d'un rêve / Yawmiyat hilm. 1984. 110 minutes. Docudrama.

The Extras / Les figurants / al-Kumbars. 1993. Distributed in the United States by Arab
Film distribution. 100 minutes.

Situations / Situations / Halat. 1997. 450 minutes. Television serial.

Top Secret / Ultrasecret / Siri li-l-ghaya. 1999. Television serial.

Najla's Love Affairs / Les amours de Najla / Gharamiyat Najla. 2002. 90 minutes.

The Hunt Feast / La fête chasse. 2005. 105 minutes. Not yet released.

The Road to Damascus / Le chemin de Damas / 'A Sham 'A Sham. 2006. 78 minutes.
Documentary.

REFERENCES

Armbrust, Walter. 2000. "The Golden Age before the Golden Age: Commercial Egyptian Cinema Before the 1960s." In *Mass Mediations: New Approaches to Popular Culture in the Middle East and Beyond,* edited by Walter Armbrust, 292–327. Berkeley: University of California Press.

ArteEast. 2006. "The Extras," film festival web site, *The Road to Damascus: Discovering Syrian Cinema,* http://www.arteeast.org/cinemaeast/syrian-06/syrian06 -films/theextras.html. Accessed October 7, 2011 (the page has been removed from Arteeast web site).

Boëx, Cécile. 2011. "La contestation médiatisée par le monde de l'art en contexte autoritaire: L'expérience cinématographique en Syrie au sein de l'Organisme général du cinema, 1964–2010." PhD diss., Institut d'études politiques d'Aix-en-Provence, France.

cooke, miriam. 2007. *Dissident Syria: Making Oppositional Arts Official.* Durham: Duke University Press.

Della Ratta, Donatella. 2012. "Dramas of the Authoritarian State." *Middle East Report* (*MERIP*), Interventions, February, http://www.merip.org/mero/interventions /dramas-authoritarian-state.

———. 2013. "Dramas of the Authoritarian State: The Politics of Syrian TV Serials in the Pan Arab Market." PhD diss., Humanities Faculty, Copenhagen University.

Ginsberg, Terri, and Chris Lippard. 2010. *Historical Dictionary of Middle Eastern Cinema.* Lanham, MD: Scarecrow Press.

Gugler, Josef. 2011. "The Extras." In *Film in the Middle East: Creative Dissidence,* edited by Josef Gugler, 125–133. Austin: University of Texas Press.

Hatahet, Lilas. 2011. "Nabil Maleh: The Loneliness of the Long Distance Runner," *Variety Arabia,* June 9, http://varietyarabia.com/Docs.Viewer/eaeda7ca-6de5-4df4 -bd22-9561451bb81f/default.aspx. Accessed July 27, 2011 (this publication is no longer available online).

Joubin, Rebecca. 2013. "Syrian Drama and the Politics of Dignity." *Middle East Report* (*MERIP*) 268 (Fall): 27–29.

Maleh, Nabil. 2006. "Scenes from Life and Cinema." In *Insights into Syrian Cinema: Essays and Conversations with Contemporary Filmmakers,* edited by Rasha Salti,

84–94. New York: Arte East and Rattapallax Press. Originally published in Arabic in *Alam al-Fikri* 26 (1): 194–201.

McCourt, Frank. 1996. *Angela's Ashes*. New York: Simon and Schuster.

Mina, Hanna. 2004. *Fragments of Memory: The Story of a Syrian Family*. Translated by Olive Kenny and Lorne Kenny. Austin: Center for Middle Eastern Studies, University of Texas.

Salamandra, Christa. 1998. "Moustache Hairs Lost: Ramadan Television Serials and the Construction of Identity in Damascus, Syria." *Visual Anthropology* 10 (2–4): 227–246.

———. 2004. *A New Old Damascus: Authenticity and Distinction in Urban Syria*. Bloomington: Indiana University Press.

———. 2011a. "Spotlight on the Bashar al-Asad Era: The Television Drama Outpouring." *Middle East Critique* 20 (2): 157–167.

———. 2011b. "Arab Television Drama Production in the Satellite Era." In *Soap Operas and Telenovelas in the Digital Age: Global Industries, Hybrid Content, and New Audiences,* edited by Diana I. Rios and Mari Castaneda, 275–290. New York: Peter Lang.

———. 2012. "Prelude to an Uprising: Syrian Fictional Television and Socio-Political Critique." *Jadaliyya,* May, http://www.jadaliyya.com/pages/index/5578/prelude -to-an-uprising_syrian-fictional-television.

———. 2013a. "Arab Television Drama Production and the Islamic Public Sphere." In *Visual Culture in the Modern Middle East: Rhetoric of the Image,* edited by Christiane Gruber and Sune Haugbølle, 261–274. Bloomington: Indiana University Press.

———. 2013b. "Syrian Television Drama: A National Industry in a Pan-Arab Mediascape." In *National Broadcasting and State Policy in Arab Countries,* edited by Tourya Guaaybess, 83–95. Basingstoke: Palgrave Macmillan, 2013.

———. Forthcoming. "Syria's Drama Outpouring between Complicity and Critique." In *Syria from Reform to Revolt: Culture, Religion and Society,* edited by Christa Salamandra and Leif Stenberg. Syracuse: Syracuse University Press.

———. *Waiting for Light: Syrian Drama Production in the Satellite Era.* Unpublished book manuscript.

Salti, Rasha. 2006. "Critical Nationals: The Paradoxes of Syrian Cinema." In *Insights into Syrian Cinema: Essays and Conversations with Contemporary Filmmakers,* edited by Rasha Salti, 21–44. New York: Arte East and Rattapallax Press.

Wedeen, Lisa. 1999. *The Ambiguities of Domination: Politics, Rhetoric and Symbols in Contemporary Syria*. Chicago: University of Chicago Press.

———. 2013. "Ideology and Humor in Dark Times: Notes from Syria." *Critical Inquiry* 39 (Summer): 841–873.

Jocelyne Saab at the Vesoul International Film Festival of Asian Cinema 2012.

2

Jocelyne Saab

A LIFETIME JOURNEY IN SEARCH OF
FREEDOM AND BEAUTY
(LEBANON)

Dalia Said Mostafa

Jocelyne Saab is one of Lebanon's best-known filmmakers at home and abroad. In the context of Arab cinema, her cinematography is versatile, varied in style, and unique in outlook. Her first engagement with filmmaking was through the documentary genre, where she has produced over thirty films since 1973 (Hillauer 2005, 173). Like many Lebanese filmmakers of her generation, it was during the early years of the Lebanese civil war (1975–1990) that Saab's films took root. The context of war, ironically, made possible her contribution as a war reporter, journalist, photographer, and filmmaker. Saab has also produced feature films (which will be the focus of this chapter), and she has won many awards and prizes in both regional and international festivals.

Saab was born in 1948 in Beirut and studied economics in Paris. In the early part of her career, she worked as a journalist and, with the breakout of the civil war, became a war reporter. In 1975 she made her first long documentary, *Lebanon in the Tempest* (*Lubnan fil Dawwama*), which won the Arab Critics' Award. In 1981, she was the second unit director with Volker Schlöndorff's movie on the Lebanese civil war, *Circle of Deceit.* She produced her debut feature film, *A Suspended Life,* in 1984. The film was selected for the Director's Fortnight at the Cannes International Film Festival. In 1994, she made her second feature film *Once Upon a Time, Beirut,* a tribute to the memory of her city; and three years later, she shot in Vietnam a documentary film, *Lady from Saigon* (*La dame de Saigon*). Saab wrote the scripts of all her films except *A Suspended Life*, which was written by Gerard Brach. She co-produced many of her films with her company Balcon Production. Saab has also had photography and installation exhibitions in Dubai and Singapore. In 2010, she released her latest feature film, *What's Going On?* which she filmed in Beirut.[1]

In a 1994 interview Saab reminisced that she came from a bourgeois family and grew up in a "sheltered world between home, school, and a few close friends" (Hillauer 2005, 173). As she was growing up in a politically charged society such as Lebanon, the first thing that intrigued her was the plight of the Palestinians: "It was our reality—they were in the city, in the country, and Israel was just around the corner. When I went to Paris to study, I became interested in the Arab world. I wanted to know who I was" (ibid.). Saab adds that she belongs to a "generation that was educated in French schools. We didn't have contact with our origins. We were the generation that started looking for our roots to see why we lost them" (ibid.). It is not surprising, then, that Saab's feature films focus in essence on questions of identity formation and coming-of-age experiences. Her cinematic lens aims to explore the cultural roots of her characters, who are drawn from both the bourgeois and low-income classes. The filmmaker follows her characters in their journeys to gain knowledge about their Arab heritage and civilization and to carve an independent life for themselves. Thus, one major theme in her four features is the journey of self-discovery of the characters, particularly of the young women, to come to terms with a sense of belonging to the society they inhabit.

In the early 1970s when Saab ventured into the sphere of war reportage and documentary films, it was unconventional for an Arab woman to cross such male-dominated boundaries (Hillauer 2005, 174). Yet Saab was courageous enough to cover heated topics ranging from Muammar Gaddafi's politics (she interviewed him in 1973 in her documentary *Portrait of Qaddafi / Portrait de Khadafi*) to the 1973 October war, to Kurdistan Iraq, the conflict in the Sahara, the situation of the Palestinian refugees in Lebanon, the impact of the civil war on low-income sectors in Lebanon as well as on children, and the history of some of the southern Lebanese villages, in addition to a variety of topics related to the political dynamics of the Middle East. In the 1980s, Saab continued to film some important documentaries about Beirut, for example *Beirut My City* (*Beyrouth ma ville / Beirut Madinati,* 1982), which won a number of international prizes (ibid. 178), but she also traveled to Egypt and filmed four documentaries in a row in 1986: *The Architect of Luxor* (*Egypte: l'architecte de Louxor*), *The Ghosts of Alexandria* (*Egypte: les fantômes d'Alexandrie*), *The Cross of the Pharaohs* (*Egypte: la croix des pharaons*), and *The Love for God—Fundamentalism* (*Egypte: l'amour d'Allah—l'intégrisme*).[2]

The variety of issues and themes Saab has addressed in both her documentary and feature films points to a vibrant and unconventional filmmaker in style and outlook. As a result, she has triggered much debate and controversy throughout her journalistic and cinematic career. For example, Islamist Amal fighters tried to kidnap her once in 1983, and she was banned from entering Egypt for seven years and from entering Morocco for seventeen years after she released her documentary *The Sahara is not for Sale* (*Le Sahara n'est pas à vendre*, 1977), which focused on the Polisario movement (Saab 2011a). In Beirut during the war, Saab was not allowed to cross from the east to the west side where her family lived: "It was not only what I said, it was how I said it" (Hillauer 2005, 174). As a result, during the early part of her work in Lebanon in the 1970s, she felt quite isolated:

> Everybody was disturbed by what I was doing—and the more I worked, the more alone I felt. [. . .] I was living as a European and they were kidnapping foreign people more and more often. So I couldn't stay. I already lived in a mental or inner exile in Lebanon. Then came the physical exile to France. Physical exile was terrible because you have to imagine a new world. [. . .] You have to change, you can't go on living in a nostalgia (ibid. 174–175).

Moreover, like many Lebanese filmmakers, Saab has had to struggle to fund her films. She established her own production company, Balcon Production, but many of her films have been co-produced with foreign companies. Even with foreign funding, sometimes it was a challenge to cover all the costs. Saab had to borrow money from her assistants to survive, and the crew had to stay at her place to cut down the costs when shooting *A Suspended Life* (Saab in Khatib 2008, 38–39). Foreign funding also imposed constraints. The dialogue in her films *A Suspended Life* and *Once Upon a Time, Beirut* is in part in French rather than Arabic, "because it's an obligation from the National Fund for Cinema [in France] who funded the films: we can give you a lot of money if all the language is in French" (Saab in Khatib 2008, 40).

ON WOMEN AND CITIES

Jocelyne Saab remarks that when the civil war broke out in 1975, she took her camera and started shooting on the streets of Beirut. Within a decade, she had compiled a huge amount of visual material on the city. She says: "Sometimes I feel my eyes are filled with snapshots of those years" (Khoury 2011). When asked about how she made the move from documentary to feature films, she commented: "This is what I do, I make images. First, they were war images, and then I started to invent them, because when everything was destroyed in front of my eyes, I couldn't collect the real anymore. I had to reinvent everything. This is how I moved into fiction" (Saab 2009). In 1976 she produced her documentary *The Children of War* (*Les enfants de la guerre* / *Atfal al Harb*) on the children who survived the 1976 Phalanga militias massacre during the war in northern Beirut's quarantined area. Saab recounts that she woke one morning and "Hamra Street was covered with my photos on a magazine condemning me to death. J'ai eu très peur . . . mais j'ai continué (I was so scared . . . but I continued)."[3]

Jocelyne Saab is one among a number of Arab filmmakers who have paid close attention to the representation of city life in both her documentary and feature films. While "searching for beauty in the midst of boredom and destruction," she made three documentaries on Beirut: *Beirut, Never More* (1976); *Letter From Beirut* (1978); and *Beirut My City* (1982).[4] Later on, in her four feature films, Saab articulated her cinematic aesthetics with a focus on the relationship between the city (Beirut, Cairo) and the experiences of her characters (particularly the female characters), while depicting their search for freedom and beauty in the space of these cities.

Saab's three feature films in/on Beirut may be seen as a trilogy. They present the stories of her female characters as integral to Beirut's story over a period spanning close to thirty years: *A Suspended Life* is set in 1982 while the civil war was at its height, followed by *Once Upon a Time, Beirut* in 1994 after the end of the civil war, and lastly *What's Going On?* in 2010, fifteen years after her last feature in Beirut. In this way, each film captures a certain image of the city at a particular historical juncture by creating female protagonists who reflect the city's characteristics, as if each of them is looking in the mirror to see Beirut from her own perspective. Saab's cinematic "trademark" lies in how she interweaves the plight as well as the dreams and aspirations of the women in the films into the fabric of the city.

SAAB'S BEIRUT

In *A Suspended Life* (*Une vie suspendue* / *Ghazl al Banat*—2, 1984), we see West Beirut ravaged by war and destruction, leaving Samar (who is around the age of thirteen or fourteen) surrounded by extraordinary situations. Samar reappropriates Beirut's streets and alleys through endless walks, trying to make sense of everything and everyone that comes her way. She carves herself a space in the war-torn city when she comes across a massive abandoned pink house and finds in it countless scattered ornaments, as well as old pictures and neglected pieces of furniture. The place haunts her with its unfamiliar setting. It is as if she has come face to face with a treasure house of memories, of past times which she did not live. And she finds something to hold on to—an impossible relationship with the owner of the house, the artist Karim, who is about fifty.

The film is a coming-of-age narrative, a depiction of Samar's exploration of her sexuality as well as her social identity. Samar is originally from the South. After the breakout of the civil war, her family was forced to leave their village and move to Beirut. Samar's mother knows that her daughter is no longer a virgin, and she wants to restore "virginity" through an operation, so her daughter can get married. Samar does not share her mother's concern, but she accepts her wish and undergoes the operation. When she meets the rich and highly educated Karim, Samar is immediately aware of the social and cultural gap that separates their worlds. She tells Karim that the war could not be a bad thing— had it not been for the war, she would have never met him. She tells him about her father, about the resemblance she finds between him and Karim: they both talk to themselves frequently, and they are both artists (her father is a tile maker and builder). Karim replies that Samar's father is the real artist because he wants to build and beautify the city. Ironically, both these characters are killed in the war, while Samar, her mother, and her siblings survive.

In the last sequence of the film, Samar tells Karim that she is in love with him, and that he does not have to love her back. They climb the stairs of a deserted lighthouse to watch the moon and the stars. Karim asks Samar how old she is, and she replies: "I am four thousand or five thousand years old. I am a city. I am Beirut, holding an eraser in one hand and a chalk in the other hand. With the chalk, I write stories of children, and I create streets, and I build palaces; and with my other hand, I erase the children, and I erase the streets, and I erase the palaces."[5] Samar's experience of Beirut has integrated her story into the fabric of the city. Beirut is made and remade by her children, her men, and her women, like Samar. When Karim asks her what she would like to do when she grows up, she replies: "We might be dead by then, who knows?" Toward the end of the film, when Karim is suddenly shot dead by a sniper, Samar runs to the spot where he lies and stands by his body, waiting for the sniper to shoot her too. Samar, however, does not die. She is led by the neighborhood children to a beach where they carry on playing their games. Samar is still a child after all. The film ends with the children playing at the beautiful beach where we do not see any trace of the war, but it also subtly suggests how the lives and futures of these children are suspended like the life and future of Beirut. The war has created a permanent wound that might need a lifetime to heal.

In Saab's three features on Beirut, the war's long-term impact on the city and its inhabitants is reflected through various cinematic techniques and literary motifs and metaphors. In *A Suspended Life,* the violence of war as seen through Samar's eyes can alter lives and impede the future of the young generation. Saab remarks about this film: "My first feature film was inspired by the siege of Beirut in 1982. I encountered the internal destruction and so I wrote the story of this little girl who was of the war generation. It was a story of the violence I was fighting and of the tolerance I was advocating. We filmed it under bombings. Cinema is life and I wanted to make a film that reflected the reality around me" (Khatib 2008, xxi).

While Saab captures visually the fragmentation of the city space as a result of war in *A Suspended Life,* in *Once Upon a Time, Beirut* (*Il était une fois Beyrouth—histoire d'une star / Kan ya ma Kan, Beyrouth,* 1994), there is a shift in the filmmaker's perception of the city after the war had ended. Here, Saab attempts to reconstruct Beirut as a story in the historical memory since the early part of the twentieth century. The filmmaker follows the technique of a film-within-film narrative, interweaving footage from 1940s to 1980s French, American, British, and Arabic films that have portrayed Beirut in one way or another, linking them in perspective to her two female protagonists, Yasmine and Leila. In the film, the tales of these two young women are inextricably linked to Beirut's story, precisely as Samar's position and experience were embedded in the larger narrative of her city during the war. But while Samar's journey is primarily geared toward an exploration of her sexuality during a time of political turmoil, Yasmine and Leila's journey is directed toward an understanding of the history of Beirut, a city they were away from during the war years. In fact, it can be argued that Yasmine and Leila display characteristics of the young Saab herself, when she was reflecting on her roots, her bourgeois background, and her French education.

Once Upon a Time, Beirut was one of the first feature films to be made and released by a Lebanese filmmaker following the end of the civil war (Khatib 2007, 157). In it, Saab delves into the visual memory of Beirut throughout the larger part of the twentieth century by constructing the story of Yasmine and Leila, who come back to Beirut after the war. They are twenty years of age and have spent most of their lives away from Beirut (rather mentally than geographically, as Saab indicates, since the war generation is portrayed here as ignorant of the city's history as a result of the civil war).[6] They speak French more than they speak Arabic. Upon their "return" to Beirut, or rather their state of "awakening" to satisfy their desire to "know," they decide to visit Mr. Farouk, who is known to have a huge film archive. They were told that Farouk is "Beirut's living memory." Farouk's studio symbolizes a treasure house or a magical world that houses the city's artistic memory (in a metaphorical way, drawing a link to Karim's house of paintings in *A Suspended Life*). Yasmine and Leila start selecting the films they want to watch to learn about the history of Beirut, and Farouk tells them: "I'm going to show you Beirut, the city of love." As Samar learns at Karim's house about a past she had not lived in the city, Yasmine and Leila learn at Mr. Farouk's studio about the visual representation of the city in film, or about a Beirut they did not know. The two films complicate the relationship between the younger Lebanese generation and their city's history through focusing on these young women's journeys in search of knowledge about themselves as women, as well as about the "truth" of the nation's identity and their relation to the homeland, an endeavor Saab has pursued throughout her cinematic career—that is, to explore the roots of Lebanese and Arab civilization.

Once Upon a Time, Beirut is divided into several parts, thus creating multiple layers of meaning. Each part of the film is summarized by a revealing theme written on a title card, which appears before the action as in old silent movies. Each part is meant to show a facet of Beirut through the eyes of Yasmine and Leila. Thus, each segment is reinvented through the new interpretation of events provided by the two women. However, the events are narrated not in chronological order but in a fragmented manner, while creating a large collage of Beirut and how the two protagonists fit themselves within its scheme. As Khatib (2007, 158–159) puts it, Saab makes the two women "jump across time . . . Her deliberate composition of a fractured sense of time, where history is not reconstructed chronologically, but almost haphazardly, acts as a hint at the complex identity of Beirut and the intersection of representations across time and space."

The film is laden with footage from a wide array of movies that have shown Beirut in many different ways throughout the years. One of the revealing scenes toward the end of the film is when Yasmine and Leila drag Chouchou's donkey through the streets of Beirut back to Farouk's studio, as Chouchou tells them that his donkey has swallowed a history book.[7] The two protagonists refer to the donkey as "the history teacher," commenting, "Even the donkey has learned the lesson." The film ends with footage from an old French film starring Omar Sharif, where he ridicules a group of sheikhs who are trying to explain to their students the meaning of "truth." Sharif makes fun of their efforts, while declaring: "Truth is a monkey. It can pull all sorts of faces."

Saab brings together fragments of pictures and stories and shows Leila and Yasmine engaging with a history of the visual imagination of Beirut, and commenting on or criticizing what they see and hear. A large mosaic picture of Beirut emerges, with a variety of colors, viewpoints, and motifs. Saab makes this important observation while summing up the story behind her film:

> For a long time, Beirut was the West's Oriental "favorite." It had no rival in the Near East. It was a city for people from all cultures, a place of business, pleasure, and drama, but also a place of myths. For a long time, it basked in this image, not overtly bothered by certain realities. But, although the myths associated with Beirut did so much over the years to enhance its wealth and fame, they were also largely responsible for its downfall. The idea here is to review these great myths, which for forty years now have contributed to shaping the image of Beirut, to look into the city's past and find the reasons it became a star. And finally, to show the real-life rifts, the heartbreak, and decline (Hillauer 2005, 180).

As Leila Fawaz (1997, 253) remarked, "Jocelyne Saab's *Once Upon a Time, Beirut* projects with subtlety both the shallowness and beauty of pre-war Lebanon, but it also has a note of optimism missing from *A Suspended Life,* filmed during the war." This note of optimism is seen through the lens of Yasmine and Leila when they leave Mr. Farouk's studio at the end of the film determined to carry on the search for their country's lost memories and heritage.[8]

With her latest film *What's Going On?* (*Shou 'amm Beyseer?* 2010), Saab offers viewers an altogether different perspective on Beirut. Here, stories of Beirut and its lovers are all coming out of a huge book of poetry. Saab was inspired to make the film when UNESCO nominated Beirut the Book Capital of the Year, and the Lebanese Ministry of Culture appointed her as "cinematic ambassador." In the film we do not see any traces of the trauma associated with the war, but we see Beirut through a refreshing lens: a great, historic city, a big house of mythology, love, and poetry. It is an idealized image of the city and can be seen as a poetic "love letter" from the filmmaker to her city.

In an interview on Lebanese TV after the release of the film in Beirut, Saab explained that the film follows a "surrealist" cinematic approach, as she wanted to divert from the conventions of storytelling and to represent Beirut this time as a popular tale such as may be found in *One Thousand and One Nights.*[9] She added that she was deeply influenced by classical Arabic poetry in this film,

Samar and Karim at his house among his paintings in *A Suspended Life*.

Dunia dancing, with Cairo in the background, in the final scene of *Dunia*.

and hence she framed the story around Jalal—a writer/dressmaker—who mixes these two professions in creating his characters. Jalal the writer aims to teach one of his characters, Nasri, how to search for the woman's soul in order to reach the essence of love of Woman. Jalal creates his characters as a dressmaker creates patterns, and he "dresses up" each of his characters with certain features as if he is making "types" out of them.

Saab also mentioned that her intention was to show a Beirut that the Lebanese do not see any more in this age of globalization, where everything looks the same. She wanted to focus on the beautiful areas of Beirut as immersed in history, poetry, and culture. For example, she shows Burj al Murr (which is associated in the collective memory with the division of Beirut into two zones during the war) in a new light by representing it as "Souk 'Ukaz," a great book market where people come from all over the world to read books and exchange ideas.[10]

Each of the women whom Nasri meets teaches him something about the woman's soul: there is the goddess Lilith, who is descended from old mythology, and who tells Nasri about the value of equality between men and women: "I am Lilith, woman of Destiny. Equal creature and equal bride." The role is played by the well-known Lebanese poet Joumana Haddad, who wrote the film's script together with Saab. Then there is the woman who loves farming and plants, and lives surrounded by a big garden that she has grown herself. The heart of the third is in pain; she is afraid they might change her heart so she would not be able to fall in love again. The role is played by Kholoud, who is of mixed African and Lebanese descent, conveying Saab's comments about how the Lebanese have mixed with other cultures and civilizations throughout their history.[11] It is Kholoud whom Nasri falls in love with, and whose pure heart the writer/dressmaker Jalal is envious of and tries to steal, emphasizing the element of fantasy in the film. Finally, there is the free woman, the sex worker, who was only thirteen when she was married off to a sixty-five-year-old husband. She tells of divorcing her husband after many years of living together because he constantly reminded her of the war and its atrocities. Rather than stay with him, chained to the traumatic past, she wanted to move forward.

Saab has commented that in essence all the women in the film constitute one Woman, or they are all a manifestation of one particular woman whose heart is taken outside of her.[12] Her heart is bleeding and hurt. This woman with her big heart is the City. Thus, the writer creates the young man's character (Nasri) in relation to Woman/City, which he does not know and seeks to explore. Nasri is situated in relation to Woman, who symbolizes the renewal of life. Saab further explained that the sex worker is the one emancipated woman in the film, because she has decided to change her destiny. Similar to her city Beirut, she is exhausted and wants to be liberated from all forms of exploitation. She is the one who wears a gun as a necklace—the gun has lost its significance as a weapon in post-war Beirut and has become a mere accessory. The film calls upon the viewer's imagination; it is a return to the "book" and to thinking about identity. It is a recreation of a "dull" city as something beautiful and exciting: "The city has become dull. I'm the one who has filmed the city as beautiful, the beauty which no one is able to see anymore," according to Saab. There needs to be imagination when trying to reconstruct a city and an identity. Therefore, as Saab goes on to say, the film needs to be viewed on the big screen in order for the audience to realize its aesthetics.

Saab uses minimal dialogue, emphasizing how music communicates meaning and how the inner voices of the characters mix with the rhythm of music. For example, Saab uses the song "Sabali" (Patience) by the famous Mali band Amadou and Mariam, when Kholoud fights for her love. The song conveys the value of patience, suggesting, according to Saab, that if you learn to be patient, you will learn how to love and find true love.[13] The choice of film conveys the value of world civilizations coming together through poetry, music, and culture. Saab also remarked that perhaps one of the most significant lines of dialogue between Nasri and Kholoud is when he says to her, "I want to make love to you," and she answers, "Not before you bring back to me the gardens of the city."[14] Finally, it is Lilith, the goddess of poetry, who descends upon the city shrouding it in verse, rather than war and destruction.

In *What's Going On?* Saab tries to forge a new identity for Beirut as a city of love and poetry, deeply rooted in mythology and history. It is a very different representation from what we have seen in her two previous films on Beirut. It is as if Saab has finally reached an image of the city that she can make peace with. Perhaps Nasri summarizes to an extent Saab's endeavor in this film when he says: "To learn is to remember, and in order to remember something you need to have learned it beforehand."

DUNIA'S WORLD . . . DUNIA'S CAIRO

In 2005, while living between Cairo and Paris, Saab produced her film *Dunia: Kiss Me Not on the Eyes (Dunia: Balach Tboussni fi 'Aynaya)*. The film was selected in the world competition at the Sundance International Film Festival and was the opening feature at the Singapore International Film Festival in

2006 (Hillauer 2005, 173). The very title of the film suggests that love is a central theme. "Kiss Me Not on the Eyes" (*Dunia: Balach Tboussni fi 'Aynaya*) is a famous song by the late Egyptian singer and composer Mohammad 'Abdel Wahab, who was known for his passionate love songs. It did not come as a surprise to find Saab embarking on a feature film set in Cairo with *Dunia*. Already in *A Suspended Life* and *Once Upon a Time, Beirut,* there was a notable influence of Egyptian cinema on the language, humor, and style of the characters, who imitate Egyptian actors in the way they talk and act. Also, in *Once Upon a Time, Beirut* there were numerous references to Egyptian films shot in Lebanon before the war.

In *Dunia,* however, Saab addresses the role and position of her female protagonists along new lines of interpretation. *Dunia,* the Arabic word for *life* or *world,* is the name of the main protagonist, played by the well-known Egyptian actress Hanan Turk. Dunia's story is intertwined with the everyday events of the big city. The camera roams around Cairo, following Dunia and her friends in the streets and alleys, inside their small flats and in the places where they meet for entertainment. As Saab has commented, "From the first shot of the film, you feel as if you have been 'thrown' into Cairo, into its markets, and into its *dunia* (world)" (Bakhat 2006; my translation). We follow the stories of these women through their intimate conversations while driving around the city.

With *Dunia,* Saab confronted the issue of female genital mutilation in Egypt. From the first scenes of the film, there is a particular emphasis on Dunia's feelings about her body. She was subjected to circumcision as a child. The film interweaves the feelings of detachment felt by the victims of such a practice with the potential to redefine one's relationship to the body and sexual identity through love and art. Dunia's relationship with her body is rather ambivalent, and she is fascinated by the theme of pleasure and sexual desire in classical Arabic poetry, which becomes the subject of her master's thesis. The film portrays Dunia's struggle to come to terms with her bodily desires, sensations, and movements through dance, through the memory of her late mother, who was a famous belly dancer, as well as through music, poetry, and lovemaking. Professor Bechir teaches her "not to be afraid of words," while her dance instructor teaches her "not to be afraid of her body."

For raising such a taboo issue as female genital mutilation, the film was harshly attacked in Egypt. In a 2005 interview, Saab details the problems she had encountered with the Egyptian censors (Hillauer 2005, 181–182), which turned into a "battle" between the filmmaker and the Egyptian authorities. The film was finally released in Egyptian cinemas after Saab appealed to then Egyptian president Hosni Mubarak. However, during the press conference following its screening at the Cairo International Film Festival in 2005, Saab and Hanan Turk were subjected to ruthless criticism (Hassan 2005; El Sirgany 2005). An article in the Egyptian press called for Saab to be put to death.[15] Saab has commented that many journalists saw *Dunia* exclusively in terms of the issue of female circumcision, but that the film essentially portrays a love story. Saab says: "The drama is built from within the psychology of these young circumcised women . . . it is a disturbed sexuality. The whole movie is a projection of what we can be because it shows an image of a young woman who chose herself, and who could be free. This is what they didn't tolerate also in the movie" (Saab 2009).

In the film, the characters try to reshape both the public and private spaces they interact with through their continuous search for various means of free expression. In a huge metropolis like Cairo, how can women and men still be subjected to oppressive traditions and restrictions imposed by the family, society, or the state? What are their means to break free? Dunia's answer is to be able to define her bodily and sexual desires and to express herself through dance. The film portrays the relationship between the characters as a product of their specific urban context. The viewer is encouraged to consider and think about the relationship between the protagonists and how they perceive their physical and social position in the city. The film ends with a dream-like scene of Dunia dancing—perhaps her dance of liberation—on a plateau with a panoramic view of the city behind her, after she and Bechir have fallen in love, even though she is still married to Mamdouh. As Gaul (2011) observes about Dunia's last dance scene, "It is not until the final scene that we see Dunia (all of Dunia) dancing uninterrupted, not for a competition or for a lover, but for herself, with Cairo in the background. The film achieves its resolution not with a relationship or on a stage, but in a performance through which Dunia finally embodies the ideas she has struggled with, unties her mother's scarf from her wrist, and sends it into the wind." Dunia becomes a symbol of her mother city, Cairo. Her quest for independence and freedom as a young woman living on her own in a huge metropolis points to the possibilities that can be found in this city. The city changes when its inhabitants seek to change it, and when their social and economic relations transform.[16] As Lilith immerses Beirut in love and poetry, so Dunia embraces Cairo with her dance and sensuality.

CHANGE AND CONTINUITY IN SAAB'S WORK

Jocelyne Saab has produced a wide range of cinematic and artistic output oscillating between the documentary genre, fiction, photography, and art installations. She has created a vast repertoire of documentary films about politics, society, and culture in the Arab world. In her four feature films, she has established two important lines of critical inquiry: an exploration of womanhood in Arab societies, which remains an enduring theme in Arab cinema; and a reinvention of the intimate relationships we form with the cities we live in. Saab features women from a younger generation in pursuit of freedom from taboos and social restrictions. They pursue new interpretations of life; they are creative and inventive; they are attached to their history and heritage. These young women discover a new way of living because they experience new challenges in the present. While looking into the ways they shape their societies, Saab captures the process of these women maturing. Saab's feature films have enriched the representation of the intricate relationship between woman and city in Arab cinema. Her oeuvre points to a process of maturity in perspective and outlook, a wide array of cinematic stylistics, and a potential continuity in addressing unconventional issues.

NOTES

1. Biographical information on Saab's life and films are drawn from three main sources: her website: http://www.jocelynesaab.com (accessed on 10 September 2014); Rebecca Hillauer, *Encyclopedia of Arab Women Filmmakers,* trans. by Allison Brown et al. (Cairo: American University in Cairo Press, 2005, 173–182); and several email correspondences between the author and Jocelyne Saab in July 2011.

2. For a filmography of Saab's documentary and feature films up to 2005, see Hillauer (2005, 177–178).

3. Saab, correspondence with the author, July 2011.

4. Saab, correspondence with the author, July 2011.

5. All quotations from Saab's films are my translation from the Arabic.

6. Saab, correspondence with the author, July 2011.

7. Chouchou is an iconic Lebanese actor famous for his satiric sitcoms. His real name was Hassan 'Alaa el Din. In *Once Upon a Time, Beirut,* it is Chouchou's son, Khodr, who plays his father's character.

8. See also Khatib (2008, 59–60).

9. Saab, interview on Lebanese TV. At http://www.youtube.com/watch?v=Dwt4110LVnk (accessed on June 20, 2011; no longer accessible online).

10. Ibid.

11. Ibid.

12. Saab, correspondence with the author, July 2011.

13. Saab, interview on Lebanese TV.

14. Ibid.

15. In an interview with Cynthia Karena (2007), Saab told of the major obstacles she had to overcome to produce *Dunia* in Egypt and of the death threat that ensued.

16. We have seen concrete manifestations of these transformations on a mass scale since the Egyptian revolution began on January 25, 2011, particularly when we consider the leading role that women have played throughout the revolutionary process and onward.

FILMOGRAPHY OF JOCELYNE SAAB

This list is limited to the films by Saab discussed in this chapter. For a more comprehensive filmography up to 2005, see Hillauer, 2005, 177–178.

Portrait of Qaddafi / Portrait de Khadafi. 1973. 52 minutes. Documentary.

Lebanon in the Tempest / Lubnan fil Dawwama. 1975. 75 minutes. Documentary.

The Children of War / Les enfants de la guerre / Atfal al Harb. 1976. 10 minutes. Documentary.

Beirut, Never More. 1976. Documentary.

The Sahara is Not for Sale / Le Sahara n'est pas à vendre. 1977. 90 minutes. Documentary.

Letter From Beirut. 1978. Documentary.

Beirut My City / Beyrouth ma ville / Beirut Madinati. 1982. 35 minutes. Documentary.

A Suspended Life / Une vie suspendue / Ghazl al Banat—2. 1984. Distributed in the United States by Arab Film Distribution. 90 minutes.

Egypt: The Architect of Luxor / Egypte: l'architecte de Louxor. 1986. 20 minutes. Documentary.

Egypt: The Ghosts of Alexandria / Egypte: les fantômes d'Alexandrie. 1986. 17 minutes. Documentary.

Egypt: The Cross of the Pharaohs / Egypte: la croix des pharaons. 1986. 20 minutes. Documentary.

Egypt: The Love for God—Fundamentalism / Egypte: l'amour d'Allah—l'intégrisme. 1986. 17 minutes. Documentary.

Once Upon a Time, Beirut / Il était une fois Beyrouth—histoire d'une star / Kan ya ma Kan, Beyrouth. 1994. Distributed in the United States by Arab Film Distribution. 104 minutes.

Lady of Saigon / La dame de Saigon. 1997. 60 minutes. Documentary.

Dunia: Kiss Me Not on the Eyes / Balach Tboussni fi 'Aynaya. 2005. Distributed in the United States by Alexander Street Press. 108 minutes.

What's Going On? / Shou 'amm Beyseer? 2010. 80. minutes.

REFERENCES

Bakhat, Islah. 2006. "*Dunia* Jocelyne Saab Tahuttu al Rihal fi Freiburg" [*Dunia* Jocelyne Saab arrives in Freiburg]. *Swissinfo*, March 18, 2006. Available at http://www.swissinfo.ch/ara/detail/content.html?cid=5073524. Accessed on September 10, 2014.

El Sirgany, Sarah. 2005. "*Dunia*: A World of Controversy Wells Up in Cairo." *The Daily Star*, December 8, 2005. Available at http://www.dailystar.com.lb/Culture/Arts

/Dec/08/Dunia-a-world-of-controversy-wells-up-in-Cairo.ashx#axzz1QUsDNxBs. Accessed on September 10, 2014.

Fawaz, Leila. 1997. Film Reviews. *The American Historical Review* 102 (1) (February 1997): 252–253.

Gaul, Anny. 2011. "From Dance to Transcendence." *Jadaliyya*, June 13, 2011. Available at http://www.jadaliyya.com/pages/index/1808/from-dance-to-transcendence. Accessed on September 10, 2014.

Hassan, Jameel. 2005. "Nadwat Film *Dunia* lil Mukhrija al Lubnaniyya Jocelyne Saab" [Seminar on the film *Dunia* by the Lebanese director Jocelyne Saab]. *Al-'Asefa*, December 10, 2005. Available at http://www.a13asefah.com/forum/index.php ?showtopic=3563. Accessed on June 12, 2011.

Hillauer, Rebecca. 2005. *Encyclopedia of Arab Women Filmmakers*. Translated by Brown, Allison, et al. Cairo: American University in Cairo Press.

Karena, Cynthia. 2007. "Grace and Ecstasy: An Interview with Jocelyn Saab." *Metro Magazine: Media and Education Magazine* 152 (April): 78–81.

Khatib, Lina. 2007. *Kan ya ma Kan Beirut* (*Once Upon a Time, Beirut*). In *The Cinema of North Africa and the Middle East,* edited by Gönül Dönmez-Colin, 157–166. London: Wallflower Press, 2007.

———. 2008. *Lebanese Cinema: Imagining the Civil War and Beyond*. London: I. B. Tauris.

Khoury, Sanaa. 2011. "Jocelyne Saab: Sinimai'yyat al Hobb wa Beyrouth al Zaman al Harib" [Jocelyne Saab: Filmmaker of Love and the Fugitive Times of Beirut]. *Al Akhbar*, February 11, 2011. Available at http://www.al-akhbar.com/node/4224. Accessed on September 10, 2014.

Mostafa, Dalia S. 2009. "Cinematic Representations of the Changing Gender Relations in Today's Cairo." *Arab Studies Quarterly* 31 (3) (June): 1–20.

Saab, Jocelyne. 2009. Jocelyne Saab, *Dunia* Q&A. Available at http://www.youtube .com/watch?v=gmN5Ou9fCzs. Accessed on September 10, 2014.

Michel Khleifi at the Dubai International Film Festival 2009.

3

Michel Khleifi

FILMMAKER OF MEMORY
(PALESTINE)

Tim Kennedy

From his first film, *Fertile Memory* (*La mémoire fertile* / *Al-Dhakira al-Khisba,* 1980), Michel Khleifi displays the narrative-documentary style that he goes on to develop to such great effect. He also announces some of the major themes that permeate his later work: the centrality of the land to Palestinian identity; the preservation of collective memory and culture; the difficulty of telling the history of the nation; the common humanity of Arabs and Jews; the trauma of defeat, displacement, and exile; and his critique of the weakness and paralysis of what he considers to be an archaic Arab society.

Stylistically his films subtly mix reality and fiction—*Fertile Memory* and the shorter *Ma'loul Celebrates Its Destruction* (*Ma'loul fête sa destruction,* 1984) fashion fictional spaces from fragments of the political reality of defeat and disorder; the feature *Wedding in Galilee* (*Noce en Galilée* / *Urs al-Jalil,* 1987) steers a fictional narrative through the tensions of an incipient uprising against the reality of military occupation; and the formally innovative *Canticle of the Stones* (*Le cantique des pierres* / *Nashid al-Hajjar,* 1990), the dreamlike *Tale of the Three Jewels* (*Le conte des trois diamants* / *Hikayatul jawahiri thalath,* 1994), and his exploration of memory, *Zindeeq* (2009), create an often uncomfortable tension between fiction, myth, and the actuality of oppression and active resistance.

Though Khleifi is not unique in this respect, his films employ objects—photographs, graves, ruins—and evoke the different senses—sound, smell, touch, and color—to great effect as subjective markers of memory. His camerawork creates a sense of unified space out of the fragmentary Palestinian environment, and he uses the physical terrain not just as spectacle or as a backdrop but as a central protagonist in the Palestinian narrative: a narrative in which love of the land is local and personal.

But no discussion of Khleifi's work can ignore the daunting context of making films about Palestine: the difficulty of obtaining what needs to be international funding for topics not well understood outside the Middle East; the fight against unrelenting anti-Palestinian propaganda; the lack of support in the Arab world; the negligible distribution channels in Palestine and the Middle East; the obstruction of distribution in the West; the lack of technical expertise and training in cinema in Palestine; the distancing effect of his own exile; and, above all, the physical difficulties of filming in constantly changing circumstances of violence, curfews, travel restrictions, and political interference.[1] Though he has always been able to operate with minimal resources, making the films he has wanted has been a continual struggle.[2]

Born in Nazareth in 1950, Khleifi worked as a car mechanic for some years before leaving Palestine in 1970 with the intention of moving to Germany to train with Volkswagen.[3] On the way, he visited a cousin in Belgium who encouraged him to stay. Already very interested in the arts, Khleifi discovered that he could join the Institut National Supérieur des Arts du Spectacle (INSAS) in Brussels in the theater and television section without the baccalaureate. However, he needed to study French. A year or so later, he was admitted to the degree course. He graduated in 1975 with a thesis on forms of cultural expression in Palestine. From there, he joined the Belgian state television company and first returned to Palestine in 1978 to work on a series of more or less conventional documentaries about the Occupied Territories.

Looking back, he elaborates that he was "convinced . . . that culture is the most important commodity for [him] and for every Arab" and that "education is the essential element in [the] struggle and the most significant basis for change."[4] This may be a slight gloss on an unformed early idealism; nonetheless, a preoccupation with the dual struggle of Palestinians, not only against occupation and denial of their history and culture but also against the constrictions of traditional social structures, has been central to his filmmaking career.

LAND AND MEMORY

His initial experiences of filming in Palestine drove Khleifi to try to find a different form of cinematic representation. He claims that the resulting film, *Fertile Memory*, was "for—and not about—the women of Palestine . . . a film for Palestine" (Khleifi 2006, 49). For almost the first time ordinary people, two women in this case, were to be heard and the banalities of their everyday lives uncovered. That he was able to imbue these banalities with significance is evidenced by the film's success at a number of film festivals and the early international critical attention it achieved.[5]

Khleifi's stylistic explorations at this point include his discreet opening up of a space in which the women are able freely to express their personalities. Not usually revealed in Arab cinema, this is an inner space of the home, which an ambiguous conclusion suggests is an essentially feminine vision of resistance. Yet, by alternating between the two women's stories, comparing their responses to events—one active the other passive—Khleifi expands this to a unified political space that links the personal and the national.[6]

Khleifi released his second film, *Ma'loul Celebrates Its Destruction,* in 1984/5. *Ma'loul,* a village near Nazareth, was cleared and virtually destroyed in 1948. On its site, the Jewish National Fund created a forest of remembrance to mark the end of British rule and the creation of the state of Israel. Former Palestinian villagers are allowed to visit the site once a year on Israeli "Independence Day," and many families take this opportunity to picnic in the ruins.

The film mixes sequences of the displaced villagers searching the ruined buildings for their former homes with scenes where a group of refugees discuss a mural depicting the village as it was nearly forty years earlier. Both groups revisit the village as a grave and recount its frozen image as if tracing out the profile of a lost loved one. They cannot mourn in a normal way: the very personal loss of home is inextricably linked to the larger and more profound loss of homeland. The fact that their "loved one" still lives yet is unattainable induces a deep and apparently irresolvable melancholia.[7]

Khleifi's innovations here are to explore the uncertainty and unreliability of memory—the former villagers, retracing their steps, cannot quite be sure of their discoveries; the refugees argue over where a particular home should be on the mural—and to relate individual memories to the collective memory. He not only affirms Palestinian presence on the land with his elegiac evocation of the past, but, for the first time in Palestinian film, he also exposes the stultifying effect on memory and on action induced by the trauma of defeat and occupation.

REPRESENTING PALESTINIANS

Until the late 1970s virtually the sole cinematic representation of a Palestinian narrative were the films produced under the auspices of the PLO.[8] Though these did not reach a wide audience in either the Arab world or the West, they achieved an almost mythical status for many Palestinians and were instrumental in refuting Israel's denial of Palestinian identity. However, by perpetuating nostalgic images of an idyllic past life before 1948, blaming defeat on others, and portraying failure as triumph, they avoided any critique of the shortcomings of Palestinian society. At the same time, Western and Israeli cinema continued to pour out overwhelmingly negative images of Palestinians and Arabs.[9] It was not until Israel invaded Lebanon in 1982 that media coverage began "to halt if not to reverse the process of stereotyping and dehumanizing the Arabs" by "personalizing and humanizing the victims" (Ghareeb 1983, 182).

The importance of Khleifi's first two films is that they represent a significant breakthrough in Palestinian filmmaking. Khleifi had been searching for a new way of representing Palestinians, one that focused on individual lives and exposed the injustices of their situation. In contrast to ubiquitous images of Palestinians as violent terrorists, he argues, "We had to provide the world with another way of talking about us" (2006, 46). But he also insisted on showing different facets of Palestinian society and its many flaws and faults. Thus, in his next three films, as he attempts to explore the traumatic effects of defeat, he argues for the necessity of accepting responsibility for that defeat. He lays bare the stifling effect of traditional patriarchal power structures on women and the younger generation. And he investigates different forms of resistance to oppression, including the preservation of memory and culture.

CONFLICT AND COOPERATION

Despite his early success with *Fertile Memory,* and though his next film was set to be the first feature ever made by a Palestinian inside historical Palestine, Khleifi encountered major funding difficulties that delayed production until 1986/7. Ultimately, *Wedding in Galilee* has become Khleifi's most respected film to date, winning many awards and widespread critical approval and academic attention.[10] It has achieved significant theatrical, video, and DVD distribution as well as frequent showings at international film festivals.

The film revolves around the fictional story of a village in Galilee under curfew imposed by the Israeli military. The mayor (*mukhtar*) is forced to seek permission from the governor for his son, Adel, to be married in a ceremony that tradition demands would last well into the night. The Israeli governor reluctantly agrees on condition that he and his staff are invited, seeing this as an opportunity to gain intelligence on the unrest in the area. At one level, the film proceeds as a brilliant "portrait of a people, a celebration of their memories" where the village is a "storehouse of tradition" (Rosen 1988, 7). But Khleifi's aim is far more complex: examining power structures both within the community and between Palestinians and Israelis, and revealing their inherent tensions.

On returning to the village, the mukhtar is quickly established as master of his household through Khleifi's subtle geometrical design of circling figures and camera movements. As he enters the family courtyard, Adel and his daughter Sumaya and youngest son Hassan are drawn inexorably and perhaps unwillingly into his visual field. The camera slowly tracks forward with him and circles as he greets his wife, Umm Adel, and family, enfolding them all. This circular motif is repeated in the unhurried circling shot that follows Umm Adel as she supervises the preparation by neighboring women of food for the wedding. Her connection to each of them accentuates the communal nature of their activities. Neighbors deliver gifts for the family, accompanied by rhythmic singing and circular dancing of the *dabke*. Then an intricate sequence begins, showing the ritual washing of bride and groom for the wedding intercut with inserts of an old woman making bread. Alternating between the two scenes of preparation of the bride and groom, the pace quickens in anticipation of their union.

These sequences, with their elaborating symbols of food preparation, marriage, and fertility, imply unity, regeneration, and permanence in the Palestinian community. But this is gradually subverted as tensions within the family and village are exposed: the mukhtar's brother refuses to attend the wedding, seeing the Israeli presence as a humiliation. A group of young men, led by the fiery Ziad, reject political compromise with the Israeli authorities and make plans to attack the Israelis. Sumaya disdains tradition, refuses to be subservient to the male villagers, and mocks the power of her father. In this way, Khleifi explores the struggle between modernity and traditional power relationships. On the one hand he acknowledges the important role of tradition in sustaining national identity, on the other he maintains that it holds back development of the nation. His metaphorical circles may be interpreted as cultural boundaries, defining who is included and who excluded, but they also create an enclosure signifying the binding (and stifling) force of tradition and the family. Sumaya's unsettling, uncontrollable energy evoked by her direct and linear movements always threatens to break out of the confines imposed by these circles.

Thus, *Wedding in Galilee* challenges traditional ideas of a unified patriarchal society—the mukhtar's power in the village and family is shown to be limited. And masculinity itself is questioned: the mukhtar has had to allow the Israelis to enter—or penetrate—the village, as a result of which Adel is unable to consummate the marriage; and Ziad's plot against their presence peters out in farce. In contrast, Sumaya playfully assumes authority by trying on her father's headdress, and the bride, Samia, takes over the male role when faced with her husband's impotence. Where *Fertile Memory* disclosed the innate strength of women in Palestinian society, here Khleifi seems to argue that a shift has taken place in the locus of power from male to female. He thus affirms Shohat's assertion that in women's central but difficult position in nation building, they frequently have to assume both male and female identities (Shohat and Stam 1994, 277–278).

Yet Khleifi is also responsible for perpetuating the common stereotypical idea of the nation as female: idealized as virgin, as mother, and as the beloved. And he creates differently sexualized spaces in *Wedding in Galilee:* the exterior, masculine world of political conflict in which all is noise, action, and movement; the transitional world of the wedding couple in which sexual tension drains color and sound and leaves the pair in a sterile, white setting; and the mysterious, warmly colored interior world of the women's quarter. Over the course of the film, Khleifi cuts between the action in these strikingly contrasting spaces, exploring the different senses (sound, smell, touch, and color) for their male and female attributes.

Khleifi argues that, far from suggesting that male and female worlds are, or should be, intrinsically separate, he is exploring the dialectic between strength and weakness. For him, the failure of traditional male-dominated Arab society is due to its rigid and archaic structures and its disregard for women's rights.[11] As in *Fertile Memory,* he implies that the feminine side of Arab society is much stronger and more purposeful than the masculine, and he claims that he opens up a political space in which women are seen to contribute significantly to the expression of national identity. In general, I agree that these justifications are substantiated throughout Khleifi's work.

Wedding in Galilee also initiates another shift in rhetoric: now it is the Israelis who are shown to be outsiders in Palestine. The grandfather mockingly places the Israeli presence in the context of previous transitory colonial occupations by the Turkish and British; soldiers are left speechless in the village; and Khleifi challenges Israeli claims to the land. Whereas the soldiers travel in jeeps, camouflaged by their dark glasses and uniforms, seemingly unconcerned with land or landscape, the villagers display a profound bond with the land.

Despite conjuring rising tensions between the villagers and soldiers, Khleifi displays optimism at this point about coexistence between the two communities if only the military presence were to be removed. Sumaya provocatively tells one of the soldiers, "You will have to take off your uniform if you want to dance." Another, female, soldier who faints is swept off by the village women to their quarters, where in a mysterious, transformational sequence her uniform is removed and she is dressed in soft Arab clothes. And the mukhtar, cooperating with the soldiers, rescues his prize mare from a minefield, gaining their respect in the process. Khleifi's explanation is that he "wanted to have a go at the Manichean rigidity" on both sides of the Arab–Israeli divide and to show that cooperation was possible (2006, 50). Even so, the film concludes in uncertainty as the villagers signal an uprising against military rule by contemptuously throwing gifts into the path of the departing Israeli governor and his soldiers. Released in 1987, this ending prefigures the first Palestinian uprising or Intifada. It also anticipates a new responsibility for the young as they are precipitated into the heart of the conflict with Israel.[12]

Stylistically, *Wedding in Galilee* represented a significant breakthrough in Palestinian film. The fluid camerawork, the calculated rise in suspense in the different plot lines, and the merging of fiction and realism showed the world a different face of Palestine and the Palestinians. The film's technical sophistication and beauty raised hopes that the struggle for freedom from oppression could be advanced through cultural exposure.

LOSS AND DISPLACEMENT

Under normal circumstances the success of *Wedding in Galilee* would have been expected to open up new opportunities for Khleifi. However, the coincidence of its release with the onset of the Intifada altered the context entirely. Filmmaking in the region generally became extremely difficult as a result of the disruption and, though international media attention was at last drawn to the area, at best its coverage of events was superficial and reductive.[13] Khleifi, whose dual Israeli-Belgian citizenship enabled him to travel to Palestine, felt it was imperative to find a better way to narrate the suffering of the Palestinians, "above all, children who were dying under the army's bullets" (2006, 53).

He wrote the scenario for a film about an unnamed Woman who returns from exile to research the concept of sacrifice, especially as it applied to the deaths of such children. In Jerusalem she meets a former lover, a writer recently released from prison. *Canticle of the Stones,* released in 1989/90, once again interweaves different threads: this time poetic staged scenes between the Man and Woman with documentary sequences and interviews. Though the main concern of the film is the suffering of the Palestinian people under Israeli repression, the form that Khleifi chose—a "poetic, impressionistic" portrait—also supports reiteration of many of the themes that run through his work.

The use of formal Arabic for the continuing, intermittent dialogue between the lovers makes the text highly "accented," in Naficy's terms, emphasizing both protagonists' liminal position in this society.[14] And, as Alexander perceptively points out, this "mirrors a dialogue Khleifi himself conducts with Palestinian society as both a native of Palestine and an exile returning to his homeland" (2002, 170–171). As the film progresses Khleifi makes us aware that the Woman is an outsider. She is confined to angled views, views through car windows, views through doorways and from gardens. Though she is the motivating force for many of the scenes, Khleifi does not quite hide the fact that it is he who conducts the interviews—occasionally his voice appears on the soundtrack—while the Woman is always outside the frame. Thus, he creates a doubled awareness of separation—of the isolation of the exile from both the outside world and the homeland—a more powerful and direct statement than he had achieved before.

His themes of memory and of the bond between Palestinians and the land continue with a sequence of an old woman who tells the story of her family's dispossession in 1948 and their subsequent move to the West Bank. Her house on the edge of an encroaching Jewish settlement is a vivid articulation of her memories. Every bit of space is taken up with old photographs, paintings, furniture from her previous life, a framed calendar, relics, ornaments, and rugs. The very act of crowding her possessions into an inappropriate space serves to emphasize the fracturing of her life and her loss and displacement.[15] But her home is intimately connected to its immediate landscape—the "home-land" becomes an extension of the home. Thus, the old woman's expression of love for her home and for the surrounding land transmutes into love for the land of Palestine. Again, this intrinsic, intimate love that we saw in the earlier films is set against the Israeli idea of the house as a commodity, subsidized to encourage immigration and settlement.

Finally, the concept of failed masculinity, encountered in *Wedding in Galilee,* is taken further in the shape of the Man: an elusive figure, appearing and disappearing and frequently filmed against the light so that his features are weakened. Juxtaposition of his story with stories of school closures, of children being shot, of soldiers breaking the arms of women and children, and of bullet injuries incurred during the Intifada, implies his failure to prevent these things happening. The children, on the other hand, have become knowing in the artifacts of war, something that will come to the forefront later on in *Tale of the Three Jewels*.

Canticle of the Stones was first shown in 1990 at Cannes, where it received a mixed response.[16] This may in part be attributed to the formal approach selected by Khleifi. Whereas *Wedding in Galilee* is motivated by the viewpoint of various individuals, *Canticle of the Stones* is particularly problematic in this respect. Though it is a powerful film, the lovers' scant relationship to events in the refugee camps—which may be interpreted as an expression of their impotence before the tragedy of the uprising—exposes the work's seams too obviously, lessening the effect of what it has to say about Palestinian society.

DREAMS OF THE CHILDREN

Khleifi's patent concerns with his position as an exile, of being between two worlds, were exacerbated after the release of his next film, *Order of the Day* (*L'ordre du jour*), in 1993. Described as an "anthropological" look at the bureaucracy of Brussels, the film was not a success. This response, together with Arab responses to his earlier films, seems to have affected Khleifi quite badly; he states he was left feeling like an intruder in Europe as well as being regarded as an agent of Western culture in the Arab world (2006, 56). Nevertheless, he returned to Palestine for his next project, *Tale of the Three Jewels*, the first feature to be shot entirely in the Gaza Strip. Originally commissioned by the BBC and the One World Group of Broadcasters as a fifty-minute television film, a full 35mm version was funded by French television ARTE, the Belgian Ministry of the French Community, and the production company Sindibad Films.[17] The film was made under extreme conditions as the Intifada continued and violence increased. However, the film crew remained loyal, and filming was completed in less than two months of the bitterly cold winter of 1994.[18]

As Khleifi recounts, the challenge he set himself was to "produce a modern tale using the traditional form of an oriental tale" (2006, 57). Thus, it tells of the innocent love between two twelve-year-olds, Yusef, from a Gaza refugee camp, and a mysterious gypsy girl, Aida, and develops into a fantastical quest for three jewels missing from a necklace: Yusef must find the jewels in order to win the love of Aida. This fable is interspersed with sequences depicting the daily reality of life in Gaza under occupation: poverty, violence, confinement, limited opportunities, and despair. In particular, Khleifi tries to illustrate the traumatic effects of violence against children and the sorrow of lost childhood.

While breaking new ground by moving into dreams and fantasy, many of Khleifi's earlier concerns are again evident. The camerawork cloaking the landscape in a loving embrace and Aida's rapt scrutiny of insects, birds, plants, and the weather underline the intense connection of Palestinians to the land and nature. Loss of power and defeat are signaled by the deranged figure of Yusef's father, the blindness of an old neighbor, and his brother's position as a fugitive. And, as in other Khleifi films, the young "learn" history from their elders. Fairy tales, dreams, and fantasies make up Yusef's world. He is assailed by the memories of his neighbor, the stories of his mother, his sister's account of Palestinian history, and an old grandmother's tales of Jaffa before the war.

The richness, plenty, and fertility of Palestine is symbolized by the repeated flashes of color from golden oranges, especially in the scene where Yusef hides in a crate in a desperate attempt to escape and follow his quest for the jewels. In a poetic dream sequence, his old neighbor regains his sight and becomes a prophet, the jewels are transformed into three drops of blood, symbolizing "time, space, and the flesh," or as we might say, history, land, and the people, which Yusef, the Palestinian child, clasps in his hand, uniting them. In this way, Khleifi asserts the Palestinians' right to be remembered, and their right to record their tenure of the land.

In another ambiguous ending, Yusef awakes from his dream and finds himself still in the orange crate in the orchard after curfew. As he emerges and runs home, he is shot and apparently killed by soldiers; but he recovers as his mother and Aida come to find him. Of all the readings of this ending, perhaps the most convincing comes from Gertz and George Khleifi, who argue that it is a reassertion of Palestinian identity in the face of whatever force and repression brought to bear against the people.[19]

From the seemingly unified space occupied by the two women in *Fertile Memory*, Khleifi has been concerned with constructing an unrestricted space out of fragments of Palestinian life. The sequence of the mukhtar in *Wedding in Galilee* steering his prized horse, simply by means of cries and calls, out of an Israeli minefield is, perhaps, the peak of his accomplishment. But here, he tackles a more direct case: the prison of Gaza and the liminal space of the refugee camps.[20] In these confined spaces, the camera, while recording the soldiers, the barbed wire and watchtowers, seems to be able to float. As Gertz and George Khleifi note, "The camera and poetic editing of the film hurdle the obstacles, burst into open nature, and construct a large space in lieu of the cloistered and cramped one where the characters live" (2008, 94). Yusef escapes into his dreams and the stories told him by Aida, his birds fly freely, the sky is open and unrestricted. Style, rather than just simple narrative elements, achieves the rendition of a space that can be called Palestine.

Tale of the Three Jewels has had much positive coverage by critics in the years since its release; however, its reception at Cannes in 1995 was subdued. As al-Qattan perceptively points out, this may be partly explained by the context of the peace talks initiated under the Oslo Accords of 1993 (2006, 172–176). Though these dragged on intermittently without reaching a conclusion, the mere fact that negotiations were underway created a new paradox for Palestinian filmmaking. On the one hand there was greater international awareness of the situation in Palestine and, perhaps, a wave of euphoria and goodwill toward the people. On the other, there was an apparent wish to avoid acknowledging the continuing conflict and to hide behind the comforting veil of an elusive "peace process."

BACK TO REALITY

Khleifi's vision in *Wedding in Galilee* of the possibility of cooperation between the Israeli and Palestinian communities in Israel, and his construction of a "virtual" national space to include the Occupied Territories and Gaza was seen by some other filmmakers to be over-optimistic.[21] In most Palestinian films after 1987 there are virtually no direct encounters between the two communities. The Jewish presence is impersonalized in summarizing symbols: the Israeli flag, uniformed soldiers hiding behind dark glasses, barbed wire, tanks, bulldozers, helicopters and jet fighters. Palestinian physical space is characterized by both visible and invisible barriers, and the sound-space experienced by Palestinians is represented as insecure. Films are studded with diegetic rural sounds: goatbells, wedding songs, the songs of village women and children, ululation; or urban sounds of street vendors, popular music, groups of musicians. Yet the alien is inescapably present in the noise of helicopters, fighter jet planes screeching overhead, sirens, loudspeakers shouting commands, and Israeli radio and television programs.

However, Khleifi continued to explore the possibility of coexistence in his next film, a documentary, *Forbidden Marriages in the Holy Land* (1995). In this,

Groom and bride in *Wedding in Galilee.*

Yusef and Aida in *Tale of the Three Jewels.*

he interviews a number of interfaith couples, questioning how they have addressed religious or cultural differences in their marriages. Some have seen signs of hope in these marriages and the way the different communities have dealt with them. Others are more pessimistic, observing that Arab society appears to remain rigid while Israeli society has become ever more conservative. Though well received at various film festivals and retrospectives of Khleifi's work, the film has not been widely screened.

The treatment of *Three Jewels* and *Forbidden Marriages* by broadcasters and film festivals, the general climate of avoidance of the reality of the Israeli–Palestinian struggle, and his disaffection with the artistic direction of cinema in general and Palestinian cinema in particular, led to a fallow period for Khleifi from the mid-1990s.[22] However, he continued teaching at INSAS, lecturing on Palestinian cinema, and training Palestinian filmmakers. A sense of reality did not return until the Oslo peace process foundered at the Camp David Summit of 2000. The subsequent rise in tension, exacerbated by provocative Israeli activities at the Al-Aqsa mosque in Jerusalem, exploded into the second Intifada that quickly spread to the Occupied Territories and Gaza.[23] One consequence of the ensuing violence is that both sides have been driven further apart. Gaza is caged off, the separation barrier and wall cuts off Israel from the Occupied Territories, and roadblocks and checkpoints for Palestinians have proliferated. This is a time when Palestinian filmmakers have turned to produce what Gertz and George Khleifi call "roadblock movies"—films limited to "blocked areas and border zones" (2008, 136). These events brought Khleifi back into active filmmaking with *Route 181: Fragments of a Journey in Palestine-Israel* (2004), made in collaboration with Jewish-Israeli filmmaker Eyal Sivan. This is a film that explores the liminal space between Arab and Jew in Israel and, as a consequence, exposes tensions that cannot be papered over by the one-sided peace process.

The filmmakers set out in 2002 to retrace the route of the partition line between notional Israeli and Palestinian states that was established by UN Resolution 181 of 1947. Traveling from south to north they interviewed and filmed Arabs and Jews living in close and not always comfortable proximity. The unhurried pace of the resulting film, extending over four and a half hours, enables them to reveal the nuanced complexity of these communities. Though we meet a variety of people, choice of the route dictates to a certain extent the fact that the majority are Jewish-Israelis, living often on what once was Arab land and in former Arab villages. Their proximity to Arab-Israeli neighbors increases friction, and some Jewish interviewees reveal their racism, intolerance, rage, and fear, making clear their view that Arabs are not wanted in Israel. Khleifi has argued that the intention of the film is not to poison the Palestinian–Israeli dialogue by exposing these harsh truths but to get both sides to recognize their faults and responsibilities.[24]

On release in 2004 the film received negative reviews in the United States, and it has failed to achieve distribution there; one of two scheduled screenings at the Festival du Cinéma du Réel in Paris was canceled as the film was said to encourage "anti-Semitic and anti-Jewish statements and acts in France," and the filmmakers came under direct attack from various French and American intellectuals.[25] However, there was also strong support from others, including Jacques Derrida and Etienne Balibar, and numerous more constructive reviews and analyses have also appeared.[26] The DVD package has enabled the film to be fairly widely disseminated.

Route 181 is an important film, but as an oral history of a particular place and time it leaves little room for the subtle construction of political space that is the trademark of Khleifi's earlier work. The relentless progress from one stop to the next is episodic and only connected through the device of looking back momentarily before moving on. But, as Bashir Abu-Manneh rightly observes, "Khleifi and Sivan record on film their search for elements of future society already immanent in the present." The aim of their journey is not to expose to our shocked eyes the seemingly irreconcilable distance between these two societies, but rather to suggest that reconciliation can be achieved through "a joint journey of discovery and exposition" of the past (Abu-Manneh 2004).

AN EXILE'S LOVE FOR HIS COUNTRY

Khleifi returned to narrative filmmaking with his latest film, *Zindeeq*, a self-referential story released in 2009. Here, Mohammad Bakri plays an unnamed Palestinian filmmaker who goes back to his homeland from Europe to document testimonies from witnesses of the 1948 expulsion. A young local woman, Racha, accompanies him as his sound engineer.

Filming in Ramallah is interrupted by news that one of his nephews has killed a neighbor, thus instigating a vendetta against his family in Nazareth. Despite his sister's pleas for him to stay away, he decides to return to see what he can do to help. The rest of the film, shot mainly at night, follows him on his journey and through the dangerous back streets of his hometown, where he is denied shelter and is constantly in danger. Much of the time he is alone in his car except for the images on his camcorder, his dreams, fantasies, and ghosts.

Behind these bare bones of a plot lies a valiant attempt by Khleifi at finding a new way of recounting Palestinian history. Despite Racha's comment that "the story has been told, what more is there to tell?" Khleifi's intricate film shows that history is not one story but a multitude of stories that cannot be folded into a single or a personal narrative.

Through the film we see fragments of interviews—live, on the viewfinder of his camera, or as replayed on screen. Always interrupted, they cannot be pieced together into a whole. These are leavened with idyllic scenes of an almost prelapsarian Palestine—a golden harvest being brought in by women in beautiful peasant costumes, and interspersed with scenes of destruction and the looming Wall.[27]

The exile and his sister wander through the graveyard in Nazareth searching for the graves of their parents; this calls to mind a vision of his mother searching in turn for the graves of her parents. He is tormented by a desire to know why his mother would not tell him what happened to the family in 1948. Finding the key to his old home, he goes inside and finds old family photos and papers and a broken cross, all of which he consigns to a fire. He is visited by an apparition of his mother and, in an inversion of the usual question, he asks, "Why did you stay? Why didn't they expel you?" The reply is subverted by a mother's concern over whether he has eaten. Finally, he leaves the house, dropping the keys into the ashes of his fire.[28]

Within this complex narration of histories, Khleifi weaves the threads of the exile's denial of belonging to Palestine and his infatuation with Racha. Many times he says, "I am not from here," or he is told, "You are not from here." He complains about the violent, divided society that Palestine has become. Many times he fantasizes about Racha, only to betray her with other women. These threads come together at the end, where he is finally recognized as being a local by the owner of a café, who makes him coffee; and then a vision of Racha, veiled and robed in white, beckons to him from the sea. The juxtaposition of the ordinary and the fantasy hints at a reconciliation not only between different factions in Palestinian society but also between the filmmaker and his country. Racha is the Palestine that has rejected him many times and that he has loved but also fatally betrayed.

Zindeeq won the Muhr Arab prize at the Dubai Film Festival in 2009 but has yet to receive the critical and academic attention it deserves. It is a rich film that warrants more detailed analysis. It shows Khleifi has lost none of his desire to explicate the trauma of the Palestinian people in their continued half-life, outside time. And it shows him prepared to explore new ways of trying to tell the Palestinian story.

The term "resistance literature" was first applied by Ghassan Kanafani to describe Palestinian literature written under occupation (Harlow 1987). By extension, graffiti scribbled nightly on the walls of occupied Palestinian towns, artworks and photographic essays displayed in exhibitions, Palestinian flags hoisted on telegraph wires, postcards and stamps sent around the world depicting symbols of the Palestinian nation, defiant murals, political posters, and of course film, are part of a "discourse of resistance" that, perhaps more than anything else, has come to define the Palestinian nation and hold it together.

Palestinian filmmakers of the 1960s and 1970s were largely concerned with encouraging resistance. Yet, even during that time of extreme turmoil, there was also an awareness of the need to preserve Palestinian culture and resist Western (and Israeli) hegemony—to create narratives of cultural resistance. From the early 1980s filmmakers tackled this problem in a number of important ways: competing with the dominant negative view of the Palestinian nation; looking for alternative cinematic forms and symbolism to enable distinct Palestinian voices to emerge; and documenting stories and recording memories, so creating works of art that resist the threat of cultural erasure.

Michel Khleifi was the first of this younger generation of filmmakers to contest the stereotyping of Palestinians, by means of revealing the humanity of the people and giving them a voice with which to express themselves. In this respect, his position as the originator of a new Palestinian cinema is unassailable. His approach to this issue has, of course, not been without its critics. It is argued that he has failed to engage sufficiently with the discursive colonial language responsible for generating stereotypes in the first place. For Alexander, it is insufficient simply to ignore stereotypes; it is necessary to displace them, to speak using a "deconstructive language that is yet comprehensible to [a foreign] audience" (1998, 326). Jayce Salloum is also distinctly critical of Khleifi's type of filmmaking, arguing that it can lead only to a kind of empathy, never to an understanding of the other culture. He sees such attempts at proving a people's humanity as "a paternalistic gesture at best, dehumanizing at worst" (Hankwitz

2002, 95). Khleifi has also been censured for creating a utopian vision of rural life in some of his films.[29]

While some of this criticism may be valid, Khleifi's vision is far from utopian. He not only lays bare the extreme conditions under which Palestinian life continues, he reveals the tensions and contradictions within this society. And I would argue that, rather than presenting his subjects as mere specimens, Khleifi provides both documentary and fictional insight into the lives and concerns of men, women, and children, making visible the complexity and richness of Palestinian society.

Certainly, Khleifi has been less concerned with radical experiments in cinematic form and style than with trying to find a new means of representing the fragmented places available to Palestinians and constructing a political space in which Palestinian identity may be expressed. Even so, by weaving together political stories, newsreels, and documentary footage with details of real and fictional everyday life, he has created a "cinematic syncretism," an artistic strategy of resistance that appropriates from but is not subordinate to dominant forms.[30] His work has a distinctive voice and demonstrates an integrity of vision that belies its seeming simplicity.

Film, which plays directly into the mind of the viewer and mimics the way our own memories are formed through half-remembered images, voices, and sounds, is a powerful means of recording memory. Whether real or fictional, and whether told through interviews, reminiscences, or autobiography, cinematic representations are imbued with a gloss of authenticity. Khleifi's film includes many examples of these forms of individual memory, and he has contributed to the struggle to reclaim the identity of the Palestinian people by telling their stories, reimagining their communities, and helping to preserve the memories of the nation.

Michel Khleifi continues to be an important figure in Palestinian cinema, not only because of his own films, but also for his teaching and his efforts to promote Palestinian films in Palestine and the diaspora. His films bear witness to events such as the demolition of houses, appropriation of land, arrests, imposition of curfews and checkpoints, encroachment of settlements, police activity, restrictions, and harassment; and they ensure these will not go unrecorded. Unafraid of exploring fractures in Palestinian society, revealing its heterogeneity, while at the same time expressing the essential unity of the community, he has sought and found different ways of affirming to the outside world the existence of a unique Palestinian cultural identity.

Khleifi's films are marked by resistance: resistance to homogenization—a determination to represent the different political and social spaces occupied by Palestinians and the effect this has on their national identity; resistance to being absorbed into other cultures; and, above all, resistance to erasure. His strategies of cultural resistance in the cinema are a bedrock in affirming the legitimacy of Palestinian rights and realities.

NOTES

I am deeply indebted to Omar al-Qattan and Michel Khleifi for comments on this chapter and to Sindibad Films for providing materials for study.

1. For a detailed discussion of the problems of making film in Israel and the Occupied Territories, see al-Qattan (2006).

2. See Khleifi's own account of early influences in his filmmaking and the various difficulties he has encountered with financing his work (2006).

3. For more detailed information about Khleifi's early years and the circumstances of his departure from Palestine see Nurith Gertz and George Khleifi (2008), Khleifi (2006), and Sindibad (2008).

4. Khleifi interview with Youssef Hijazi (2005, 1).

5. Awards for *Fertile Memory* include: the Prix de la Critique, Carthage 1980, and the Semaine de La Critique award, Cannes 1981.

6. See Telmissany (2010), and for a more detailed discussion on the construction of political space see Gertz and Khleifi (2008).

7. For the distinction between mourning and melancholia see, for example, Bresheeth (2007), Kassabian and Kazanjian (1999), and Kennedy (2007).

8. The film movement, sponsored mainly by the Palestine Liberation Organization, is detailed in Gertz and Khleifi (2008), Kennedy (2007), and Tawil (2005).

9. The "battlefield" of public discourse on Israel and Palestine is discussed in, for example, Kennedy (2007), Khatib (2006), Loshitzky (2001), and Shaheen (2001).

10. Awards include: the International Federation of Film Critics Award, Cannes 1987; the Golden Shell, San Sebastian 1987; and Tanit d'Or, Carthage 1988. For critical analyses see, for example, Gertz and Khleifi (2008), Kennedy (2006), Sabouraud and Toubiana (1987), Shafik (1998), and Shohat (1988).

11. See Khleifi interviews by Feinstein (1993) and Sabouraud and Toubiana (1987).

12. Kimmerling notes that the image of young, unprofessional fighters, ready to confront Israeli soldiers openly and head-on, began to dominate news of the conflict (Kimmerling and Migdal 2003, 297–303).

13. al-Qattan provides a graphic account of the difficulties of filmmaking at this time (2006). For an analysis of media coverage see, for example, Dunsky (2001).

14. See Hamid Naficy's discussion of language (2001, 22–24).

15. Edward Said remarks on the obsession among displaced Palestinians with re-creating the interior of their former homes, an obsession which "inadvertently high-lights and preserves the rift or break fundamental to our lives" (1986, 58).

16. Press reviews were generally cold or hostile and critics were more puzzled than engaged. See al-Qattan for a discussion on the problems with screening the film (2006).

17. Sindibad Films is the production company for the films of Michel Khleifi and Omar al-Qattan.

18. For more detail about the difficulties of filming at this time, see al-Qattan (2006) and Johnson (1996).

19. See Gertz and Khleifi (2011) and also Khatib (2006) for a more extensive analy-sis of the film.

20. Israel partially handed over governance of the Gaza Strip in 1994 to the Pales-tinian Authority. Since then the tiny area, with a population of around two million, has been under varying degrees of blockade—in effect it is an open prison. Israel con-trols the borders—including proxy control of the Egyptian border, the air space, and access by sea. Israel restricts movement into and out of the region, it limits fishing to a narrow coastal zone, it frequently refuses to pay tax revenues to the Palestinians, and it prevents the delivery of foreign aid. Periodic attacks by Hamas incur disproportion-ate, collective punishment by Israel on the civilian population of Gaza.

21. For example see the work of Rashid Masharawi and Elia Suleiman.

22. See al-Qattan (2006) and Khleifi (2006) for a discussion of distribution issues and their views on cinema during this period.

23. For a reasonably balanced account of events leading up to the Intifada, see the Mitchell Report of 2001.

24. Interview with Youssef Hijazi (2005).

25. For the filmmakers' reaction to this attack, see Sindibad (2004).

26. See, for example, Murphy (2004) and Porton (2006).

27. The country scenes are archive images from Khleifi's earlier documentaries.

28. The significance to Palestinian history of the key to the house is discussed in more detail in Seed (1999).

29. See, for example, Elia Suleiman's comments in Porton (2003), Rapfogel (2003), and Shohat (1988).

30. See Shohat and Stam on this mode of representation in anticolonial cinemas (1994).

FILMOGRAPHY OF MICHEL KHLEIFI

All films except *Zindeeq* are distributed by Sindibad Films at *sindibad.co.uk*. That dis-tribution is worldwide except for the films that have U.S. distributors as indicated.

Fertile Memory / La mémoire fertile / Al-Dhakira al-Khisba. 1980. Distributed in the United States by Kino Lorber. 99 minutes. Documentary.

Ma'loul Celebrates Its Destruction / Ma'loul fête sa destruction. 1984. 30 minutes. Documentary.

Wedding in Galilee / Noce en Galilée / Urs al-Jalil. 1987. Distributed in the United States by Kino Lorber. 113 minutes.

Canticle of the Stones / Le cantique des pierres / Nashid al-Hajjar. 1990. Distributed in the United States by Arab Film Distribution at *arabfilm.com.* 110 minutes.

Order of the Day / L'ordre du jour. 1993. 115 minutes.

Tale of the Three Jewels Le conte des trois diamants / Hikayatul jawahiri thalath. 1994. Distributed in the United States by Arab Film Distribution at *arabfilm.com* and *Amazon.com.* 107 minutes.

Forbidden Marriages in the Holy Land. 1995. Distributed in the United States by Arab Film Distribution at *arabfilm.com.* 66 minutes. Documentary.

Route 181: Fragments of a Journey in Palestine-Israel (co-director Eyal Sivan). 2004. 272 minutes. Documentary.

Zindeeq. 2009. 85 minutes.

REFERENCES

Abu-Manneh, Bashir. 2004. "Journey Towards a Route in Common." *Middle East Research and Information Project.* MER231, Spring 2004, http://www.merip.org/mer/mer231/journey-towards-route-common. Accessed April 2014.

Alexander, Livia. 1998. "Palestinians in Film: Representing and Being Represented in the Cinematic Struggle for National Identity." *Visual Anthropology* 10 (2–4): 319–333.

———. 2002. "Let Me In, Let Me Out, Going Places and Going Back." *Framework* 43 (2): 157–177.

Bresheeth, Haim. 2007. "The Continuity of Trauma and Struggle." In *Nakba: Palestine, 1948, and the Claims of Memory,* edited by Ahmad H. Sa'di and Lila Abu-Lughod, 161–187. New York: Columbia University Press.

Dunsky, Marda. 2001. "Missing: The Bias Implicit in the Absent." *Arab Studies Quarterly* 23 (3): 1–30.

Feinstein, Howard. 1993. "Arab Films at Pesaro Festival." *Cineaste* 20 (2): 42–43.

Gertz, Nurith, and George Khleifi. 2008. *Palestinian Cinema: Landscape, Trauma and Memory.* Edinburgh: Edinburgh University Press.

———. 2011. "*Tale of the Three Jewels:* Children Living and Dreaming amid Violence in Gaza." In *Film in the Middle East and North Africa: Creative Dissidence,* edited by Josef Gugler, 209–217. Austin: University of Texas Press.

Ghareeb, Edmund. 1983. "A Renewed Look at American Coverage of the Arabs: Toward a Better Understanding?" In *Split vision: The Portrayal of Arabs in the American Media,* edited by Edmund Ghareeb, 157–194. Washington, D.C.: American-Arab Affairs Council.

Hankwitz, Molly. 2002. "Occupied Territories: Mapping the Transgressions of Cultural Terrain." *Framework* 43 (2): 85–103.

Harlow, Barbara. 1987. *Resistance Literature*. New York: Methuen.

Hijazi, Youssef. 2005. "Film as a Political Work of Art." *Qantara.de,* http://en.qantara
.de/content/interview-michel-khleifi-film-as-a-political-work-of-art. Accessed
April 5, 2014.

Johnson, Lisa. 1996. "Imagination in the Shadow of the Intifada." Review. *The Bulletin*
(Brussels), April 12, 1996, 24–29.

Kassabian, Anahid, and David Kazanjian. 1999. "Melancholic Memories and Manic
Politics: Feminism, Documentary, and the Armenian Diaspora." In *Feminism and
Documentary,* edited by Diane Waldman and Janet Walker, 202–223. Minneapolis:
University of Minnesota Press.

Kennedy, Tim. 2006. "Wedding in Galilee." *Film Quarterly* 59 (4): 40–46.

———. 2007. "Cinema Regarding Nations: Re-imagining Armenian, Kurdish, and
Palestinian national identity in film." PhD thesis, Department of Film, Theatre &
Television, University of Reading, Reading, UK.

Khatib, Lina. 2006. *Filming the Modern Middle East: Politics in the Cinemas of Hollywood and the Arab World*. London: I. B. Tauris.

Khleifi, Michel. 2006. "From Reality to Fiction—From Poverty to Expression." In
Dreams of a Nation: On Palestinian Cinema, edited by Hamid Dabashi, 45–57.
London: Verso.

Kimmerling, Baruch, and Joel Migdal. 2003. *The Palestinian People: A History*. Cambridge, Massachusetts: Harvard University Press.

Loshitzky, Yosefa. 2001. *Identity Politics on the Israeli Screen*. Austin: University of
Texas Press.

Mitchell, George J. 2001 "Sharm El-Sheikh Fact-Finding Committee Report," http://
eeas.europa.eu/mepp/docs/mitchell_report_2001_en.pdf. Accessed April 2014.

Murphy, Maureen Clare. 2004. "Review: *Route 181: Fragments of a Journey in Palestine-Israel.*" *The Electronic Intifada,* June 2004, http://electronicintifada.net
/content/review-route-181-fragments-journey-palestine-israel/3464. Accessed
May 2014.

Naficy, Hamid. 2001. *An Accented Cinema: Exilic and Diasporic Filmmaking*. Princeton, NJ: Princeton University Press.

Porton, Richard. 2003. "Notes from the Palestinian Diaspora: An Interview with Elia
Suleiman." *Cineaste* 28 (3): 24–27.

———. 2006. "Roads to Somewhere: Paradise Now and Route 181." *Cinema Scope* 7 (3).

al-Qattan, Omar. 2006. "The Challenges of Palestinian Filmmaking (1990–2003)." In
Dreams of a Nation: On Palestinian Cinema, edited by Hamid Dabashi, 110–130.
London: Verso.

Rapfogel, Jared. 2003. "A Report of Dreams of a Nation—A Palestinian Film Festival."
Senses of Cinema Issue 25, http://sensesofcinema.com/2003/festival-reports/dreams
_of_a_nation/. Accessed April 2014.

Rosen, Miriam. 1988. "Wedding in Galilee." *Cineaste* 16 (4): 50–51.

Sabouraud, Frédéric, and Serge Toubiana. 1987. "La Force du faible: 'Noce en Galilée,' entretien avec Michel Khleifi." *Cahiers du cinéma* 401: 111.

Said, Edward. 1986. *After the Last Sky: Palestinian Lives.* London: Faber and Faber.

Seed, Patricia. 1999. "The Key to the House." In *Home, Exile, Homeland: Film, Media, and the Politics of Place,* edited by Hamid Naficy, 85–94. London: Routledge.

Shafik, Viola. 1998. *Arab Cinema: History and Cultural Identity.* Cairo: University of Cairo Press.

Shaheen, Jack G. 2001. *Reel Bad Arabs: Arab and Muslim Stereotyping in American Popular Culture.* Northampton, MA: Interlink.

Shohat, Ella. 1988. "Wedding in Galilee." *Middle East Report* 154: 44–46.

Shohat, Ella, and Robert Stam. 1994. *Unthinking Eurocentrism: Multiculturalism and the Media.* London: Routledge.

Sindibad. 2004. "Film *Route 181* censored by French Culture Ministry." *The Electronic Intifada,* March 2004, http://electronicintifada.net/content/film-route-181-censored-french-culture-ministry/5017. Accessed April 2014.

———. 2008. "Michel Khleifi—Palestine's Film Poet." *This Week in Palestine* (117), http://archive.thisweekinpalestine.com/details.php?id=2357&ed=149&edid=149. Accessed September 1, 2014.

Tawil, Helga. 2005. "Coming Into Being and Flowing Into Exile: History and Trends in Palestinian Filmmaking." *Nebula* 2 (2): 113–140.

Telmissany, May. 2010. "Displacement and Memory: Visual Narratives of al-Shatat in Michel Khleifi's Films." *Comparative Studies of South Asia, Africa and the Middle East* 30 (1): 69–84.

Elia Suleiman while shooting *Diary of a Beginner* in Havana, about 2011.

4

Elia Suleiman

NARRATING NEGATIVE SPACE
(PALESTINE)

Refqa Abu-Remaileh

Elia Suleiman is a pioneering filmmaker who has captured the absurdities of Palestinian life with a twist of humor and a deep dose of irony. His deceptively simple style has attracted audiences worldwide and won him recognition at major international film festivals. Both viewers who are more familiar with the sociopolitical Palestinian context of the films and those who are not have indulged in the pleasure of uncovering a multitude of layers, references, and allusions. Critics have likened Suleiman's film style to those of Jacques Tati, Buster Keaton, and Jim Jarmusch. However, Suleiman has expressed in a number of interviews that his influences came from elsewhere—from Asia, particularly the films of Yasujiro Ozu and Hou Hsiao-Hsien.[1]

This chapter will begin with a short biography, moving on to an analysis of key elements of Suleiman's filmmaking style, focusing on his three long fiction films.

BIOGRAPHY

Elia Suleiman was born in 1960 into a Nazareth that had become part of the new Israeli state in 1948. In his late teens, Suleiman was compelled to leave Nazareth. Reasons for his sudden departure are captured in his most recent film, *The*

Time That Remains. Living in exile, Suleiman began to experiment with film-making, creating what he calls a "complicatedly simple" style of multilayered static frames, choreographed action, little dialogue, and nonlinear narratives (Butler 2003, 67). His early New York experiments paved the way for his three long fiction films: *Chronicle of a Disappearance, Divine Intervention,* and *The Time That Remains*.

Suleiman collaborated with Lebanese-Canadian video artist Jayce Salloum in *Introduction to the End of an Argument / Muqaddimah li-nihayat jidal* in 1990. A critique of Western representations of the Middle East and a subversion of stereotypes, *Introduction* is a collage of layered images and sounds, with clips from mainly Hollywood films, documentary footage from the West Bank and Gaza, and assembled news coverage. In 1991, in the midst of the first Gulf War, Suleiman shifted gears and went solo, writing, directing, and acting in his short film *Homage by Assassination* (*Homage par assassinat / Takrim bil qatl*). The film sets many of the stylistic foundations that become Suleiman's hallmarks in his long fiction films. *Homage,* set during the first Gulf war and featuring a young Suleiman trapped in his New York apartment trying to reach his parents in Nazareth, was also an introduction to his silent on-screen persona, which in his later films becomes known as "E. S." Suleiman considers *Homage* to be his departure point: "I owe everything to *Homage,* it was the mess that exploded—the Big Bang."[2]

Like others during the brief euphoric moment following the signing of the Oslo Peace Accords in 1993, Suleiman decided to return to his homeland. He settled in Jerusalem and began a teaching stint at Birzeit University in Ramallah. To capture some of the new realities he was experiencing, Suleiman reworked a script he had begun writing in New York, eventually securing enough funding to make it his first long fiction film. *Chronicle of a Disappearance* (*Chronique d'une disparition / Segell ikhtifa,* 1996) put to the test the techniques Suleiman experimented with in *Homage.*[3] The result was a minimalist diary-like narrative featuring scenes of an episodic nature and an unconventional treatment of the Palestinian ideal of return. *Chronicle*'s aesthetic structure set the trend for many of Suleiman's later films.

Between *Chronicle* and the release of his second long fiction film, *Divine Intervention,* in 2002, Suleiman directed a documentary film with Israeli film-maker Amos Gitai, *War and Peace in Vesoul* (1997),[4] and a couple of short films: *The Arab Dream* (*Rêve arabe / al-Hulm al-arabi,* 1998), which explores themes of place, home, and exile,[5] and *Cyber Palestine* (2000), Suleiman's contribution to the Palestinian Authority's Bethlehem 2000 Project. *Cyber Palestine* anticipates an approaching new millennium in Bethlehem, transposing the biblical story of Mary and Joseph by fast-forwarding the characters to modern-day Palestine. In the larger scheme of his works, Suleiman considers *Cyber Palestine* as a "dress rehearsal" for some of the techniques he uses in his later films, for example the slow motion shot, used to astounding effect in the sequence of a woman crossing a checkpoint in *Divine Intervention*.[6]

Divine Intervention (*Intervention divine / Yadun ilahiyya*, 2002) became Suleiman's best-known film after it received the prestigious Jury Prize at the 2002 Cannes Film Festival. The film captures the fragmented reality of Palestinians with new psychological depth, depicting the repercussions of the ongoing conflict on personal relations and the claustrophobic conditions it creates, prompting people to lash out against each other. Following *Divine Intervention*, Suleiman contributed a short film, *Irtebak*, to the Cannes Film Festival 2007 compilation *To Each His Own Cinema* (*Chacun son cinéma*), featuring a silent Suleiman in a series of awkward moments at a film festival.

The dark humor of the first two long fiction films ripples through *The Time That Remains* (*Le temps qu'il reste / al-Zaman al-baqi*, 2009) while also inviting scenes of wonderful tenderness and humanity. The film follows in the aesthetic footsteps of *Chronicle* and *Divine Intervention*, and this has prompted critics to see the three as a trilogy. *The Time That Remains* is Suleiman's most ambitious and expansive film, historically spanning the creation of the state of Israel in 1948 through to the second Intifada and the siege of Ramallah in 2002. The inspiration for this film was not only Suleiman's "notebook and pen" (Wood 2006)—events that he had observed or stories he had been told by others that he noted down—but also his father's diaries and his mother's letters to her family in Jordan. Having finally broached the difficult subject of the 1948 Nakba in *The Time That Remains*, Suleiman has hinted at setting his next long fiction film outside of Palestine, and basing it on his experiences in New York and Paris.

As with other Palestinian and independent films, securing funding is a constant struggle that has made and broken film projects. While there is no Palestinian film industry to support film production, Israel has an established infrastructure for filmmaking. The lack of a Palestinian film infrastructure, including the number of functioning screening facilities, makes distribution difficult, and has often meant that the very people the films are about do not get a chance to see them, while international audiences and Palestinians in the diaspora can catch them on international film festival circuits. Despite that, filmmakers have tried to find ways of screening films, via mobile cinemas, ad hoc screening facilities, or at better-equipped venues, such as the al-Kasaba theatre in Ramallah.[7] Working without an institutional framework, however, opened up avenues for more individual experiments that gave rise to auteur and independent filmmakers such as Michel Khleifi, Rashid Masharawi, and Suleiman, among others.

As a Palestinian citizen of Israel, Suleiman has had access to Israeli film funding, which he received for *Chronicle of a Disappearance,* and for which he was heavily criticized by the Arab world. At the time, Suleiman saw the funding controversy as a "civil rights fight" (Erickson 2003)—the Israeli Fund for Quality Films had not previously funded an Arab or Palestinian film. Suleiman made his point, but he was not actually awarded the full amount of the grant. His film went on to win a prize at Venice and was eventually screened in Israel, to the pleasure of Israeli left-liberal cinephiles and to the dismay of those at the Israeli film fund, who "hated the film entirely" (ibid.).

Going down the Israeli funding route proved cumbersome, as it trapped Suleiman between trying to prove a point to the Israelis and being subjected to criticism from every other angle. With no local, uncontroversial film industry to support his work, Suleiman turned to co-productions, financing his films using external funding, especially via European producers, as well as private Arab and Palestinian sources. This interstitial mode of production, according to Hamid Naficy's description of "accented cinema" (Naficy 2001, 40), is the path many exilic and diasporic filmmakers resorted to. In this way, Suleiman was able to operate both within the cracks in the system and outside it, while also being located "at the intersection of the local and the global" (ibid., 46).

Taking a closer look at aesthetics, structures, and techniques, the next part will offer an analysis of the genre-blurring techniques that create ambiguity about whether Suleiman's films are documentary, autobiography, or fiction imbued with an ahistorical façade. I will then move on to argue that the films see both the past and present through a view from the margins. Such a view is shaped by a reluctance to narrate, as will be illustrated in the anti-interview examples, and springs out of the negative space in and around conflict and historical events. The following two sections will present a look at self-reflexive techniques and the creation of an overarching metafictional space that produces strong nonverbal links among Suleiman's films. The last section will zoom out to the dualities of contradiction created within Suleiman's narratives, of absence and presence, silence and language, and appearance and disappearance.

REPRESENTING AN ETERNAL PRESENT?

In the context of the Palestinian–Israeli conflict, where reality can indeed be stranger than fiction, Suleiman resorts to genre-blurring techniques to capture that absurd reality. "What happens when reality becomes too fictive to be fictionalized, too unreal to accommodate any metaphor?" asks Hamid Dabashi (2006b, 11). Suleiman is no stranger to paradoxical realities that are reflected through a merging of genres, creating films that are described as "hovering above that boundary between fiction and documentary" (Bresheeth 2001, 24). The effect is one of ambiguity, raising questions as to whether Suleiman's films are documentary, autobiography, or fiction. At one level, the films combine aspects of all three genres. On a second level, Suleiman's films are less about adhering to one genre or the other, and more about experimenting with aesthetics and techniques that uncover different forms of narration and communication. In this sense, the films aim to narrate without direct narration, and tell stories without directly telling them.

Up until *Divine Intervention,* this kind of genre-blurring appeared to be linked to the way the films seem trapped in a kind of eternal present with no reference to the past, history, or future. The starkly ahistorical façade of many of Suleiman's films and the preoccupation with seemingly banal day-to-day events are characteristic of other contemporary Palestinian fiction films, prompting some critics to see the abandonment of history as a trend. In their study of Palestinian cinema, Nurith Gertz and George Khleifi divide Palestinian cinema into four periods, tracing a trend of "forgetting history rather than constructing it" (Gertz and Khleifi 2008, 60).

Arguments scholars have presented to explain the intense focus on the present revolve around a history of trauma, a state of temporality, and refugee and exilic conditions that sanction the linear structuring of history in narrative (ibid., 2). According to Gertz and Khleifi, Palestinian cinema moved toward forgetting history in the 1960s. Thereafter, films turned to the local and the immediate and refrained from touching on the series of events that led to the painful past. In contrast, Haim Bresheeth argues, in an essay on cinematic representations of the Nakba, that there is a "prevalence of Nakba themes" (Bresheeth 2007a, 161) in recent Palestinian films. However, Bresheeth views these films (including Suleiman's) through the lens of documentary filmmaking, and suggests that through representations of the second Intifada the films display a "continuity of pain and trauma . . . as well as a continuity of struggle" (ibid., 161). Bresheeth then focuses on how the films tell stories through trauma, memory, and identity, turning melancholia to mourning.

Although the films Bresheeth selects for his study invoke and allude to 1948,[8] none are direct fictional representations or reconstructions of the events of the Nakba. They are rather a testament to the fact that the impact and the emotions of that traumatic history were not forgotten. Along similar lines, *Chronicle of a Disappearance* and *Divine Intervention* can be seen as studies of a present scarred by a history of "forced *public* amnesia," as Bresheeth describes it (Bresheeth 2001, 32), where the conditions of remembering and commemorating are inhibited to this day. Navigating through the silences of history and memory, these two films can be seen as present-day nonverbal exercises in excavating the psychological and emotional from a landscape of conflict and trauma. Indirect references to the "repressed past" and history are more apparent here through aesthetics, structure, technique, and music. While never directly alluded to in dialogue, the historical to some extent shapes the form and structure of the films. For example, both *Chronicle* and *Divine Intervention* have a two-part structure that alternates between Nazareth and Jerusalem. These alternations can be read as references to the historical fault lines of the wars of 1948 and 1967. These divisive wars split up Palestinians from each other and from their land, and are represented by interrupted journeys, checkpoints, and discontinuous spaces that never connect.

An increased preoccupation with a Palestinian present, which, according to Gertz and Khleifi, began in the 1980s, continues into the contemporary period, to which Suleiman belongs. The latter half of this period saw the rise of independent production and the auteur filmmaker, where the focus on the present was no longer strictly aligned with and financed by the national struggle. This is a good description of Suleiman and his films: the auteur filmmaker, scenes of an incessant present, and nonalignment with a particular nationalist vision. However, Suleiman's most recent film, *The Time That Remains* (2009), is the first long fiction film to directly engage with the events of 1948, and by extension the spectrum of Palestinian history. *The Time That Remains* takes the viewer back to the Nazareth of the 1948 Nakba, not through metaphors, allusions, and symbols, but through historical and personal events. In an interview, Suleiman describes *The Time That Remains* as a "period film" (Smith 2011). Even with its period sets and costumes, the film is also, as one critic put it, "mercifully free of histrionics" (Lane 2011). Although the film can be seen as a departure from Suleiman's eternal present films, I argue in the next section that it can also be seen as an expression of continued aesthetic experimentation with form, narrative, and unconventional storytelling.

THE VIEW FROM THE MARGINS: NARRATING NEGATIVE SPACE

The Time That Remains is roughly based on a chronology of Palestinian history, but it is not a film structured with a view to creating a comprehensive historical narrative. "I am not telling Palestinian history at all," Suleiman asserts in an interview, "I am an artist, not a historian. It's very simple, I am not somebody who has come to archive."[9] Instead, the film follows in the same footsteps of the nonlinear and fragmented narratives of *Chronicle of a Disappearance* and *Divine Intervention*. Just as *Chronicle* and *Divine Intervention* are not simply documentary reconstructions of daily events, *The Time That Remains* is not a documentary reconstruction of historical events. It is a film of carefully chosen moments, angles and views, which happen to be placed in an overtly signified historical context. It is a film of epic and historical qualities that avoids what Suleiman calls "sensationalism, the bombastic, and predictable scenes" (Jaafar 2010). With its sparse supply of dates, the film brushes over entire decades without comment, choosing to focus on the unfamiliar and moments of surprise. It does not document well-known facts and incidents, but rather hits on "tones that are usually on the margins," as film critic Ali Jaafar notes (ibid.), leaving it up to the viewers to make their own connections to the better-known aspects of Palestinian history.

A good example of this "view from the margins" is the sequence in a Nazarene olive grove in 1948, where E. S.'s blindfolded father, Fuad, is seen kneeling under a tree. A brief close-up shows an Israeli soldier putting a gun to his head, but instead of getting closer to the action the camera retreats to a long shot as he is beaten and his body is thrown over a wall. Suleiman keeps a critical distance within his frames. In order not to sensationalize, he tells the story from "a place with contemplation and a certain serenity" (Suleiman 2010), from an angle that is never too far and never too close. Rather than operate solely in the realm of history, *The Time That Remains* explores the points at which, according to critic Anthony Lane, "a small world intersects with a wider one" (Lane 2011). While aspects of the wider world are visually revealed in their historical context in the film, the very same aspects weigh heavily on the frame of the small worlds that make up the claustrophobic present of *Divine Intervention* and *Chronicle*.

Gertz and Khleifi, in their periodization of Palestinian cinema, did not anticipate the possibility of structuring history through emotions, the personal, and
the nonverbal rather than through a "sequential national narrative" (Gertz and
Khleifi 2008, 60). In fact, Suleiman's personal rationale for invoking the events
of the Nakba of 1948 is based on his own cinematic growth: "I was filled with
insecurity about touching on that business for 10 or 15 years. This is an episode
that I have thought about for such a long time but that I don't think I was ever
mature enough to approach—not cinematically, and not as a person. Only in
this film did I dare to do it, I can say, with all the doubt and risk-taking" (Cutler
2011). Suleiman's statement points to the idiosyncrasies and personal nature of
contemporary Palestinian film, which makes it difficult to identify movements
or trends. However, within the microcosm of his own body of work, Suleiman
creates strong resonances, interlinkings and trends. In these films, the framing
of the shots, the editing of the film, and its structure are just as important as
what is seen, said and heard within the frames. The marginal view is thus medi-
ated by the film's aesthetics, structure, techniques, and music.

The scenes that I will refer to as the anti-interview scenes in *Chronicle* are
an example of this marginal view. Although not intended as such, these scenes,
in many ways, resemble documentary interviews. The interview, especially in
Palestinian documentary films, is a trope often used to relate an oral history of
the Palestinian–Israeli conflict, with a particular focus on the experiences, suffering, and human tragedy of the 1948 Nakba. But instead of personal testimonies, in *Chronicle* the viewer witnesses a surprising reluctance to narrate. It is
perhaps precisely because Suleiman is not a documentary filmmaker, combined
with the diary-like structure of the film, based on a series of "appointment
with . . ." segments, that Suleiman opens up a window of nonverbal and visual
possibilities to shed light on a troubled society.[10] Suleiman's anti-interview
scenes are a look through the cracks of a society caught between an ongoing
conflict and a repressed history. What they highlight is the negative space
around events, through which the contours of those events can be glimpsed.[11]

Through this technique of negative shading, the anti-interview scenes paint
personal testimonies of the day-to-day minutiae around the larger history of
the Palestinian–Israeli conflict. A striking example is the opening scene of
Chronicle. It features E. S.'s aunt, who walks into a static frame, sits on a couch
at the center of that frame, and speaks directly to the camera—all elements
of a documentary interview. What is unexpected is the subject matter and
content of her monologue. A seasoned viewer of Palestinian films would have
presumed the aunt would recount her experiences of the 1948 Nakba and the

family struggles thereafter. But as soon as she sits down she begins to denigrate the neighbors, the very same people she is about to go pay her condolences to. Ironically, she ends her diatribe with: "It's better if one stays silent and doesn't say anything." The rest of the film follows her advice, and is weighted by a silence heaving with the same tensions and bitterness as the opening monologue. Thus, antithetical to the nature of the interview, there is instead a withdrawal from direct forms of narration. This style of staccato narration aims to leave the audience with more to unveil through frames, repetitions, and fragments than it is willing to reveal itself.

The ambiguity of these scenes is compounded by the use of words such as "segell" (a record) in the Arabic title of *Chronicle,* which invokes documentary precision. Rather than being a record of the national struggle, the word is translated into a filmmaking technique that zooms in on the micro-level struggle of everyday Palestinian life inside Israel. By resorting to the nonverbal, these scenes ultimately question the construction of conventional narrative through use of language and create what Linda Mokdad describes as "a remarkably ironic tension in his films regarding the role of orality" (Mokdad 2012, 197).

The remaining silence of the film is punctuated by a number of other surprising monologues. A Russian Orthodox priest stands atop the Mount of Beatitudes, overlooking Lake Tiberias, lamenting the fact that the place where Jesus is said to have walked over water has become a "gastronomic sewer, filled with excrement, shit of American and German tourists, who eat Chinese food." At first sight of a priest, the viewer may anticipate pointed comments on interfaith dialogue and coexistence. Instead, the priest is confessing to losing faith and cursing the tourist industry that is stripping the land of its holiness. For those who pay attention to credits, another surprise is in store: unlike many of the other characters in *Chronicle,* where Suleiman's mother plays the mother, his father the father, and his aunt the aunt, the priest is not a real priest. In a breach of the authenticity pact a documentary strikes with the viewer—the assurance that the person interviewed is who they are said to be—the priest turns out to be an Ukrainian actor and musician. This twist has the effect of putting viewers on alert in terms of what they see, hear, and are presented with.

The scenes resembling interviews challenge the viewer's expectation of a film set in a small spot of the world that has attracted decades of media, political, and intellectual attention and analysis. Neither the aunt nor the priest says what might be expected of those characters, given the context. In this way, Suleiman creates "an image that transcends the ideological definition of what it means to be Palestinian, an image far from any stereotype" (Bourland 2000, 98). Behind such an image rises a stark reality of Nazareth as a ghetto with a population living in a claustrophobic state of stasis and impotence (Wood 2006, 217). To create such an image requires a "decentralization of viewpoint, perception, narration" (Bourlond 2000, 97) that yields multiple narrative perspectives. This decentralization, and the ruffling of the viewer's comfort zone, are evident in the anti-interview scenes and are employed through other techniques, such as the prevalence of self-reflexivity in Suleiman's films, which draws attention to the medium of film and its construction. Exposing the mechanisms of fictional construction brings the construction of other narratives into question, especially historical narratives, the linearity, assertiveness, and myths of which have both failed and occupied Palestinians for more than sixty years. Ultimately, Suleiman tries, through focusing on negative spaces and decentralizing the image, to show that no singular meanings or interpretation exist.

SELF-REFLEXIVITY

Self-reflexive techniques, which draw attention to the behind-the-scenes and mechanics of filmmaking, can be seen as part of Suleiman's pursuit of a "democratic framing" (Haider 2010) that allows multiple levels of interpretation. While he does not employ the more common self-reflexive techniques of characters looking and speaking directly to the camera, he creates the effect of watching the film as it is being made. Both Suleiman's short film *Homage* and *Chronicle* feature the film within a film effect. *Homage* shows Suleiman waiting to be interviewed on a radio show about the making of his new film—the same film the viewer is watching. A similar moment occurs in a scene in *Chronicle* that shows E. S. about to give a speech about his new film, which is again, the same film we are watching. In both these examples, E. S. is simultaneously a character in the films as well as the filmmaker who has made the films.

While there are no direct references to E. S. being a filmmaker in *Divine Intervention,* the sticky notes scenes prompt the viewer to question E. S.'s relationship to the creation of the narrative. These scenes reveal E. S. in his Jerusalem flat standing between two walls lined with well-ordered notes. Close-ups of the text on the notes show that the notes relate to scenes that the viewer has already seen or is about to see, thus corresponding to the film either retrospectively or prospectively. These notes point to clues of a possible association between E. S., the titles printed on the notes, and the scenes we see in the film. The retrospective notes relating to scenes the viewer has already seen—for example when E. S. picks up the note that reads: *yamrad al-ab* (father falls sick)

Israeli police rush to relieve themselves in *Chronicle of a Disappearance*.

Elia Suleiman as E. S. in *Divine Intervention*.

Displaying the Palestinian flag as Nazareth surrenders to the
Jewish Haganah forces in 1948, in *The Time That Remains.*

following the father in the hospital scene—gives the sense that E. S., a character
in the film, is reflecting upon earlier scenes. The prospective notes—e.g., *ana
majnun ʿashan bahibbek* (I am crazy because I love you)—which announce
scenes to come, imply that E. S. has some sort of control over the progression
and content of the scenes.

Despite the element of premeditation and the degree of control in the film
(the well-ordered notes are a metaphor), certain events are beyond E. S.'s sphere
of influence. The film shows E. S. reacting to events as they happen, changing
the position and order of the notes/scenes in response, and exposing elements
of film editing. The reference to the film's structure within the film, combined
with the use of the present tense on the notes, invokes a sense of immediacy,
giving the viewer the feeling of being part of the making of the film. This kind
of self-reflexivity draws attention to the creation process, highlighting the possibilities of manipulation and narrative as a subjective and personal instrument. More than "unearthing the story" of Palestine, Haim Bresheeth reads

Suleiman's techniques as a response to the suppression, erasure, and socialized forgetfulness (Bresheeth 2001, 36).

Drawing attention to the construction of narrative, the films use all aspects the medium provides to tell fragments of stories through mute imagery that avoids singular claims, instead revealing a world of multiplicity, diversity, and questioning. Suleiman writes in *Theorizing National Cinema* about the dangers of representing "one clotted truth": "A one truth is a stagnant truth. Real as it can get, it becomes our only reality and we become its prisoners" (Suleiman 2006, 204). Suleiman is interested in creating a democracy of viewing. In an interview he explains: "I want to make my films as embedded and layered as possible for the spectator to have the democracy of viewing this image aesthetically and not linearly. I don't want to feed the spectator."[12] In this way, Suleiman is also exposing the viewer to the artifice of narrative construction, questioning narratives questions around claims, especially in creating a film world that allows a diversity of potential truths, releasing its meanings from rigid, preconceived, or ideological interpretations.

THE METAFICTIONAL DIMENSION

Suleiman's works are self-reflexive not only within each fictional unit, but also toward his filmic production as a whole, creating a parallel metanarrative and a metafictional world alongside both Suleiman's life and his films. The structural nods between *Divine Intervention* and *Chronicle* are an example. *Divine Intervention*'s clean-cut abbreviated structure is an evolution of Suleiman's experimentations in *Chronicle,* which adopts more or less the same two-part Nazareth/Jerusalem vignette-based structural form. The subtle referencing between the two films is not restricted to structure; it is also apparent in characterization and recurrent themes, which also extend to *The Time That Remains.*

Suleiman's silent on-screen persona, E. S., directly links all of his feature films. E. S. has consistent characteristics throughout the films, appearing as a silent, passive, and detached filmmaker character, but also as a "defiant witness" (Dabashi 2006a, 158) who "sees, hears, and knows everything" (ibid., 151). In *The Time That Remains,* E. S.'s character is imbued with a deeper sense of melancholy than in previous films, and according to Suleiman is "no longer completely neutralized," beginning to show "slight dramatic reactions and sadness."[13] His silence and inaction capture the frustration of living *in absentia,* watching, waiting, witnessing but not being able to do much. Ironically, such an observational marginal stance sits in contrast to the high degree of control

Suleiman exerts over the film image, which is where the real power lies. The presence of a character-as-witness, a character that is perhaps observing the film while the viewer is watching it, adds another layer to the film's self-reflexivity. Suleiman's parents are another link. In all three films, they either appear as themselves or are played by actors. A number of other characters also appear in all three films. For example, E. S.'s cousin and companion with whom he sits in front of the Holyland souvenir shop in *Chronicle* reappears as the same character in *The Time That Remains*,[14] and the man with the large moustache appears as the car mechanic in *Chronicle,* as the neighbor with the American van in *Divine Intervention,* and as E. S.'s father's fishing companion in *The Time That Remains.*[15] The consistent appearance of characters and actors links the films, creating an overarching metafictional world.

Taking Suleiman's body of work as a whole, not only do characters become increasingly familiar, but so do spaces. His parents' home and the cast of characters in Nazareth all become intimately familiar to the viewer, who is witness to their evolution, growth, and passing on over time. In an interview, Suleiman talks about creating a different kind of global collective memory springing from the local and personal in his films: "It is interesting to me when the memory becomes a collective one not only in a specific location but worldwide" (Cutler 2011). By seeking the universal through the experience of the local, Suleiman aims to create not just films that become a metaphor of Palestine, but rather films where Palestine becomes a metaphor for the world (Smith 2011). These self-reflexive metanarratives contribute to the blurring between fiction and reality. Suleiman's use of autobiographical elements, such as casting his parents and representing their and his lives, as well as casting himself as a character, makes it difficult to distinguish the autobiographical from the fictional.

PRESENT ABSENTEES

Genre-blurring techniques reflect the ambiguities of Palestinian life inside Israel—a life suspended, neither fully Palestinian nor Israeli, caught between an absurd reality that does not recognize Palestinian presence, and the traumatic history of how Palestinians remained in their homeland only to find themselves occupied. Palestinians inside Israel in particular experience two virtual countries making claims for the same space and becoming, as Bresheeth puts it "two parallel universes disregarding each other" (Bresheeth 2001, 38).[16] Living in such a condition forces a constant questioning of the representation of reality, seen as a construction, consisting of narratives of myth, fantasy, and a selective history.

What Suleiman's ever-present silent narrator is in fact recording is a phenomenon of presence through absence and disappearance. This is another negative space technique—a structural pun on the paradoxical term "present absentees" imposed by the Israeli government onto a quarter of Palestinians living inside Israel. The term, which appears in the subtitle of *The Time That Remains: Chronicle of a Present Absentee,* is a label given to Palestinians who were forced to flee their homes during the 1948 war but managed to return to Israel. Their property was duly confiscated by the newly created state, and they were not able to return to their homes, despite being present within its borders. These Palestinians were considered present on the land but absent from their homes under the Israeli Absentee Property Law of 1950. A Custodian of Absentee Property was assigned by the state to protect these properties, which in practice meant handing them over to newly arrived Jewish immigrants.

The comic raid scene in *Chronicle* exemplifies the visual manifestation of the absurdity of being simultaneously present and absent. The film meditates on this particularly Palestinian paradox in conjunction with the Zionist slogan "A land without a people for a people without a land." In this scene, Israeli policemen raid E. S.'s Jerusalem flat but do not notice him, despite his trying to block their passage and following them around. In their assignment report, it becomes clear that they are more interested in E. S.'s property than in him as a person. Hijacking the soundscape via reports exchanged on the two-way radio after the raid, they name all objects of importance in his flat, mentioning him last as "the guy in pajamas." In effect, they record his nonexistence despite his presence on the screen. The viewer, however, also witnesses the scene and becomes aware of the disjunction between the visual and the aural, i.e., the difference between what we see and what we hear in the Israeli report. In a similar scene in *Divine Intervention,* E. S.'s father's property is seized by the Israeli authorities. While they record the value of objects in his house, the disembodied voice of a woman on the two-way radio orders them to "go for the valuables." In the midst of all this, judging by his treatment at the hands of the policemen, E. S.'s father is as good as transparent, standing there watching a football game on TV.

A few scenes after the raid in *Chronicle,* Adan, E. S.'s female double, causes a commotion in Jerusalem and makes a farce out of the Israeli security machinery, controlling their airwaves by using their own language, Hebrew, even going as far as singing the *Hatikvah,* the Israeli national anthem. The anthem speaks of Jewish desire to return to Jerusalem. The ingenuity of this twist is that, as sung by the Palestinian Adan, the anthem can be read in its original sense as "the anthem of the oppressed who have lost Jerusalem, who have lost the land, who have disappeared," writes Bresheeth (2007b, 177). She eventually gets caught and captured but disappears, to be replaced by a mannequin.

Through the female characters in *Chronicle* and *Divine Intervention,* both of whom appear to be E. S.'s fantastical projections and a counterweight to his own inactivity and escapism, Suleiman questions the concept of action and resistance. After the woman disappears in *Divine Intervention,* she reemerges at the end of the film in the guise of a *fida'i* ninja who fights off Israeli Special Forces. But this depiction of resistance is clichéd and idealized. Suleiman reinforces this view in his comments: "It's totally artificial and the audience should be laughing" (Porton 2003, 24), and suggests that despite the woman's apparent heroism, she is only an image: "She comes out of the target and she returns to the target" (White 2010, 45).

According to Bresheeth (2002, 75), E.S. is the character who speaks not through action but through "passages of expressive silence." While Suleiman is not himself a present absentee, he is the "absent other" (Bresheeth 2007a, 176) returning from exile in New York to a double exile in Nazareth (he is a stranger in his own home) and ending up in a worse exile—Jerusalem under occupation. "Instead of finding an old and cherished self," Bresheeth writes, "Suleiman is gradually and painfully disappearing—a simile of the disappearance of Palestine, and of the Palestinians" (ibid., 178). In light of the woman's disappearance, the viewer begins to wonder whether resistance lies in E.S.'s steadfastness in remaining present on the screen despite his silence and dwindling levels of activity.

But E. S. does not disappear—he is seen again in *The Time That Remains*—nor does Palestine. In a title card in *Chronicle,* E. S. types "*al-damir al-mustatir taqdiruhu filastin*" (the hidden conscience of estimated Palestine). For Arabic speakers, this phrase invites a grammatical interpretation of the sentence: "The implied pronoun is understood to be Palestine." Thus, the implied pronoun is a reference to a hidden one used to identify an agent. In this case, E. S. estimates the agent to be "Palestine." Suleiman's character E. S. highlights the power of the nonverbal and the unspoken, carrying a heavy silence that speaks louder than the various modes of communication that failed him. Thus, the silenced Palestine becomes inevitably present through its absence. Suleiman believes that "the things we say are so minute compared to the things that are unsaid" (Suleiman 2010). Attracted to the power of silence in destabilizing power, Suleiman also sees the crevices it creates as an invitation for the viewer's own participation. In the end E. S.'s strength lies in using silence to juxtapose "two versions of reality—one present and the other absent, each concealing yet exposing the other" (Gertz and Khleifi 2008, 181).

NARRATING THE ABSURD

Representing the suspended and often absurd lives of Palestinians has led Suleiman down a path of experimentation, eventually giving rise to the nonlinear, fragmented and silent narratives of his fiction films. This chapter is a brief insight into the visual richness the films offer for analysis. It began by looking at how Suleiman's most recent film, *The Time That Remains,* challenges the notion that Palestinian fiction films do not directly engage with the history of the past by representing the 1948 Nakba. I argued that in fact *The Time That Remains* is less about historical representation and more interested in uncovering different forms of narration and communication, in aesthetic continuity with the present-day narratives of *Chronicle of a Disappearance* and *Divine Intervention.* The ambiguity of genre—whether *The Time That Remains* is a period film, or whether *Chronicle* and *Divine Intervention* are documentaries, autobiographies, or fiction—is the result of experimentation and Suleiman's refusal to adhere to conventional forms. The blurring of genres goes hand in hand with a shift of perspective. While it is clear that *The Time That Remains* deals with historical material, it purposely leaves out big chunks of history. It represents the story through moments of surprise, viewed from within the cracks of the conflict and the emotions of history. I argued that just as *The Time That Remains* does not attempt a historical reconstruction of events in the documentary sense, the same applies to the treatment of the present in *Divine Intervention* and *Chronicle.*

Although set up to resemble documentary interviews, the examples of anti-interviews in *Chronicle* illustrate a reluctance toward straightforward narration and storytelling. The rare verbal interjections in this mostly silent film question narratives constructed through use of language, and by extension those with truth claims such as historical narratives. Combined with the nonverbal, fragments of the film fill in the negative space around the story, outlining the contours of the conflict without directly addressing it. This is Suleiman's narration from negative space, the view from the margins, and his decentralized image, springing from unusual moments in the cracks of daily life and history, avoiding sensationalism, and offering multiple levels of meanings and interpretation, but no singular truths. The decentralized peripheral image in Suleiman's films—which ruffles the viewer's comfort zone—draws attention to itself as a film image. Self-reflexive techniques expose the way narratives are constructed, whether through the film-within-a-film effect as in *Homage* and *Chronicle* or through the sticky notes scenes of *Divine Intervention,* which act as the storyboard of the film that is being viewed. The films also refer and allude to each other in a metafictional, self-reflexive manner, through recurrent structural patterns, techniques, characters, themes, and aesthetics. The parallel fictional world turns familiar spaces and faces into a global collective memory through which Palestinian presence is reaffirmed and becomes a metaphor for the world. *The Chronicle of a Present Absentee* may be taken as a fitting subtitle for the process that first began by chronicling a so-called disappearance and evolved into a process of recording presence through absence. Ultimately, Suleiman's strategy of simultaneously concealing and exposing parallels the paradoxical situation where the Palestinians are willed to disappear but continue to be present despite acts of recording their nonexistence.

After the release of *The Time That Remains,* it can be said that Palestinian fiction film no longer shies away from representing the tragic events of the Nakba of 1948. Rather it is the representation of a future that continues to be the black hole in contemporary Palestinian cinema.

NOTES

1. Elia Suleiman, interview with the author at the BFI London Film Festival, October 16, 2009. Other influences Suleiman mentions include Edward Said, Hannah Arendt, the Frankfurt School of Philosophy, Primo Levi, John Berger, and the Syrian poet Adonis.

2. Ibid.

3. Ibid. "I remember that the first version I wrote," Suleiman remarked, "was an interesting script but at the same time very narrative. It was a story about a family. What you saw in *Chronicle* is the deconstruction of that narrative. I was heading elsewhere. I needed to start work to know what was needed—I still had a lot of insecurity about throwing myself in the poetic frame."

4. The documentary features Elia Suleiman and Amos Gitai on their way to the Vesoul festival in France. They share their thoughts on war and peace in the Middle East and their somewhat comical experiences at the festival.

5. For more on the film see Anne Bourlond (2000).

6. Elia Suleiman, interview with the author at the BFI London Film Festival, October 16, 2009. Suleiman dismisses *Cyber Palestine* as "not terribly cinematic—it is very anecdotal. You can see I am not in that film. There is nothing real; it's a religious story. It's not really my style, I mean, it is not really studied in an aesthetic sense."

7. Suleiman speaks about screening his film in Ramallah in the Jason Wood interview (2006). In addition, see the section titled "The Cinema and Its Audience" in Gertz and Khleifi (2008, 34–37).

8. The films Bresheeth analyzes are: *Ustura* (Israel, 1998), *Jenin, Jenin* (Israel/Palestine, 2002), *Egteyah* (Israel/Palestine, 2002), *Divine Intervention* (Palestine, 2002).

9. Elia Suleiman, interview with the author at the BFI London Film Festival, October 16, 2009.

10. "There is all the difference between document and documentary. I think what I do is to document," Suleiman stressed in an interview with the author at the BFI London Film Festival, October 16, 2009.

11. Negative space, in art, is the space around a subject. It is a technique whereby the emphasis is placed on the space around a subject rather than the subject itself. By shading the space around a subject, a silhouette of that subject emerges, drawing attention to the shape around it.

12. Elia Suleiman, interview with the author at the BFI London Film Festival, October 16, 2009.

13. Ibid.

14. Appears as a character named "Jamal" in the credits played by Jamal Daher.

15. Appears as Lutof Nweiser in the credits. Among other recurrent character/actor examples, Palestinian filmmaker and scholar, George Khleifi appears in both *Divine Intervention* (as the collaborator) and *The Time That Remains* (as mayor of Nazareth)

16. Bresheeth also writes about how the Zionist narrative annuls, conquers, and subdues a Palestinian party, history, and story; see p. 35.

FILMOGRAPHY OF ELIA SULEIMAN

Introduction to the End of an Argument / *Muqaddimah li-nihayat jidal*. Co-directed with Jayce Salloum. 1990. Distributed in the United States by Arab Film Distribution. 45 minutes. Documentary.

Homage by Assassination / *Homage par assessinat* / *Takrim bil qatl*. 1991. Distributed in the United States by Arab Film Distribution. 18 minutes. In *The Gulf War, What Next?* / *La guerre du Golfe . . . et après?*

War and Peace in Vesoul. Co-directed with Amos Gitai. 1997. Distributed in France by Agav Films and K-Films. 83 minutes. Documentary.

The Arab Dream / *Rêve arabe* / *al-Hulm al-arabi*. 1998. 20 minutes.

Chronicle of a Disappearance / *Chronique d'une disparition* / *Segell ikhtifa*. 1996. Distributed in the United States by International Film Circuit. 88 minutes.

Cyber Palestine. 2000. 15 minutes. Part of the Bethlehem 2000 Project.

Divine Intervention: A Chronicle of Love and Pain / *Intervention divine* / *Yadun ilahiyya*. 2002. Distributed in the United States by Avatar Films and Arab Film Distribution. 90 minutes.

Irtebak. 2007. 6 minutes. In *To Each His Own Cinema / Chacun son cinéma/* (60th Cannes Film Festival).

The Time That Remains / Le temps qu'il reste / al-Zaman al-baqi. 2009. Distributed in the United States by IFC Films. 109 minutes.

Diary of a Beginner. 2012. 17 minutes. In *7 Days in Havana / 7 jours à la Havane / 7 días en La Habana.* Distributed worldwide by Wild Bunch.

REFERENCES

Bourlond, Anne. 2000. "A Cinema of Nowhere: An Interview with Elia Suleiman." *Journal of Palestine Studies* 29 (1): 95–101.

Bresheeth, Haim. 2001. "Telling the Stories of *Heim* and *Heimat,* Home and Exile: Recent Palestinian Films and the Iconic Parable of the Invisible Palestine." *New Cinemas: Journal of Contemporary Film* 1 (1): 24–30.

———. 2002. "A Symphony of Absence: Borders and Liminality in Elia Suleiman's *Chronicle of a Disappearance." Framework* 43 (2): 71–84.

———. 2007a. "The Continuity of Trauma and Struggle: Recent Cinematic Representations of the Nakba." In *Nakba: Palestine, 1948, and the Claims of Memory,* edited by Ahmad H. Sadi and Lila Abu-Lughod, 162–183. New York: Columbia University Press.

———. 2007b. "Segell Ikhtifa: Chronicle of a Disappearance." In *The Cinema of North Africa And The Middle East,* edited by Gönül Dönmez-Colin, 169–178. London: Wall Flower Press.

Butler, Linda. 2003. "The Occupation (and Life) through an Absurdist Lens: An Interview with Elia Suleiman." *Journal of Palestine Studies* 32 (2): 63–73.

Cutler, Aaron. 2011. "Elia Suleiman." *Bomb Magazine,* January 18, http://bombmagazine .org/article/4802/. Accessed August 31, 2014.

Dabashi, Hamid. 2006a. "In Praise of Frivolity: On the Cinema of Elia Suleiman." In *Dreams of a Nation: On Palestinian Cinema,* edited by Hamid Dabashi, 131–161. London: Verso.

———. 2006b. "Introduction." In *Dreams of a Nation: On Palestinian Cinema,* edited by Hamid Dabashi, 7–22. London: Verso.

Erickson, Steve. 2003. "A Breakdown of Communication: Elia Suleiman talks about *Divine Intervention." Indiewire,* January 15, http://www.indiewire.com /article/a_breakdown_of_communication_elia_suleiman_talks_about_divine _intervention. Accessed August 31, 2014.

Gertz, Nurith, and George Khleifi. 2008. *Palestinian Cinema: Landscape, Trauma and Memory.* Edinburgh: Edinburgh University Press.

Haider, Sabah. 2010. "A Different Kind of Occupation: An Interview with Elia Suleiman." *Electronic Intifada,* February 1, http://electronicintifada.net/content/different -kind-occupation-interview-elia-suleiman/8654. Accessed March 3, 2015.

Jaafar, Ali. 2010. "The Time That Remains: Elia Suleiman." *BFI Sight & Sound Magazine,* June 20, http://www.bfi.org.uk/news-opinion/sight-sound-magazine/interviews /time-remains-elia-suleiman. Accessed August 31, 2014.

Lane, Anthony. 2011. "Unhappy Days." *The New Yorker,* January 17, http://www .newyorker.com/arts/critics/cinema/2011/01/17/110117crci_cinema_lane?current Page=all. Accessed August 31, 2014.

Mokdad, Linda. 2012. "The Reluctance to Narrate: Elia Suleiman's *Chronicle of a Disappearance* and *Divine Intervention.*" In *Storytelling in World Cinemas,* edited by Lina Khatib. Vol. 1, *Forms,* 192–204. London: I. B. Tauris.

Naficy, Hamid. 2001. *Accented Cinema: Exilic and Diasporic Filmmaking.* Princeton: Princeton University Press.

Porton, Richard. 2003. "Notes from the Palestinian Diaspora: An Interview with Elia Suleiman." *Cineaste* 28 (3), Summer: 24–27.

Smith, Damon. 2011. "Elia Suleiman, *The Time That Remains.*" *Filmmaker Magazine,* January 5, http://www.filmmakermagazine.com/news/2011/01/elia-suleiman-the -time-that-remains.

Suleiman, Elia. 2006. "The Hidden Conscience of Estimated Palestine." In *Theorising National Cinema,* edited by Valentina and Paul Willemen Vitali, 202–207. London: British Film Institute.

———. 2010. "Elia Suleiman Masterclass." *The Fabulous Picture Show,* January 14, al-Jazeera Network, www.aljazeera.com/programmes/fps/2010/01/2010111959577754 .html. Accessed August 31, 2014.

White, Rob. 2010. "Sad Times: An Interview with Elia Suleiman." *Film Quarterly* 64 (1), Fall: 38–45.

Wood, Jason. 2006. "A Quick Chat with Elia Suleiman." *Kamera,* http://www.kamera .co.uk/interviews/elia_suleiman.html. Accessed August 31, 2014.

———. "Elia Suleiman." 2006. In *Talking Movies: Contemporary World Filmmakers in Interview,* 216–221. London: Wall Flower Press.

Youssef Chahine and Yousra on the set of *The Emigrant,* about 1993.

5

Youssef Chahine

DEVOURING MIMICRIES OR JUGGLING WITH SELF AND OTHER (EGYPT)

Viola Shafik

ANECDOTES AND EXAGGERATIONS

When I was approached to contribute this chapter—I have to confess—I did refuse at first. So much has been already said about Youssef Chahine (Yusuf Shahin), and so many have written about him, for decades, including myself. At one point I stopped dealing with him; I moved to other subjects, despite the fact that his enigmatic figure has accompanied my film curating and writing career from the very beginning, and even on the private level I could hardly neglect his effect, having acquired a number of dear friends including my husband on his film sets. So, why not write about him, about "Jo," as his friends call him, him, one of the most congenial and charming directors of Egypt's cinematic Golden Age?

Doubtless the general iconic exaltation of Chahine's personality and work—regardless of his de facto enormous achievements—is one thing that made me start turning my attention away. I became so used to his overwhelming presence, his name looming through almost every announcement of Egypt-related film events, screenings of film retrospectives, reviews on Egyptian cinema, particularly in Europe, that I went fishing elsewhere. This, and the slight feeling of disappointment that had seized me since he entered his very last working phase; so different from the daring, charming—and entertaining—early Youssef Chahine. What happened?

You may think I am exaggerating. Sure, I do; for I cannot deny there is always something recognizably, unmistakably "Chahinian" about his works, regardless of their quality and difference over time, the mark of an auteur in the deepest Truffaut sense, a continuous marker that holds together and amalgamates even a strongly commercial, mainstream-oriented oeuvre of outstanding directors. Yet the question remains, how to nail down this personal "Chahinian" character? Critics have resorted to all kinds of descriptions: they juxtaposed him to his hometown, Alexandria, in "Chahine l'Alexandrin" (Bosséno, ed., 1985); they praised him for his political involvement (Khayati 1996), his realism (Farid 1992), his originality (Fawal 2001); they highlighted his "baroque" aesthetics (Larouche 1984), adding to that his immense fascination with popular film or, to be more precise, with early Hollywood musical. And in fact, a proper description should probably contain all of that.

With regard to more analytical or academic approaches, there is good reason to view Chahine as a politically oriented yet individualist auteur filmmaker who traded his neorealist roots for the nouvelle vague (Tesson 2008), to perceive him as a spearhead of postcolonial African cinema (Murphy and Williams 2007), and to discuss him as an example of counter-hegemonic cinema in relation to the "unfinished" modernist national Arab project (Khouri 2010).

What stands out in all these attempts, however, is that they agree on his hybrid patchwork cinema and his personal credo in diversity and cross-cultural humanism. Thus, I would like to highlight Chahine's aesthetic and thematic variety, his stylistic mishmash, or what Shohat and Stam (1994, 310) call the "anthropophagic devouring of varied cultural stimuli in all their heterogeneity" of Third World cinema when reacting to the West's Eurocentric orientation. Much of Chahine's artistic and political inspiration comes precisely from this constellation: drawing from a hegemonic West, devouring its impact and transcending it into cultural resistance, thereby reshaping his own oscillating political and cultural identity.

The particular features that hold Chahine's work together have formed interrelated clusters of subjects, motifs, and undercurrents—to name only one example, the motif of the prodigal son and the encounter with the sexual, religious, cultural, and ethnic Other (condensed most notably in the allegory of the urban hodgepodge, namely his hometown Alexandria) and, last but not least, subtle homoeroticism. On a more formal level the director has shown a recurrent inclination toward music hall and grand spectacle. His development may nevertheless be divided into three interrelated phases of continuous change: first, his adaptation of classical Hollywood genre cinema, merging secondly into the so-called "revolutionary" realism of the Nasserist era, to be eventually complemented and in part extinguished by individualist authorship in his third phase.

FROM HOLLYWOOD TO POLITICS

Hollywood, and particularly the musical spectacle of the 1940s, is doubtless the starting point from which Chahine's overall work departs and to which it ultimately returns on the real-life as well as on the fictional level. Chahine was born in Alexandria into a Christian family of Levantine-Lebanese origin in 1926. Educated at the city's prestigious Victoria College, he left in 1946 to study method acting at the Pasadena Playhouse near Los Angeles, where he shifted his interest to directing. On his return he met the Egyptian film pioneer and camera man Alvise Orfanelli, who seems to have opened for him the doors to the field and with whom he shot his second film, *Son of the Nile* (*Le fils du Nil / Ibn al-Nil, 1951*). Chahine started out with mainstream comedies, musicals, and even melodramas for a then booming national film industry. His very first film, *Baba Amin,* also known under the title *Father Amin* (*Papa Amine / Baba Amin,* 1950), and *Mortal Revenge,* also known under the title *The Blazing Sun* (*Soleil éclatant / Sira' fi-l-wadi,* 1954) are his most distinguished films of this period.

Baba Amin stands out for its relative stylistic coherence and its warm human approach. The middle-aged family father, Amin, lives with his wife, little son, and almost grown-up daughter in a petty bourgeois neighborhood of Cairo. He receives regular visits from a certain Mabruk, who eventually talks him into investing his life savings in an enterprise that promises fantastic returns. However, Mabruk disappears with the money and leaves Amin in huge trouble. He is now unable to pay for the mortgage on his house, the wedding of his daughter, and the bicycle he promised his son. Grief-stricken, the father dies, only to return as a ghost watching over the disasters his carelessness has engendered. After some dramatic turns, among others his daughter resorting to singing in a night club, Amin wakes up to find that it was all a nightmare; Mabruk reappears, and the money is even returned.

The film was based on an idea by the director scripted by Husain Hilmi. It recycles elements of Charles Dickens's *A Christmas Carol* (1843), such as the figure of the ghost and the motif of the dreamed death, but now the story is set in the fasting month of Ramadan, which in Egypt is a festivity similarly family-oriented as is Christmas. In some respects it anticipates the typical Chahine universe with its most recurrent characters and themes—that is, the economic crisis that hits a family, the embattled father, and the child witness (Bosséno 1985a). Plot and a masterful mise-en-scène radiate a lot of charm and fine humor, due also to highly successful casting, featuring two of the most distinguished film and theater actors of the time, Mary Munib as the mother and Husain Riad as the father, in addition to Fatin Hamama, who was to become the undisputed queen of melodrama, as the daughter.

In a way *Baba Amin* remains exceptional for that period, as in the following years many of Chahine's films lack the consistency of his first film, even though he had the opportunity to try out and increase his professional skills in different genres, ranging from spectacle to Bedouin film, thriller, melodrama, and musical. Only occasionally did he create a masterpiece; such was *Mortal Revenge,* with which he introduced his Alexandria compatriot Michel Chalhoub (Shalhub) to the silver screen as Omar Sharif ('Umar al-Sharif). Chalhoub/Sharif had never acted before and seems to have met the director accidentally in a Cairo café.

Mortal Revenge is a melodramatic thriller. Chahine successfully combined action elements such as chases and shootings with a typical melodramatic plot, namely love obstructed by class difference. Produced after the Nasserist coup d'état in 1952 and the first land reform, the film was part of a cinematic wave that denounced the old feudal system and its representatives, the pashas. The social struggle was epitomized in this case in a violent showdown set in the picturesque ancient Karnak temple. A handsome peasant son and engineer (Omar Sharif) and his beloved, the pasha's daughter (Fatin Hamama), are attacked by the pasha's greedy and abusive nephew, representing the old order, which gets wiped out on this occasion.

The same year a subsequent Chahine film, the spectacle *The Devil of the Desert (Le démon du désert / Shaytan al-sahra',* 1954), was released. It paid homage to a quite genuine Egyptian film genre, the Bedouin film, which was already at the verge of extinction. Chahine used some of the Orientalist repertory of early Hollywood films and combined it with an anticolonial subtext by representing an Arab Bedouin tribe confronting a tyrant king.[1] This film, like the director's subsequent musicals, was not highly regarded by the critics, nor even by the director himself, who considered it just a good exercise that helped him to accomplish his historical spectacle *Saladin Victorious* ten years later (Bosséno 1985b).

Chahine's musicals of the 1950s were quite obviously made to serve audience expectations and hardly made any realistic reference to social or political conditions. Such is the case of the melodramatic musical *The Lady on the Train* (*La Dame du train / Sayiddat al-qitar,* 1952), starring singer Layla Murad. While the film includes some cinematically interesting scenes, it is otherwise spoiled by a hardly believable plot of a woman duped by her greedy husband into being declared dead, thus depriving her of her daughter, who soon afterward fails to recognize her mother when she sees her by chance. The same may be said for two musicals featuring Farid al-Atrash, *Farewell to Your Love* (*Adieu mon amour / Wada't hubbak,* 1956) and *My One and Only Love* (*C'est toi mon amour / Inta habibi,* 1957), which furthermore were very poor in setting, cast, and characters. Ironically enough, in particular Chahine's more accomplished "commercial" films, such as the beautifully shot adaptation of the opera *Carmen, Lovers' Call* (*L'appel des amants / Nida' al-'ushshaq,* 1960) and *A Man in My Life* (*Un homme dans ma vie / Rajul fi hayati,* 1961) were less successful than the musicals at the box office.

The year 1963 saw the nationalization of the film industry, of studios and movie theaters, and the reorganization of the public film sector. Private producers, distributors, and film directors saw their existence jeopardized as the effects of these measures were compounded by bureaucracy, nepotism, and patronage. Some of them headed to Lebanon, boosting output there while production rates in Egypt sharply declined. Chahine too left temporarily for Lebanon, where he directed two films, first a musical, *The Seller of Rings* (*Le vendeur des bagues / Baya' al-khawatim,* 1965) with the Rahbani brothers and the iconic singer Fayruz adapting one of their operettas to the screen. The film was set in a Maronite (Christian) Lebanese environment in Mont Liban and displayed strongly folkloristic elements. Its almost entirely chanted dialogues set it apart from the patchwork style of Chahine's Egyptian musicals, where several on-screen turns by a star singer were usually held together by a fragmented and weak plot. Chahine's second Lebanese production, *Golden Sands* (*Sables d'or / Rimal min al-dhahab,* 1967) was a rather trivial love story between an Arab Bedouin girl and a Spanish torero set in Morocco, Lebanon, and Spain and lacking any realism or credibility.

Mastering the rules of mainstream film genres was always a necessity for Youssef Chahine. The mainstream vocabulary remained omnipresent even when he had first started experimenting with realism, as in *Cairo Central Station* (*Gare centrale / Bab al-hadid,* 1958), or later when producing his musical *The Return of the Prodigal Son* (*Le retour de l'enfant prodigue / 'Audat al-ibn al-dal,*

1976). The latter film stands out not only because it uses the unconventional musical style of the then young Lebanese singer, Magda al-Rumi, an outsider to the Egyptian star system, in a lead role, but also in combining her songs with group performances by workers, thus creating a sort of socialist musical.

Chahine's penchant for mainstream elements, particularly the use of songs and dances, persisted in his more radical auteur films, most notably his biographical series. In those works it is particularly Ginger Rogers and Fred Astaire who stand quite symbolically for Chahine's fascination with the cinematic spectacle in general and the American musical in particular. Their dance scenes are copied in *Alexandria . . . Why?* (*Alexandrie pourquoi?* / *Iskandariyya . . . lih?* 1978) and used as inspiration in *Alexandria Again and Forever* (*Alexandrie encore et toujours* / *Iskandariyya kamam wa kaman,* 1990); the name Ginger even stands in to tell us the story of Chahine's first love in *Alexandria . . . New York* (*Alexandrie . . . New York* / *Iskandariyya . . . New York,* 2004).

REALISM AND POLITICS

For good reason, francophone film historiography (Thoraval 1975) particularly linked Chahine at first to the country's politically committed realist wave of the 1950s and 1960s that developed after the deposition of the Egyptian king in 1952, the foundation of the Egyptian republic, and complete national independence[2]—or to what Ella Shohat defined much later as anticolonial post-independence "Third-Worldist" cinema. Chahine had already shown interest in realism at an earlier stage, most notably with *Cairo Central Station* (1958) and to a certain extent even with *Son of the Nile* (1951), which starts out as a rural coming-of-age story but ends up as a nightclub drama. Yet Chahine cannot be singled out as the driving force behind Egyptian realism.

But then the very notion of Egyptian realism is problematic. Egyptian realism of the time was praised by national and international critics for being more authentic and in the socialist vein of the time, the antipode to the dream factory and its popular genres, farce-comedy, melodrama, musical, and thriller. Yet, such views neglected the fact that Egyptian realism, despite its overt alignment with nationalist anticolonial and quasi-socialist ideas, could never do without stars and relied heavily on mainstream genre elements, such as thriller and melodrama. Most of the first-wave Egyptian realism could be properly labeled "rhetorical realism," based on intention rather than any formal cinematic naturalism or quasi-documentary observation. *Cairo Central Station* comes close to the latter, but even this film was spiced with some comic scenes, musical inserts, a suspense-oriented plot that seeks a final dramatic resolution, and the glamorous presence of film star Hind Rustum in the role of a poor soft drink seller working at Cairo Central Station. The other lead role, however, was held by Chahine himself, playing the handicapped newsboy Qinawi, who falls in love with Hanuma. Emotionally and sexually deprived, he turns against her the moment he learns that she has only eyes for virile and strong Abu Sri'. In his rage he decides to abduct her, but he injures another girl instead. The main plot is enriched by several side stories, some of which pay tribute to socialist ideas—for example, the porters who try to form a syndicate under the leadership of Abu Sri'. Other parallel strings are highly stylized and quite comic, such as the Upper Egyptian lost in the crowd, or simply entertaining, like the group of young modern Egyptians whose singing and dancing is used as a pretext for a musical number. The strongest realist aspect of this film, however, remains the undisputedly haunting figure of Qinawi, whose poverty cast him from his village onto the crowded and at times hostile tracks of the railroad station platform—a marginalized, obsessive character who heralds the many other individualist and obsessed heroes that have populated Chahine's subsequent self-scripted auteur phase.

Yet it is precisely starting from the late 1950s that Chahine showed first signs of a general politicization, expressed in the anticolonial *Jamila the Algerian* (*Djamila / Jamila al-Jaza'iriyya*, 1958), which presented the ordeal and trial of a famous female Algerian mujahida or resistance fighter, and continued in *New Day* (*L'aube d'un jour nouveau / Fajr yaum jadid,* 1964), focusing on the *prise de conscience* of an upper class woman who falls in love with an academic from a lower-class background.

Jamila the Algerian was made at the height of Egypt's pan-Arab Nasserist phase, a period characterized by its strongly nationalist and anticolonial rhetoric in a time that saw the non-alignment conference held in 1955, which encouraged its members, most notably India and Egypt, to stay clear from the Cold War between the United States and the USSR, followed by the nationalization of the Suez Canal in 1956 that initiated the tripartite attack on Egypt by Israel, France, and Great Britain. In this context, the film demonstrated solidarity with a fellow Arab country, Algeria, in the middle of a ferocious national liberation war, and contributed to the third-worldist anticolonial rhetoric of the time. Casting Egyptian film star Magda, who used to appear in melodramatic love stories as the famous Algerian mujahidda, paid tribute to genre requirements by representing a suffering female heroine, with a man—French lawyer Maître Jacques Vergès, represented by Mahmud al-Miligi—coming to her rescue. At the same time, the heroine's plight and its surrounding circumstances did not unfold with the same disturbing realism and poignant analysis of Gillo Pontecorvo's *The Battle of Algiers* (1966), for example, but remained more or less in the vein of a black-and-white agitprop drawing, a mere sign of pan-Arab and anticolonialist solidarity.

Chahine's historical spectacle *Saladin Victorious* (*Saladin / al-Nasir Salah al-Din,* 1963) is part of the same pro-Nasserist anticolonialist agenda, even though the director was not on board with that project from the very beginning. Based on a screenplay developed by three lauded Egyptian novelists and scriptwriters, Nagib Mahfouz (Mahfuz), Yusuf Siba'i, and Galal Sharqawi, along with the filmmaker 'Izz al-Din Zul-Fiqar, who was supposed to direct this partly state-produced film at first, this work represents an ode to nationalist and unitary pan-Arabism like no other. It became, moreover, one of the most remarkable historical spectacles of Egyptian cinema, due to Chahine's skill in handling fierce battle scenes, but also because of the careful set and costume design realized by Wali al-Din Samih and Shadi Abdessalam.

In an indirect allusion to the country's political leader, Gamal Abdel Nasser, reflected in its Arabic title, the film focused on Saladin's struggle against European crusaders, with Richard Lionheart as his most distinguished opponent. It is no wonder that the narrative was not particularly accurate in describing the details of the crusades but offered a rather apologetic nationalist statement instead, depicting the Kurdish war lord Salah al-Din al-Ayyubi as a pan-Arab national hero defeating the crusaders, not simply by means of his military skills but by wisdom, righteousness, and dignity.

Chahine's enthusiasm for the nationalist and pan-Arabist experiment did not last. In an interview in 1971, on the completion of *The Sparrow* (*Le moineau / al-'Usfur,* 1971), he stated, "Today for example I could no longer direct Saladin. Its goal was to generate an emotional tension that is no longer sufficient. What you need today is analysis." According to the director's own account, it was in particular the events of June 1967, the so-called Six-Day War, that cemented his politicization, a war during which Egypt was defeated by Israeli forces, who were able to seize Sinai, the rest of Palestine, and the Syrian Golan Heights (Shafik 1989, 38). This historical event, which traumatized the whole Arab world and abruptly woke it up from its post-independence nationalist euphoria, incited Chahine's sense of responsibility, crystallizing in one of the most strongly Marxist-oriented anti-feudal realist epics of the Egyptian screen, *The Earth* (*La terre / al-Ard,* released in 1970) adapted from a novel by 'Abd al-Rahman al-Sharqawi.

In the aftermath of this defeat and the subsequent disillusionment, which led in the 1970s to the lifting of many socialist measures taken earlier to ease the gap between rich and poor, this work seems almost anachronistic. Ideologically the narrative of *The Earth* was one of Chahine's most uncompromising, in the sense that it did not distract from the violent class struggle it depicts through a story of romance. Moreover it was his last clearly so-called realist work. It focuses on a strong and wise peasant character, Abu Swailam (played by Mahmud al-Miligi), who unites the villagers to fight for their rights against the influential local landowner. Yet in the end solidarity and resistance are crushed, leaving the peasants' harvest destroyed and the leader of the insurrection tortured to death. *The Earth* has much in common with early Soviet cinema, its black-and-white photography, its realistic setting, and the eye for the small details such as the rugged clothes and the plight reflected in the faces of the poor, creating a sort of male Mother Courage legend, all the more memorable for being unprecedented in Egyptian film history.

THE ARAB AUTEUR

Dissecting his country's political and social situation either through realism or other genres, Chahine could never be fully identified with any genre until he became one of the Arab world's first and most distinguished auteur filmmakers, who not only insisted on a personal, individual film language, but tried also to assert their control on the very means of production. The defeat in 1967, and then Nasser's demise in 1971 and the gradual abandoning of his regime's policies, such as non-alignment and social welfare, profoundly affected Chahine, like many artists and intellectuals of his time. The post-independence nationalist dream crumbled and disillusionment spread. It is in this time frame that Chahine started to insist on a more personal approach to film subjects, to be sensed first in the psychological thriller *The Choice* (*Le choix* / *al-Ikhtiyar*, 1970), for which he wrote the screenplay, and continuing in *The Sparrow* (1971). *The Choice* deals with the killing of a much liked, joyful, and down-to-earth sailor, moving on to the drama of his intellectual and respected twin brother, who becomes mentally disturbed and eventually schizophrenic after he unsuccessfully seeks to acquire his dead brother's personality.

The Sparrow dissects the reasons for the 1967 defeat. In contrast to Chahine's earlier films, it is enriched with several parallel stories and numerous subjective moments, such as fantasies and nightmares. The panoramic film introduces a group of friends who are linked through their close relation to Bahiyya, an elderly woman who hosts them and tries to uplift them whenever they feel depressed. The group comprises the journalist Yusuf, who traces the secrecies of an arms-dealing mafia; Sheikh Ahmad, a kind of leftist fundamentalist; Johnny, a pessimistic drunkard; and the fiancé of Bahiyya's daughter Ra'uf, the son of an important state official. They are united first in helping the journalist in his investigation and then in their common experience of a collective debacle. Like many Egyptians at the time, they watch Nasser's historic televised speech on June 9, 1967, when he declared his resignation, and are shocked by the quick and unexpected military defeat. This is the film's most dramatic and pivotal scene, and it crystallizes the shattering of collective hopes that characterized the previous period in Egyptian and Arab history. It shows footage of Nasser's sad face and strongly measured voice in this speech, conveying the emotional quintessence of that historical era. While the leader declares his resignation, Sheikh Ahmad bursts out uncontrollably in tears. Bahiyya gets up and hurries out shouting: "No, we are going to fight, we are going to fight!" The film ends with doors and windows opening behind her, and people flooding out to fill the streets. In the background the corrupt official yells into the phone: "Who are those people, if they are not ours, who are they?"

Bahiyya's character is clearly metaphorical. She stands for "Mother Egypt." This allusion is reinforced by a song by Sheikh Imam that frames the film and starts with the lines "Masr yamma ya bahiyya" (Egypt, oh mother beautiful). With her and its dramatic ending *The Sparrow* evoked quite unmistakably the allegory of a female nation, in this case a nation not just facing the prospect of losing its leader, but finding herself betrayed by the new class of functionaries. Unwilling to accept her own defeat, Bahiyya asks her leader to stay, insisting on her determination to fight. The call to arms inherent in this scene was the reason Chahine's film was prohibited by Sadat's censors. For Sadat, the new self-declared "Father of the Nation" who came to power in 1970, wanted to conceal Egypt's future military intentions in order to take Israel by surprise and was not interested in any spontaneous call to arms. Thus *The Sparrow* was released only in 1973, after the October or Yom Kippur War.

The Sparrow introduced lasting changes to its director's vision. First of all, Chahine replaced the pivotal lone hero with a range of different characters (Shafik 1989, 38). It seems that the disillusionment of the defeat and the subsequent disappointment with the Nasserist experiment had engendered vexed identities, scattered perceptions of reality, expressed in an increasingly radical individualist film language. When his autobiographical masterpiece *Alexandria . . . Why?* appeared in 1978, it became a trendsetter for a new generation of Arab

Farid Shawqi and Hind Rustum in *Cairo Central Station.*

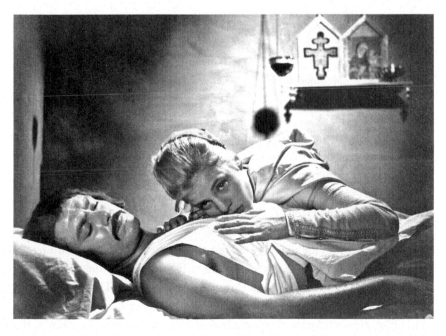

Salah Zul-Fiqar and Nadia Lutfi in *Saladin Victorious.*

Mahmud al-Miligi as Abu Swailam in *The Earth*.

filmmakers who departed from earlier notions of Third-Worldist anticolonial ideology that had been embraced by Arab state productions, toward a more independent art-film movement that put a strong emphasis on regional as well as individual existence and found its most acclaimed representatives during the 1980s in Nouri Bouzid from Tunisia, Mohamed Malas from Syria, and Michel Khleifi from Palestine. For Chahine, *The Choice* and *The Sparrow* were a turning point not only on the stylistic level but also on the professional. If his realist films had been only moderately successful at the box office, *The Choice* made him strongly contested, while the release of *The Sparrow* had to wait for years. The director was led to look for means to change the economic preconditions of his film productions, not an easy task under the "socialist" legacy of the Nasserist regime.

Ahmed Yehia and Yosra El-Lozy in *Alexandria . . . New York*.

Between 1963 and 1971 the state made an attempt to monopolize film production and distribution, while taking far-reaching measures that affected the film economy quite negatively for almost two decades by nationalizing film laboratory, studios, and movie theaters. Even though state production never exceeded 50 percent of the country's output, overall production decreased considerably during the 1960s, and a number of the most talented directors fled the country. For, contrary to what Chahine's personal *prise de conscience* in those same years suggested, times were not necessarily open to political and ambitious artistic expressions. On the contrary, political censorship, state bureaucracy, and patronage hampered even intellectually dedicated and politically committed directors. Chahine was one of them: for example, during shooting, his Russian co-production *The People and the Nile* (*Les gens du Nil / al-Nas wa-l-Nil,* 1968;

released in 1972) was jeopardized when Chahine dared to change the script, whose author, Musa Sabri, was a high-ranking state official and chief editor of al-Ahram (Nasrallah 1985).

Youssef Chahine looked for alternatives primarily in terms of foreign funding. In this he was unlike other gifted directors of the time, most notably the unique Shadi Abdessalam ('Abd al-Salam); this most radical Egyptian art filmmaker refused to accept foreign money for the production of his ingenious historical project *Akhenaten,* which for that very reason has remained uncompleted to this day. Chahine was able to establish his own means of production thanks to co-production and the help of his family, first of all financial assistance from his brother-in-law, who rendered him less dependent on the Egyptian market. His family's production house, Misr International, today under the direction of his nephew, was able to develop into a dynamic enterprise which, after running a studio and several formerly nationalized movie theaters, among other enterprises, relies also on local film distribution.

One of the pillars of this enterprise is the system of co-production. In 1971 and in 1976 Chahine received funds from the Algerian ONCIC (Office national pour le commerce et l'industrie cinématographiques) for *The Sparrow* and *The Return of the Prodigal Son.* He eventually was able to acquire French financial support for *Adieu Bonaparte* (*Wada'an Bonaparte,* 1985), due to his friendship with producer Humbert Balsan and French Minister of Culture Jacques Lang. All that finally secured him a steady and strong foothold in France, where he received funds for every film he directed henceforth. Since then his films have had only mediocre success in Egypt, but they have aired on European TV channels and circulated on European film festivals, leading to a Lifetime Achievement Award at the Cannes Film Festival in 1997.

ENCOUNTERING THE OTHER

It is certain that his increased acceptance in Europe has contributed to one of Chahine's major film tropes, condensing in the encounter with the Other—the religious, cultural, and sexual Other—a cinematic encounter often brought about either by military occupation or by the prodigality of his characters. Their prodigality is actually a continuation of early Chahinian motifs. These men leave home to be tragically crushed by their own limitations and those of their surroundings, or they manage to come back having dealt more or less successfully with their circumstances. They are peasants, like the main protagonists in *Son of the Nile* and *Cairo Central Station,* or errant intellectuals in *The Sparrow* and *The Return of the Prodigal Son.* Chahine's subsequent alter egos, Yahya in *Alexandria . . . Why?* and Ram in *The Emigrant* (*L'émigré* / *al-Muhajir,* 1994) are but variations of the same theme.

The continuity of these early motifs is overshadowed by the almost all-encompassing trope of the Other. This trope of cultural Other had already made its appearance in the historical spectacle *Saladin Victorious.* It reappeared and intensified in *Adieu Bonaparte,* set during Napoleon's invasion to Egypt, which added another dimension of the Other with the blossoming of homoeroticism. While in *Saladin Victorious* the Other was still bound into a post-independence nationalist discourse, in *Adieu Bonaparte* the Other corresponded to Chahine's personal agenda and world view. Yet, what both film have in common is their insistence on Arab-Muslim religious tolerance, contrasting it with strong tendencies of exclusion in the Occident.

In *Saladin Victorious* the notion of an Arab national identity is worked out cinematically, not only through polarizing Europeans and Arabs, Christians and Muslims, but also Arab Christians and European Christians. The character of 'Issa al-'Awam (Salah Zul-Fiqar), a Christian who is depicted as Saladin's right arm, is critical to establishing a secular notion of Arabism in the film. At the same time the film emphasized Arab moderation as opposed to European blood thirst. It conveyed that the Arab troops and their leader accepted and tolerated the presence of Christians in Jerusalem and all the other contested cities—a historical fact indeed, while the crusaders committed bloody massacres among Muslim civilians. Issa serves Saladin and his cause with his whole heart but is also seen to know the crusaders and their camp best, because of his hidden love for female crusader Louisa (Nadia Lutfi). The latter, due to her loyalty to her countrymen—that is, her national and religious affiliation at the time—does not dare to admit that she is attracted to 'Issa. Yet she stops participating in active fighting and turns to nursing the wounded when she understands that even though he is a Christian, 'Issa supports Muslim Saladin because of his Arab identity. Moreover, she witnesses several acts of treason among her fellow crusaders, which alienates her even more. In the end Richard Lionheart, upon his departure from the Holy Land, liberates Louisa from her moral constraints by advising her to follow her heart.

In Chahine's personal cinematic universe, ethnic or confessional deviations have been similarly paired with friendship and love. In *Alexandria . . . Why?* the hero's best friend in school is a Jew. Among his further acquaintances we find a Marxist female Jew who marries a Muslim comrade, as well as a homosexual Egyptian patriot who falls in love with a British soldier. The film thus makes a plea for a peaceful coexistence of faiths and the unconditional inclusion of the Other. The strategy Chahine uses is to diminish differences while presenting the almost mythical image of a traditionally tolerant Arab-Muslim culture. Most striking in this regard is the relationship of the French general Cafarelli (Michel Piccoli) with the two brothers Yahya and Ali in *Adieu Bonaparte,* an intensifying friendship and human intimacy that not only crosses cultural and religious borders, but culminates in same-sex admiration. Difference is ridiculed in this film, uncovered as a farce, through a striking scene in which occupant and occupier appear to reverse roles: during a masquerade, Napoleon, who has decided to wear the costume of an Arab, is shocked to discover that Ali has disguised himself as Bonaparte. This moment of comic mimicry not only destabilizes the political power relation but also underlines its temporally shifting nature.

Chahine's post-Nasserist ideological strategy has often been expressed in his calls for a culture of inclusion, a kind of heteroglossia, at home as well as abroad, while not necessarily denying religious difference. It stands in stark contrast to what was most common in Egyptian cinema, reinforced by censorship until the early 1990s—namely, to refrain from picturing Christian religious service and beliefs or other particularities, such as names and language with religious connotations, for the sake of national unity (Shafik 2007, 41). Not so Chahine: his semi-autobiographical films *Alexandria . . . Why?* and *An Egyptian Fairytale (La mémoire / Haduta misriyya,* 1982) are among the few Egyptian feature films that used explicitly Christian—albeit negatively depicted—symbols. In *An Egyptian Fairytale,* in one of the brief sequences that recapitulate childhood traumas, the director is depicted as horrified as a boy at the sight of a sculpture of the crucified Jesus; in another, the child protagonist inadvertently sets fire to the crib and fears to be punished with death "for having burnt Jesus."

Chahine's representation of difference has frequently involved the danger of being besieged by radical (religious) fanatics on one side or the other. Examples abound: scheming Muslim Brethren in *Alexandria . . . Why?*; the patriotic elder brother of Ali and Yahya who sides with the Mameluk princes, strongly disapproving his siblings' friendly interaction with the French, in *Adieu Bonaparte;* the comportment of religious fanatics who threaten Moorish philosopher Ibn Rushd (Averroës) in *Destiny (Le destin / al-Masir,* 1997); or modern Islamists who are opposed to a cross-cultural love-relation in *The Other (L'autre / al-Akhar,* 1999).

No wonder Chahine too incited Islamist opposition, which took shape in a court case launched against him by an Islamist lawyer in 1994, at the height of a wave of Islamist terrorism in Egypt. Because he adapted the story of Joseph

(Yusuf), who is considered a Muslim prophet, to the screen in *The Emigrant*, the director was accused of having infringed the country's censorship law banning any visual representation of the prophets. Interestingly, during the trial the religious affiliation of the director was not at issue. Chahine himself also never pointed to it, nor did anyone else mention, as far as I know, that he might have the right to deal with the Joseph figure from the perspective of his own Christian background.

POLITICAL INTERFERENCE AND CULTURAL DEVOURING

After his "political" turn Chahine developed a remarkable ability to sell his messages at the right time and place, if not to stir controversial public debates, as he did with *The Sparrow* and *The Emigrant*. Raymond Baker (1995, 32) goes so far as to suggest that the director at times opened up a space for what he calls "democratic interference." In his view, Chahine did not necessarily propose alternative visions inciting change, yet his "rude interference with official representations, discourses, and disciplines did help generate the kind of public space where a democratic politics able to struggle for a different future could, for some brief moments at least, take hold," with the short semi-fiction *Cairo as Seen by Youssef Chahine* (*Le Caire raconté par Youssef Chahine / al-Qahirra minawara bi-ahlihha*, 1991) the foremost example. This film—a hodgepodge of several staged actions, of a leftist turned Islamist, of a young unemployed man, offering observations of Cairo, its touristic and more private sites, combined with images of students protesting against the first Gulf War—was banned at first and incited a long public discussion on the freedom of expression, as was to be the case of *The Emigrant* as well.

The question remains whether Chahine's films, which have often been produced on the margins of the local market, could provide more than a brief and limited space for democratic politics. Moreover, his interference amounted at times to a sort of universalist humanism, as in his short contribution, *Egypt*, to the compilation film *11'09"01—September 11* (2002). This short starts out on the day after 9/11 with the director (represented by actor Nour al-Sherif) at the beach in Beirut, where he meets the ghost of an American killed in the Beirut marines barrack bombing in 1983. The beautiful young man says that he died just three days after he had met his first love. A debate ensues between the director and the American touching upon the Palestinian question and the U.S. involvement in the world that has resulted in millions of casualties, starting with Vietnam and ending in Iraq. The director takes the American to a Palestinian family to clarify to the audience why their son has taken part in a suicide bombing. Chahine draws on this encounter of sympathetic victims on both sides to call for the general necessity of remembrance and understanding.

Chahine's belief that "politics control society, and what controls politics is foreign policy" (Baker 1995, 31), as expressed in his short films *Egypt* and *Cairo as Seen by Youssef Chahine* and his critique of U.S. intervention in the region, explains also his constant open referral to colonialism and political extremism. Rather apologetic and far too often simply rhetorical, it has at times failed to satisfy the viewer's need to be provided with more substantial historical or social information and has transformed the narratives, which include some real historical characters, into allegories of current affairs. Such is the case in *Adieu Bonaparte* and *The Other*, which are in this respect quite unlike *Alexandria . . . Why?* and *An Egyptian Fairytale*.

The most telling example of this orientation is Chahine's last film, *Chaos* (*Le Chaos / Hiyya fawda*, 2007), co-directed a short while before his death with his assistant Khaled Youssef. This film sets out to expose human rights violations by Mubarak's police apparatus, but it seems to carry much more strongly Khaled Youssef's imprint, lacking the usual speedy dialogues and the typical Chahine universe. Its quite conventional dramatic story centers on a police officer who terrorizes a whole neighborhood, including a young woman whom he kidnaps and rapes when she refuses his advances. Metaphorically she stands for the raped homeland, or Mother Egypt (like Bahiyya in *The Sparrow*), the recurrent motif of anticolonial films and part of a highly popularized political discourse. The ending, which has the neighborhood rising up against the police officer, could be perceived as prophetic at the time (Gugler 2011, 12–13), yet it may be also interpreted as part of Khaled Youssef's political agenda as it parallels other moments of mass protest in his previous films, in particular the conclusion in *The Storm* (*al-'Assifa*, 2001). Indeed, Youssef appeared after the January 25 revolution as one of the most outspoken representatives of Egyptian artists.

In my view Chahine's real achievements lay elsewhere: in the carnivalesque subversions and modernist "anthropophagy" that have appeared in many of his films since *The Sparrow*. This practice was expressed precisely in his recurrent portrayal of his own and his characters' contradictory relationship with the West in general and the United States in particular, the deep ambivalence vis-à-vis the world's dominant disciplinary and colonizing powers: "Since there can be no unproblematic recovery of national origins undefiled by alien influences, the artist in the dominated culture should not ignore the foreign presence but must swallow it, carnivalize it, recycle it for national ends, always from a position of cultural self-confidence. The 'cannibalist' and 'carnivalist' metaphors have in common the appeal to 'oral' rituals of resistance, their evocation of a transcendence of self through the physical or spiritual commingling of self and other, and their call for the 'cordial mastication' and critical recycling of foreign culture" (Shohat and Stam 1994, 307).

While Ella Shohat and Robert Stam meant to characterize a certain type of Brazilian cinema, their statement enables us to grasp the stylistic variety in Chahine's work and its hybridity, which connects altogether different elements such as popular entertainment and autobiographic narration, cinematic realism and the radically individual and expressive interpretation of history at the very specific moment of de-(and re-)colonization in one and the same cinematic work. This tendency has been particularly evident in the director's autobiographies; a prime example is *Alexandria . . . New York,* his fourth autobiographical film. It pictures Yahya, his alter ego, an elderly Egyptian director who travels to New York for a film retrospective meant to honor his cinematic oeuvre, only to be reunited with the love of his youth, Ginger, who confesses to him that she has borne his son. This son, however, a gifted dancer, is unwilling to accept his Arab father, providing an opportunity for our director not only to lament America's lost grandeur, openness, and fascination but also to remember his own fight against all odds and eventual success in affirming his talent and cultural compatibility while studying abroad. This slightly nostalgic and standardized account is cemented on the narrative and stylistic level by the induction of recurrent mainstream film elements—in other words, the rules of the spectacle: the melodramatic victimization of fictional First-World Ginger, who, lacking her lover's talent, had to prostitute herself in contrast to Third-World Yahya's real-life success story, and glamorous music hall numbers reminiscent of the 1940s and 1950s.

This strategy, to tell a story of cultural resistance by means of an ironic imitation and/or kitschy exaltation of so-called Western popular film forms—melodrama, music hall, and the like—has been described by Shohat and Stam (1994, 283) as "mimicry." It is a profoundly subversive mimicry at times, if we look at Chahine's first autobiography, *Alexandria . . . Why?* This film describes the director's last high school year during World War II at the crucial historical moment when the troops of general Rommel arrived in El-Alamein, knocking at the doors of British-occupied Alexandria. It circles around his family's financial problems, which are overcome when young Yahya (Muhsin Muhi al-Din), Chahine's alter ego, obtains a much-longed-for scholarship to study acting in the United States, while offering a kaleidoscope of different multiethnic, religious, and cultural relations. Interspersed with historical newsreel footage, music hall numbers, theater plays, Shakespeare recitations, *Alexandria . . . Why?* not only quotes American cinematic models through original clips but amalgamates and appropriates them. This technique proceeds through a number of cheap local imitations, such as the awfully clumsy and low-brow dance number of some tastelessly costumed Egyptian women performing in a nightclub in front of drunken British soldiers, up to a burlesque student theater-play that makes fun of the political situation by presenting Yahya, dressed up as an Arab Bedouin, watching as one occupier after the other flocks through his desert. These kinds of ironic usages and adaptations of Western forms of representations and motifs eventually find their telling crescendo in the film's finale, with Yahya arriving at New York harbor. While he breathlessly watches the Statue of Liberty, the classic symbol of democracy, the statue suddenly presents him her toothless mouth in a nasty grin. This scene encapsulates, as no other, where Chahine's artistic and political interferences have taken place: in his practice of cinematic recycling and devouring, and in his confident, often joyful juggling with Self and Other.

NOTES

1. See my analysis of *Layla the Bedouin* (1937) as an anticolonial text (Shafik 2007, 96).

2. Egypt gained nominal independence from Great Britain in 1922, but remained factually under British occupation until 1954.

FILMOGRAPHY OF YOUSSEF CHAHINE

This list is limited to the films by Chahine discussed in this chapter. For a full filmography, see http://www.misrinternationalfilms.com/youssef-chahine-filmography.

Baba Amin / Father Amin / Papa Amine / Baba Amin. 1950. 110 minutes.
Son of the Nile / Le fils du Nil / ibn al-Nil. 1951. 120 minutes.
The Lady on the Train / La Dame du train / Sayiddat al-qitar. 1952. 100 minutes.
Mortal Revenge / The Blazing Sun / Soleil éclatant / Sira' fi-l-wadi. 1954. 105 minutes.
The Devil of the Desert / Le démon du désert / Shaytan al-sahra'. 1954. 105 minutes.
Farewell to Your Love / Adieu mon amour / Wada't hubbak. 1956. 100 minutes.
My One and Only Love / C'est toi mon amour / Inta habibi. 1957. 120 minutes.
Cairo Central Station / Gare centrale / Bab al-hadid. 1958. 73 minutes.
Jamila the Algerian / Djamila / Jamila al-Jaza'iriyya. 1958. 120 minutes.
Lovers' Call / L'appel des amants / Nida' al-'ushshaq. 1960. 110 minutes.
A Man in My Life / Un homme dans ma vie / Rajul fi hayati. 1961. 110 minutes.
Saladin Victorious / al-Nasir Salah al-Din. 1963. 145 minutes.

New Day / L'aube d'un jour nouveau / Fajr yaum jadid. 1964. 130 minutes.

The Seller of Rings / Le vendeur des bagues / Baya' al-khawatim. 1965. 95 minutes

Golden Sands / Sables d'or / Rimal min al-dhahab. 1967. 91 minutes.

The Earth / La terre / al-Ard. Released in 1970. 130 minutes.

The Choice / Le choix / al-Ikhtiyar. 1970. 110 minutes.

The Sparrow / Le moineau / al-'Usfur. 1971. 102 minutes.

The People and the Nile / Les gens du Nil / al-Nas wa-l-Nil. 1972 (shot in 1968). 86 minutes.

The Return of the Prodigal Son / Le retour de l'enfant prodigue / 'Audat al-ibn al-dal. 1976. 120 minutes.

Alexandria . . . Why? / Alexandrie pourquoi? / Iskandariyya . . . lih? 1978. 125 minutes.

An Egyptian Fairytale / La mémoire / Haduta misriyya. 1982, 125 minutes.

Adieu Bonaparte / Wada'an Bonaparte. 1985. 114 minutes.

Alexandria Again and Forever / Alexandrie encore et toujours / Iskandariyya kamam wa kaman. 1990. 105 minutes.

Cairo as Seen by Youssef Chahine / Le Caire raconté par Youssef Chahine / al-Qahirra minawara bi-ahlihha. Short docu-drama. 1991. 23 minutes.

The Emigrant / L'émigré / al-Muhajir. 1994. 124 minutes.

Destiny / Le destin / al-Masir. 1997. 131 minutes.

The Other / L'autre / al-Akhar. 1999. 107 minutes.

Egypt. 2002. 11 minutes. In *11'09"01—September 11.*

Alexandria . . . New York / Alexandrie . . . New York / Iskandariyya . . . New York. 2004. 11 minutes.

Chaos / Le Chaos / Hiyya fawda. Co-Directed with Khaled Youssef. 2007. 122 minutes.

REFERENCES

Baker, Raymond. 1995. "Combative Cultural Politics: Film Art and Political Spaces in Egypt." *Alif* 15: 6–38.

Bosséno, Christian, ed. 1985. *CinémAction* 33.

———. 1985a. "Papa Amine." *CinémAction* 33: 129.

———. 1985b. "Le démon du désert." *CinémAction* 33: 133–134.

Farid, Samir. 1992. *Adwa' 'ala sinima Yusuf Shahin* [Spotlight on Youssef Chahine's Filmmaking]. Cairo: al-Hay'a al-Misriyya al-'Ama li-l-Kitab.

Fawal, Ibrahim. 2001. *Youssef Chahine.* London: BFI.

Gugler, Josef. 2011. "Creative Responses to Conflict." In *Film in the Middle East and North Africa: Creative Responses to Conflict,* edited by Josef Gugler, 1–36. Austin: University of Texas Press.

Khayati, Khémaïs. 1996. *Cinémas arabes: Topographie d'une image éclatée.* Paris: L'Harmattan.

Khouri, Malek. 2010. *The Arab National Project in Youssef Chahine's Cinema.* Cairo: American University in Cairo Press.

Larouche, Michel. 1984. "L'esthétique de Chahine." In *Chahine et le cinéma égyptien* (*Dérives 43*), edited by Jean Jonassait, 27–50. Montreal: Dérives.

Murphy, David, and Patrick Williams. 2007. *Postcolonial African Cinema: Ten Directors*. Manchester, UK: Manchester University Press.

Nasrallah, Yousry. 1985. "Des origines à 'Adieu Bonaparte.'" Interview with Youssef Chahine. *CinémAction* 33: 104–107.

Shafik, Viola. 1989. *Youssef Chahine* (Kinemathek, vol. 74). Berlin: Freunde der deutschen Kinemathek.

Shafik, Viola. 2007. *Popular Egyptian Cinema: Gender, Class, and Nation*. Cairo: American University in Cairo Press.

Shohat, Ella, and Robert Stam. 1994. *Unthinking Eurocentrism: Multiculturalism and the Media*. London: Routledge.

Tesson, Charles. 2008. "Chahine, gare centrale" (Part of *Hommage à Youssef Chahine*). *Cahiers du Cinéma* 637: 78–81, http://www.cahiersducinema.com /Hommage-Chahine-gare-centrale.html.

Thoraval, Yves. 1975. *Regards sur le cinéma égyptien*. Beirut: Dar el-Machreq.

Daoud Abd El-Sayed, 2013.

6

Daoud Abd El-Sayed

PARODY AND BORDERLINE EXISTENCE
(EGYPT)

Viola Shafik

Classified at first as one of Egypt's "New Realists," Daoud Abd El-Sayed (Dawud 'Abd al-Sayyid) was in fact one of the least productive representatives of this wave that started in the 1980s. Like other New Realists, he faced major problems in finding willing producers to venture into more committed subjects. Yet despite his sporadic output, he developed and cultivated his own style, leaving behind any early classifications: epic in his narratives, often theatrical, though deeply lyrical, and at the same time ironic to the point of cynicism, he deserves to be labeled an auteur filmmaker even though he has never—unlike Youssef Chahine and Yousry Nasrallah—tailored his films for an international audience or for the European art house. Largely his own scriptwriter, he likes to send his protagonists on unsettling journeys and expose them to extreme or absurd situations. His evident social criticism quite often translates into parody; he hides the existential strife of his heroes and heroines behind an entertaining mainstream structure, ranging from thriller to musical. Despite his readiness to entertain, his insistence on quality and his critical mind still made producers shy away even after his major box office hit in 1991. This is why in forty years his work comprises only eight full-length fiction films (the ninth is currently in preparation) and six documentaries.[1]

Daoud Abd El-Sayed was born in 1946 into a Coptic middle-class family and was raised in Cairo. He studied film directing at the Higher Film Institute, graduated with excellence in 1967, and found employment in the state-run Film Organization. In the early 1970s he joined the National Documentary Film Center founded by Saad Nadim and Fuad al-Tuhami. During this period he directed several commissioned films, mostly of an educational nature, worked as an assistant director for Youssef Chahine and Kamal al-Shaykh, among others, and contributed to the Film Center's newsreel production. The few documentaries he was able to shoot following his own interests reflected the dilemmas of his subsequent fiction film production, which saw his ambitions always being curtailed by economic and/or political restrictions.

The Advice of a Wise Man in Matters of Village and Education (*Wasiyyat rajul hakim fi shu'un al-qarya wa-l ta'lim,* 1976)[2] was Abd El-Sayed's third short documentary and the first remarkable work in his oeuvre. It was realized under very difficult circumstances, as the National Film Center suffered from a lack of appropriate equipment and an even greater lack of financial means. Its productions had to be shot with heavy 35mm cameras at a very limited film material ratio, often less than 1:4. This meant that documentaries had to be staged and could hardly use any direct cinema style. Abd El-Sayed circumvented these limitations by scripting a fake documentary that contrasted the experience of his main interview partner, a rural schoolteacher who deplored the difficult state of education in the region of Kafr al-Shaykh, with the cynical voice-over commentary of a fictive upper-class character. The latter expressed strong reservations about the education of villagers. Moreover, the director and some of his state-employed colleagues met strong resistance when realizing critical or artistically ambitious films for economic as well as political reasons. The state-run National Film Center seems to have sought to curb its filmmakers' social and political criticism by restricting them by and large to themes concerned with fine arts and folklore (Raga' 2007, 37). Once again, these restrictions inspired Abd El-Sayed to improvise. His *Working in the Field* (*al-'Amal fi-l-haql,* 1979) became a poetic portrait of the Egyptian impressionist painter Hassan Sulayman. Abd El-Sayed used a single painting depicting work in a field on the countryside to contemplate the painter's oeuvre and the nature of creation as an act of resistance, as well as his own approach as a film director to his subject, creating a complex set of meanings.

These early short films heralded the main characteristics of Daoud Abd El-Sayed as one of Egypt's few auteur filmmakers in two ways: his interest in social criticism, and the self-reflexivity and intellectuality that made him resort often to irony, if not parody, in dealing with social or political issues. This approach marked his first full-length fiction film, *The Vagabonds* (*al-Sa'alik*, 1985), and later *Kitkat* (1991), *The Wedding Thief* (*Sariq al-farah*, 1995), and *A Citizen, a Detective, and a Thief* (*Muwatin, mukhbir wa harami*, 2001). Largely scripted by himself, these narratives were predominantly concerned with commenting on Egypt's rapid and radical social and political change either in an ironic or in a more compassionate way. A second string of narratives depicted odysseys and identity crises, individuals lost in time or space or leading a marginal existence, most notably *The Search for Sayyid Marzuq* (*al-Bahth 'an Sayyid Marzuq*, 1991), *Land of Dreams* (*Ard al-ahlam*, 1993), *Land of Fear* (*Ard al-khawf*, 1999), and *Messages from the Sea* (*Rasa'il al-bahr*, 2010). Marginal existences and social mobility became the central motifs that the director used to dissect Egypt's social and political turmoil since the end of Nasserism. These motifs were oftentimes complementary in the sense that the absurdity of the social system seemed to be necessarily reflected in the private lives of his protagonists. The depiction of turmoil and absurdity can be traced also in scripts of his that never or hardly materialized, such as *What Happened to the Moon?* (*Mal al-qamar?*), written in the second half of the 1980s, which deals with the setbacks and prosecution of intellectuals in the last year of Sadat's rule. In the same vein *Special Abilities* (*Qudrat khassa*), developed during the last decade of the Mubarak regime, is the story of a little girl of genius whose talent gets manipulated by the state's secret service. After several years in the pipeline, this film is only now in production and should be finished by the end of 2014.

A third project focusing on the Christian existence in Egypt fell prey to the increasing self-censorship exerted by members of the industry since the late 1980s. *Indian Film* (*Film hindi*) initially met with some resistance from the regime's censors. The film reflected on the experiences in youth of its Protestant scriptwriter, Hani Fawzi, in a humorous way; the Arab title, *Film hindi*, stood as a metaphor for triviality. Dealing with a sexually frustrated Christian and his friendship with a Muslim full of the joys of life, the film would have become the first Egyptian feature dealing in some depth with Christian psychology and piety. Yet, some of the responsible censors expressed the opinion that no church should be seen and no prayers heard; others wanted the protagonist Samuel to carry a more neutral (i.e., religiously unspecific) name. These objections were made in spite of the fact that, with regard to religious difference, Egyptian censorship regulations state quite generally that causing a stir or division among faith communities, classes, or the national unity is not permitted (Shafik 1998, 75).

Eventually the script was approved in 1995. However, social censorship proved to be more effective than state censorship: two popular young actors who had been cast for the lead roles withdrew because of the religious content, and so did the producer Hussein al-Qalla, who in the end felt it was too risky to produce the story. It is no wonder the project was not realized for years. Only in 2003, when it had become politically more opportune to present Egyptian Christians on the screen, was a production company found willing to support the film. Little surprise, it was the partly state-owned Media Production City, under the auspices of the Ministry of Information, which started at the time to foster a public discussion on national unity. Still, the film was to be made with a mediocre cast. By that time, however, Abd El-Sayed had already given up on his project as it could not be realized the way he had envisioned it. Eventually the film was directed by Munir Radi and released in 2003.

FAT CATS AND POOR UNDERDOGS

Daoud Abd El-Sayed's first full-length fiction film, *The Vagabonds* (1985), also faced some delay and a very tight budget. It was only made possible by the support of close friends, some of whom deferred their wages. Its epic narrative was inspired by the real-life success story of the supposedly illiterate Rashad 'Uthman, who became an influential businessman and member of parliament. The film features two deprived young men, Mursi and Salah, who survive by taking occasional jobs in the Alexandria harbor. Eventually they manage to start a trafficking business and move on to drug dealing. They become two of the most prosperous businessmen in town until they fall prey to an established, better connected entrepreneur.

This story and its realistic mise-en-scène gained *The Vagabonds* recognition as one of the most distinguished works of the Egyptian New Realism of the 1980s. The core group of this wave included Atef El-Tayeb, Bashir al-Dik, Khairy Beshara, Mohamed Khan, Daoud Abd El-Sayed, Ali Badrakhan, and Ra'fat al-Mihi. They were defined as realists because of their socially committed themes and their formal approaches: they shot on location, cut back on music, and used sober acting. At the same time their films, much like the first wave of Egyptian realism that started in the late 1940s, depended on local forms of production and followed the conventions of the Egyptian film industry, using known stars and compromising with prevalent genre standards.

The Vagabonds is essentially a "fat cats" plot, a theme widely used in action films as well as New Realist works of that period and motivated by a tide of criticism of the social effects of Sadat's Open Door Policy (*infitah*), as opposed to the quasi-socialist project of the preceding Nasser regime. Most of the films featuring this theme linked the nouveaux riches with criminal practices and decried their materialism and lack of the traditional sense of community. Moreover, fat cat narratives tended to be quite stereotypical and standardized. They exaggerated the extent of lower-class mobility and distorted the front line of social struggle, portraying the middle class as caught between the new bourgeoisie and the urban lower class.

Hence, one of the main tropes presented in *The Vagabonds* and many other New Realist films is the bourgeoisie's strong sense of existential endangerment in the face of the economic changes but also its clinging to its cultural capital, to use Pierre Bourdieu's term, as a safe haven. Abd El-Sayed depicts these two features through a parallel story of Salah courting a young intellectual woman from a bourgeois family. Through this relationship the film pictures the gap between the uneducated, quasi-criminal nouveau riche and the respectable and supposedly uncorrupted middle class. Salah cannot buy her love, and she prefers to go abroad to pursue her studies rather than marry him. His personal disintegration accelerates and he finally breaks up with his friend Mursi, who has completely succumbed to the laws of the capitalist jungle, where the economy is dominated by a corrupt network of businessmen and politicians. The film closes in line with that logic: a tragic showdown leaves Salah, the more sympathetic and romantic of the two, dead.[3]

In this Abd El-Sayed followed the established formula, materialism as opposed to friendship and social solidarity, a trope common to other New Realist films as well—for example, *The Flood* (*al-Tufan*, 1985), by Bashir al-Dik, and *Return of a Citizen* ('*Awdat muwatin*, 1986), by Mohamed Khan. However, like other Realists he departed from mainstream interpretations of this theme through a profound study of character and social environment. Not only do both tramps remain quite sympathetic until the very end, but their transgressions do not elicit unconditional critical distancing or invite moral judgment right away. Such is the case of one side line of the narrative that involves adultery. As Salah tenderly takes care of Mursi's wife while his friend serves a prison sentence, they are seduced by their physical closeness and end up making love. Their subsequent *prise de conscience* does not feed into any melodramatic turning points but remains embedded in the overall humane and loving characterization of these two particular protagonists and their humane orientation as opposed to Mursi's increasing, albeit troubled, materialism.

Like many other New Realist films, *The Vagabonds* was not a box office hit, and it took Abd El-Sayed several years to find a producer willing to finance his relatively expensive third feature, *Kitkat* (*al-Kitkat*, 1991). The film was set in a lower-class environment and therefore had to make use of an entirely studio-created setting; it is considered almost impossible to bring in heavy equipment and, more importantly, acclaimed stars into lower-class neighborhoods for long-term shooting because of security concerns. The film, based on Ibrahim Aslan's novel *The Heron*, is set in the smaller part, Kitkat, of one of Cairo's most crowded neighborhoods, Imbaba, close to the upscale Mohandessin and Dokki. The main conflict of the story revolves around the small house of blind Sheikh Husni, a congenial and joyful character. Several parties are interested in the house. Husni's unemployed son would like to sell it in order to get a visa and work permit abroad; the wealthy butcher dreams of pulling it down to construct a more profitable building. However, to everybody's surprise, it turns out that Sheikh Husni has pawned his property a long time ago to a drug dealer for a daily supply of hashish.

The film ends with a hilariously comic scene in which the blind man exposes all the other players. During a funeral, when all the neighbors are gathered in a tent to listen to the Quran, the technician falls asleep and forgets to switch off the microphone. Husni realizes what has happened and starts a conversation with a neighbor in which he exposes the neighborhood's secrets, the bad intentions of the butcher and the drug dealer, his son's love affair, and the mishaps of some other marginal characters, like the young jeweler who has been duped by his wife and his mother-in-law. The Sheikh thus defies his neighbors' plans to take advantage of him because of his physical deficiency. It is precisely because he is blind that he manages to decipher and interpret other people's interests, thereby reversing the very notion of blindness as a handicap. It is he who "sees" what everyone else is hiding, be it conspiracies, crimes, or sexual affairs.

As for the film's narrative form: I have discussed the anecdotal character of *Kitkat* elsewhere (Shafik 2007, 92). The set of not altogether interdependent stories helps to convey the tight web of relations in the neighborhood that affects each individual's fate. This depiction, along with the charming principal protagonist, made the film an unexpected box office hit, running for almost four months in Cairo's movie theaters. *Kitkat* was a turning point in the director's popularity; however, it did not speed up his production wheel. It took him another four years to direct his next film, again socially critical but also a concession to mainstream production, a musical starring belly dancer Lucy and produced by the latter's husband.[4]

The Wedding Thief (1995) is based on a short story by Khairy Shalabi (2002). Thematically it is but another social mobility story, depicting the struggle of a young couple from a shantytown on the Muqattam Hills, street hawker 'Awad and his beloved Ahlam, to collect enough money to be able to marry. However, an unconventional musical and a strong female lead distinguish the film. Unlike the other musicals of the time, *The Wedding Thief* does not present any of the known pop singers, but instead relies solely on several songs presented by a chorus with changing lead singers, two of them the lead players, who are not professional singers. Its music is likewise exceptional, a mixture of pop, classical European, and Egyptian music compsed by Abd El-Sayed's cousin Rageh Daoud (Ragih Dawud); so are the prose texts scripted by the director himself. Moreover, the slightly stylized gay and colorful setting and costumes match the fairytale elements of the story and serve to contradict the evident miserable living conditions of the characters, or at least to elevate them to an imaginary level while subverting the realist appearance.

On the narrative level the fairytale aspect is underlined by some supernatural turning points, culminating in Awad's consecutive visits to the shrine of Abu al-'Alamat (literally, Father of Signs) asking for help and for an answer whether to go ahead and marry Ahlam or to drop the idea altogether. He receives a positive sign every time, once some bird droppings on his head (a sign of good luck), another time a broken jar, or unexpected rain. The musical inserts underline this chimerical aspect as well, even though, echoing the bittersweet ending of the film, the words of the songs carry a lot of tragic potential—for example the lead song, "There is a girl who will marry and a boy who is getting settled." Instead of praising the extraordinary qualities of love, the song goes on to explain how female beauty fades after marriage, describing the multiple hardships a woman meets as she ages. The song is accompanied by images of the shantytown poor, which reinforce its message.

The same subversive strategy becomes evident in the film's final resolution, which offers a strong moment of truth. On their wedding night, when the couple has finally realized their common dream, Ahlam confesses that she has acquired the money she contributed to the wedding by dancing at a party for men. As 'Awad beats her up, she reminds him that he became a thief and a pimp to find the rest of the money. With that they break even, and instead of making love, Ahlam goes to the window and starts ululating happily as women are expected to, when a marriage has been consummated. While adhering to the core messages of the Egyptian dream factory since the 1930s—love marriage and social mobility—*The Wedding Thief* displays a high degree of skepticism about the realization of such dreams, thus moving toward deconstructing the genre rules of Egyptian realism.

PARODYING SOCIAL MOBILITY

A Citizen, a Detective, and a Thief (2001) is Abd El-Sayed's second musical. Much more than *Wedding Thief*, this film presents a clear parody of a social success story in depicting a citizen's gradual decline into cultural and religious conservatism until he becomes an acclaimed member of the new Islamist bourgeoisie. In fact, upon a second viewing, it is clear that the narration of *A Citizen, a Detective and a Thief*, as in a number of Abd El-Sayed's other films, combines the issue of social and political freedom with the radical social changes that have arisen since the 1970s as a result of the implementation of the Open Door Policy. It emphasizes the protagonists' class affiliation along with their ideological orientation through dress, behavior, language, and cultural interests.

The citizen, a cultured, rich, and handsome bachelor who is about to finish his first novel, is depicted in outfit and manners as strongly Westernized, quite unlike the other protagonists. The detective, in contrast, lives in a small, cramped rooftop flat in a lower-class neighborhood and dresses in the traditional jalabiyya, and the thief and the girl, the maid Hayat, live in the middle of a shantytown. In the course of the film, maid, thief, and detective gradually sneak into the life of the bourgeois until he becomes their business partner, allowing the thief, moreover, to impose his moralistic views by editing and publishing his novels. Social reconciliation takes also place on the sexual level, with the maid marrying the writer, and the thief wedding the writer's former girlfriend. Visually, too, the three parties come to resemble each other, adopting the same style of dress and living in the same kind of villa in one of the newly constructed affluent Cairo suburbs. They also come to adhere to the same ideas and moral precepts to the extent that the formerly liberal citizen shifts to cultural and religious conservatism and eventually grows a beard. A new brand of conservative, Islamist-oriented bourgeoisie is shown to establish itself.

Yet, in the end the appearances turn out to be deceptive as the actions of the citizen and his publisher contradict the moral standards they promote. The former thief is seen keeping up his relationship with the citizen's wife, Hayat, and the citizen is still courting his former girlfriend, the thief's spouse. When their children want to marry each other, the two families object strongly. The film's finale does not fully explain these objections or link them in an overt way

Mahmud 'Abd al-'Aziz and Nur al-Sharif as best friends in *The Vagabonds*.

to the two couples' extramarital relationships, but it implies that the parents are not quite sure about the paternity of their children.

The film thus ironically recasts the recent radical social changes in Egypt, interpreting them as a sort of ideological class struggle that evolves around taste, cultural production, and censorship. The film alludes to this battle on the narrative level, but also intertextually, by evoking a real-life debate around the popular folk (*sha'bi*) singer Sha'ban 'Abd al-Rihim, who holds the role of the thief. His allegedly trivial lower-class music style was seen to signal a deterioration of musical culture in Egypt, and he had become the object of public controversy surrounding the issue of taste. The most important issue raised by 'Abd al-Rihim's casting for the film is the question of social distinction through high- and lowbrow culture. The public discourse about his off-screen persona makes hypocrisy, not only in relation to moral values but also in relation to culture, one of the film's core motifs.

Mahmud 'Abd al-'Aziz as Sheikh Husni in *Kitkat.*

It is the thief character who defies highbrow cultural aspirations and defines the "new" taste and cultural orientation of the citizen by criticizing, destroying, and eventually reediting his literary output. The film thus manages to tackle the new conservatism that has seized Egyptian society since the 1980s and reversed many of the modernist achievements of the past. The director has chosen to parody this development, creating a satire in which the characters' double standard is central. Moreover, the plot is intercut with songs performed by the thief, which develop—particularly in the finale—an ironic and alienating Brechtian effect in the way they sum up the film's action as a game between mice and cats.[5] Last but not least, the anonymous narrator is a major source of dissociation as he constantly comments on the citizen's actions. One example is the occasion of Hayat's beating at the hands of the detective to make her return stolen goods from the citizen's house. When she falsely claims to be pregnant to stop the abuse, the narrator comments: "The citizen's battle was not over yet; by no means could he agree to leave any extension of himself in this environment

Farah and Ahmad Zaki in *Land of Fear.*

polluted by ignorance, poverty, and corruption—how could he leave his son in Hayat's womb?" While the narrator shows some understanding of and solidarity with the main character, he also mocks his behavior. His voice is instrumental in creating a critical distance from the hero and preventing emotional identification on the part of the viewer, who is asked to reflect on the action presented on screen. The citizen acts according to his code of honor, but it is exactly this code, this behavior, that will derail him in the end. Narration and action thus undertake a subversive re-signification that is one of the main characteristics of irony and parody. The latter relies on quotation and repetitive action, but with a twist. In terms of the overall action, the old dream of Egyptian cinema, social mobility, is realized in the plot, but with a crucial difference: it does not lead to the happy ending. It thus departs from the original discourse and creates a new context through recycling and remediation. For, unlike open criticism, parody can only make sense if it is formulated from within existing discourses.

This was not the first time Abd El-Sayed resorted to this form of parody. In his documentary *The Advice of a Wise Man in Matters of Village and Education,* he used the narrator in a quite similar way. In parodying the newsreels, with their seemingly objective anonymous commentator, who is usually perceived as an unbiased source of information, the director submitted the real-life documentary material to the demagogic comments of an invented character:

> The commentator in the documentary films of the time I used to call the Voice of God. It represented the natural reflection of the hegemony of the single voice within the totalitarian system, the voice that is not questioned from any side, while it presents the information with such extraordinary certainty and so well structured, as if it revealed and knew everything. It is a general observation with regard to the young generation and in particular to the school of Shadi Abdessalam: when we started to make films our predominant answer was to cancel the narrator. Yet this was largely a superficial measure. When I directed this film I had the idea to leave the commentator, yet use him as the catalyst for the basic conflict of the film, let its fascist tone take a strict position against education. What inspired me to represent this attitude was the fascist tone prevalent in the media of the time through which Sadat was distancing himself from the preceding era (Raga' 2007, 36). [Author's translation][6]

One of the political moves that supported the shift toward the so-called new morality, so heavily criticized by Abd El-Sayed in his subsequent works, was Sadat's ambivalent Islamization policy during the 1970s. In his attempts to diminish the influence of Nasserists and to suppress socialist ideology, he quietly approved Islamist tendencies and then tried to contain them by introducing the Sharia as a major source of legislation and by promulgating the Law of Shame in 1980, which served at the same time as a convenient way to censor critical ideas. The massive temporary migration of millions of Egyptians to work in the Gulf States in the early 1980s contributed to the new ideology as well. Having been exposed to the religious and ideological conservatism of their host countries, the migrants returned with not only a large amount of hard currency, but also more conservative and pro-Islamist precepts.

In relation to cinema the new morality reached its peak in 1983, with an outraged public debate sparked by the prohibition of two mediocre productions that year, *Alley of Love* (*Darb al-hawa,* by Hussam al-Din Mustafa, and *Gate Five* (*Khamsa bab*) by Nadir Galal. Even journalists spoke in favor of the verdict, demanding more respect for traditions and good morals. It is these events that form the silent background of the citizen/artist's anguish in *A Citizen, a Detective, and a Thief.*

BORDER EXISTENCES

Marginality and social mobility are the two central themes in the oeuvre of Abd El-Sayed, who has used them in order to dissect Egypt's social and political reality since the end of Nasserism. Among the films devoted to border existences, *The Search for Sayyid Marzuq* and *Land of Fear* are exceptional, on both the narrative and the thematic level. They have their plots structured around the motif of existential journeys, in which an individual tries in vain to retrieve his own identity. The same motif is also found in two less ambiguous and less ironic works, *Land of Dreams* and *Messages from the Sea.*

The motif of entrapment plays a pivotal role in the director's early feature film production *The Search for Sayyid Marzuq* (1991). The film was actually shot in 1988, but due to a conflict between its two producers the film was released only three years later and not well marketed, even though it featured Nur al-Sharif, a star of the time who had also acted in *The Vagabonds. The Search for Sayyid Marzuq* pictures the kafkaesque nocturnal journey of a man, Yusuf, who seems to not have taken notice of the passage of many years. One day he wakes up early to go to work but soon discovers that it is a holiday. He lets himself be driven by his observations, to end up at a party at the Nile shore where all of a sudden frogmen drag out a drowned person. This is where the protagonist meets Sayyid Marzuq, a businessman who invites him for a ride to tell him a story, only to leave his expensive car in Yusuf's care for a short while. Soon afterward, Yusuf finds himself detained by the police for stealing the car. Even though the misunderstanding is resolved and Yusuf is released, the police don't stop pursuing him, while Sayyid Marzuq keeps showing up unexpectedly in order to invite him for a ride, to present him with a birthday serenade, to offer him a gift, and so on.

The allegory is clear: the simple citizen who has remained passive for twenty years (i.e., since 1970, the year Nasser died) is thrown into a world he is no longer able to decipher, a world governed by violence and arbitrary rules, run by an omnipresent police apparatus serving omnipotent capitalists. The film expresses the absurdity of the social and political situation in the Mubarak era, a direct result of Sadat's Open Door Policy, through a dreamlike narrative structure where cause and effect become increasingly disconnected; characters appear and disappear for no discernible reason; they seem to lack any clear motivation; in short, they are reflecting a new reality, which the citizen is unable to handle. While some scenes take a surprising turn, those turns are not revealing.

A quintessential scene shows the protagonist being dragged out of the police station by the police officer, to find himself brought right into a gun battle. His hand still chained to a chair, he tries to take cover by any means, but ends up almost losing consciousness as he expects to be hit by a bullet any moment. He is dumbfounded when the police officer finally comes to his rescue once the shooting has ended. The officer smiles and asks him to stretch his fingers and slides off the handcuffs. The irony of this scene is twofold: the officer could have helped him to get rid of his handcuffs much earlier but chose not to; and the prisoner could have escaped the situation if he had just tried hard enough, but it did not occur to him.

Land of Dreams (1993) also involves a nocturnal odyssey, but the storyline is more realistic. It is one of the few films by the director that he did not script himself—the author in this case was Hani Fawzi, and the screenplay lacks the black humor of Abd El-Sayed's other stories of borderline existence. Its main plot centers on an elderly woman from the upscale Heliopolis suburb who has reluctantly agreed to emigrate to the United States in order to enable her adult children to follow her later. She loses her passport the day before she is supposed to leave. During her long search for her passport the whole following night, she meets various people, among others a charming elderly magician, and discovers hitherto unknown places, eventually putting her emigration in question. Starring the aging Egyptian diva Fatin Hamama in her last appearance on screen, the film meant to exploit her presence for the box office and heighten distribution chances. However, accommodating the diva with her dominating persona entailed trimming the film down to a relatively harmless mid-life crisis story.

An identity crisis lies again at the core of *Land of Fear* (1999). Unlike *Land of Dreams,* this multilayered secret agent story is much more open to a variety of existential and political readings. Moreover, it may be considered one of the most accomplished recent Egyptian films on the cinematic as well as on the narrative level. It manages to dress up the metaphysical quest for truth in a thrilling gangster film plot, featuring Ahmad Zaki as the secret agent Yahya, who in 1968, toward the end of the Nasserist era, gets orders to go under cover. In his fake life he is convicted of a crime, starts as a body guard upon his release from prison, marries a belly dancer, and makes his first steps in drug dealing. Then, in order to be admitted to the world of organized crime, he commits a murder. Yet, as governments and presidents change and his criminal record grows, he loses track of his original superiors. While over the years Yahya navigates through these radical changes and manages to stay afloat by displaying extreme ruthlessness, he loses more and more of his innocence and wrecks his relationship with the only woman, a sophisticated architect, he really loves. As she realizes that he has a secret but is unable or unwilling to share it with her, she decides to leave him. All the while Yahya keeps searching in vain for pointers that could help him quit his job and return to normality. Eventually he even becomes uncertain about his own motivations.

The biblical motif of the fallen angel is quite evident, but the film also expresses a more general sense of loss and futility linked to the country's social and political development. Again the story stretches over several decades, from the end of Nasser's rule to the present, as in *The Vagabonds* and *The Search for Sayyid Marzuq*. The identity of the secret agency that sponsored Yahya and his original identification with a cause becomes gradually obliterated as the small-scale business of drug dealers is replaced by big capital and corporations during the Sadat period. Eventually, after Mubarak's ascent to power in 1981, a complete transition to organized crime occurs.

Just as in *The Vagabonds* and *The Search for Sayyid Marzuq*, the director chooses to use a rather epic form of storytelling. Following the main characters on their paths through changing times appears to be the main motivation for the plots, while conflicts between the hero and his antagonists remain secondary in their impact on the course of events, or become primary only in the second half of the film, as is the case of the conflict between Salah and Mursi in *The Vagabonds*. In *Land of Fear*, Omar ('Umar), the rival police officer, intensifies his pursuit of Yahya only toward the film's finale. What enriches this thriller, though, is the mythologically inspired existential drama that forms the subtext of the film. It starts with Yahya's underworld name, Adam, and ends with a scene reminiscent of the Fall of Man in which Yahya, alias Adam, is offered a red apple by one of the drug dealers. This mythological orientation works hand in hand with a deep lyricism as expressed in the poetic voiceover, the narration of the main character who shares his painful memories with the viewer. It is enhanced, moreover, by the careful choice of locations (Onsi Abou Seif, lifelong friend of Abd El-Sayed, was once again art director and production designer) that help to embellish those mystical moments that the story injects into the thriller, such as an episode featuring the mysterious messenger, Mussa (Arabic for *Moses*) and set in the courtyard of the beautiful Sultan Hassan, a historical Cairo mosque.

Mussa had been tracked down by Yahya as the sender of the last letters he received from his former superiors. Yet Mussa, a post office employee, only adds to Yahya's confusion as he emphasizes that he was only a messenger (*rasul*, which in Arabic denotes the word *prophet* as well) to whom the source of his letters and the sender remain unknown. At this point the story transcends into an allegory of the human striving for truth in the face of divine messages which—according to the film—do not necessarily solve the riddles of existence or lead to redemption. The film ends in ambiguity as Yahya falls prey to a sadistic plan designed by Omar. Instead of detaining Yahya, he exposes him as a police informant, thus inviting the underworld to take their revenge on him. Yahya in vain tries to convince Omar of his own original identity and motivation. During their last confrontation, set in the hills of a golf course, Yahya compares Omar with the arrogant angel Iblis (Satan), who was asked by the Almighty to bow to Adam and became a devil upon refusing to do so. In the end Yahya remains in limbo, exposed, hunted, threatened with extinction at any moment, yearning for his redemption and, at the same time, for the power he once used to exert.

Like Yahya, the main character of *Messages from the Sea* (2010), who carries the same name, is likewise pictured to be in limbo. Abd El-Sayed realized this film after a long break, but returned to the core motif of previous borderline narratives, namely the protagonist who has to come to terms with a changed social reality. The story focuses on a young doctor who is unable to exercise his profession because he stutters. After the death of his mother he decides to move to his family's apartment in Alexandria, a decision that kicks off a journey of self-discovery. In Alexandria he discovers unusual people and places, faces hunger and deprivation, and discovers his passion for fishing. Most importantly, he meets his childhood friend and neighbor Carla, a lesbian Italian-Egyptian, and he falls in love with a mysterious woman whom he mistakes for a prostitute. She is in fact the second wife of a rich man but decides not to let on.

Two side plots contribute to the course of the events and express the futility of Yahya's quest. While fishing, he finds a strange bottle with a cryptic message he never manages to decipher. And then there is an Islamist trader of lower-class origin who enjoys catching fish by throwing dynamite in the sea. He has acquired the beautiful old building in which Yahya and Carla live in order to tear it down. While Carla and her old mother finally decide to give up and leave for Italy, Yahya finds himself being harassed by the thugs of the wealthy but uncultured Islamist. This confrontation leads to an ambiguous ending that has much in common with a dream sequence. After the thugs raid Yahya's apartment and start beating him and his lover, we see the couple sleeping in a small boat floating in the middle of the sea among a cloud of dead fish. Lacking a clear-cut classical dramatic plot structure, *Messages from the Sea* is organized around these relatively weak secondary narratives and appears quite fragmentary. Still, the film develops a strong emotional impact due to the poetic nature of many scenes and the fact that Yahya and his lover become increasingly trapped.

The difficulty of recruiting star actors for the project delayed its production for years. Star comedian Ahmad Hilmi decided, according to the director, that the lead role did not match his persona, while several actresses refused the female lead role because of her supposedly immoral lifestyle. This phenomenon of popular actors and actresses acting as moral arbiters of stories and characters has accompanied the new star generation that made its appearance in the mid-1990s. Hence, once again the director found himself struggling to get his film produced because of the very moralism he was exposing in *A Citizen, a Detective and a Thief.* In the existing system, the industry is highly dependent on its stars; a star defines the financial scope and the distribution possibilities of a film. Given the director's commitment to produce within the framework of the Egyptian film industry in order to reach his audiences, he thus has found himself at a major disadvantage.

REGIME CRITIQUE ADDRESSED TO LOCAL AUDIENCES

Abd El-Sayed has been marginalized by producers and the new star generation of the mid-1990s, and his works have rarely resonated outside the Arab world. He has fused his auteur motivation with genre cinema in order to keep audience interest alive and has compromised at times in form but, unlike others, has never hidden his political convictions, never stopped his direct and indirect attacks on the failings of Egypt's political and social system. In 2006, five years before the Egyptian revolution, when he was asked to comment on the low standard of the arts in his homeland in general, and film in particular, he responded that selective changes were no longer viable: "I believe that for any Egyptian to be able to achieve his modest hopes, this system has to collapse. No one in Egypt can live under the current circumstances. This system has to be brought down and everything has to change. They are playing around and trying to gain time. They are playing in a dead field without getting one step further" (El-Leithy and 'Abd al-'Al 2006, 26; my translation). By "they," he meant, of course, the representatives of the Mubarak regime. Since 2011 Abd El-Sayed has worked actively for the sake of change in Egypt, becoming one of the founding members of the new Egyptian Social Democratic Party. He is also one of the most acclaimed supporters of the Creative Front (*Jabhat al-Ibda'*), established in January 2012, which vowed to protect the freedom of creation and expression by any means. He moreover writes critical comments and articles for oppositional newspapers. Yet, as a filmmaker, he still faces the same problems he always had. Even though his last project, *Messages of Love,* has been waiting years for production and has received support from the Ministry of Culture, it was stalled again as the search for interested producers and actors has been difficult, if not impossible. As for its story, it is one more allegory of Egypt's social and political development, in which the granddaughter of a pasha represents the negative aspects of the neoliberal economy and Islamization. Both themes remain topical in post-revolution Egypt, a country that is still waiting to awake from the decades-long nightmare and odyssey of arbitrary rule and misadministration. At least the director was able to realize another project, *Special Abilities,* which is currently in postproduction.

NOTES

1. This chapter draws on my conversations with the director.

2. The date in parentheses always indicates the year of theatrical release, not of production.

3. Due to a mistake in translation, my previous accounts of the film wrongly state that both characters die in the end.

4. The director's filmography suggests that he made a second film, namely *The Search for Sayyid Marzuq,* the same year. The latter, however, was shot in 1988 and only released in 1991.

5. In a conversation with the author, the director affirmed his familiarity with Bertolt Brecht's methods but stated that this did not represent a source of inspiration to him in that respect.

6. It is interesting that Abd El-Sayed mentions Shadi Abdessalam ('Abd al-Salam) in this context. The production designer and film director not only created one of Egypt's most important auteur films, *The Mummy—The Night of Counting the Years* (*al-Mumya'*, 1969), but became in 1968 the head of the National Film Center's Experimental Film Unit. He produced documentaries on monuments and on the arts, trying to rely on the power of the image alone without using any commentary. It speaks for Abd El-Sayed's critical intellectuality and individualism that he would rebel with his early films even against the widely acclaimed Abdessalam.

FILMOGRAPHY OF DAOUD ABD EL-SAYED

A Dance on the Lake / Raqsa fi-l-buhaira. 1972. Documentary.
Populating the Canal Cities / Ta'mir mudun al-qanal. 1974. Documentary.
The Advice of a Wise Man in Matters of Village and Education / Wasiyyat rajul hakim fi shu'un al-qarya wa-l ta'lim. 1976. Documentary.
Industrial Security / al-Amn al-sina'i. 1976. Documentary.
Working in the Field / al-'Amal fi-l-haql. 1979. Documentary.

On the People and the Prophets and the Artists / 'An al-nas wa-l-anbiya' wa-l-fananin.
1980. Documentary.
The Vagabonds / al-Sa'alik. 1985. 124 minutes. Arabic version available at http://www
.youtube.com/watch?v=hSpw5GohUys.
Kitkat / al-Kitkat. 1991. 128 minutes.
The Search for Sayyid Marzuq / al-Bahth 'an Sayyid Marzuq. 1991. 123 minutes. Arabic
version available at http://www.youtube.com/watch?v=9zipkuPPIys.
Land of Dreams / Ard al-ahlam. 1993. 120 minutes. Arabic version available at http://
www.youtube.com/watch?v=s4DxrhSloJo.
Wedding Thief / Sariq al-farah. 1995. 120 minutes.
Land of Fear / Ard al-khawf. 1999. 135 minutes. Arabic version available at http://
www.youtube.com/watch?v=_aORA5-BKIk.
*A Citizen, a Detective and a Thief / Le citoyen et l'indic et le voleur / Muwatin, mukhbir
wa harami.* 2001. Distributed in the United States by Arab Film Distribution.
135 minutes.
Messages from the Sea / Les messages de la mer / Rasa'il al-bahr. 2010. 133 minutes.

REFERENCES

Aslan, Ibrahim. 1983. *Al-malik al-hazin.* Cairo: al-Shorouk. Published in 2009 as *The
Heron* in English translation by Elliott Colla. Cairo: American University in Cairo
Press.
El-Leithy, Safa', and Ahmad 'Abd al-'Al. 2006. *Mukhrij hunna mukhrij hunak: Dawud
'Abd al-Sayyid* [Film director here—film director there: Daoud Abd El-Sayed].
Film Realm / 'Alam al-Sinima. March: 16–27.
Raga', Muhammad. 2007. *Dawud 'Abd al-Sayid: Abwab wa rasa'il* [Daoud Abd El-
Sayed: Doors and Messages). Cairo: Sunduq al-Tanmiya al-Thaqafiya [Ministry of
Culture].
Shafik, Viola. 2007. *Arab Cinema: History and Cultural Identity.* Rev. ed. Cairo:
American University in Cairo Press.
Shalabi, Khairy. 2002. *Sariq al-farah [Wedding Thief].* Cairo: al-Hay'a al-'Ama
lil-Kitab.

Yousry Nasrallah at the Abu Dhabi Film Festival 2012.

7

Yousry Nasrallah

THE PURSUIT OF AUTONOMY IN THE ARAB AND EUROPEAN FILM MARKETS (EGYPT)

Benjamin Geer

This chapter surveys the career of the Egyptian filmmaker Yousry Nasrallah (born 1952).[1] Through an analysis of the eight feature-length films he directed between 1988 and 2012, it considers the relationships between his social background and biography, his pursuit of autonomy from the economic interests of mainstream film production, and the ways his films challenge social norms.

Autonomy can be understood in terms of the sociological theory of Pierre Bourdieu, where it has a specific meaning. For Bourdieu, the production of cultural goods often takes place in "fields." The social world of cinema is a field in this sense, like the worlds of literature, journalism, and academic disciplines.[2] A field is an arena of conflict, in which those who make cultural goods (directors, actors, critics, etc.) compete to attain dominant positions. Each field has its norms, its rules for competition, its criteria for evaluating participants. There are two main types of production in fields. The short production cycle involves responding to the present demands of the market outside the field; if vampire films are popular now, a vampire film stands a chance of making an immediate profit. This strategy has low autonomy from economic forces outside the field. In contrast, the long production cycle involves producing, partly or entirely, for an audience consisting of one's peers in the field. Since one's peers are also one's competitors, their judgment carries a certain symbolic weight, and their approval can confer prestige and legitimacy on films and filmmakers, *consecrating* them as part of the canon of art cinema.

Art cinema is made, at least to some extent, to satisfy the aesthetic criteria established by previous consecrated filmmakers. It thus has particular stylistic characteristics that distinguish it from mass-market cinema. Mass-market cinema tends to have aspects of what Bordwell, Staiger, and Thompson (1988) call the classical Hollywood style: reliable, omniscient narration, a plot driven by the characters' psychology and individual choices, techniques aimed at drawing the audience's attention away from the fact that they are watching a film, and a narrative structure based on the selective withholding of information, enabling the audience to progressively narrow down a set of hypotheses about the future.[3] Art cinema is recognizable by its differences from this norm; for example, it can have unreliable narration, its story can be driven by impersonal social forces beyond the characters' control, it can present a plethora of uncertainties that the audience can never resolve, and its actors can talk to the camera about their roles. An art film presumes an audience that possesses a particular kind of cultural competence, consisting of familiarity with the history and conventions of art cinema, and often of the visual arts in general. This competence is a type of what Bourdieu calls "cultural capital"; it is an aspect of social inequality, since it is more concentrated in some social classes than in others. Indeed, its exclusiveness is part of what makes it valuable. Thus art cinema, being relatively less marketable, has some autonomy from the demands of the market. This, in turn, gives it a degree of freedom to challenge social norms, which is harder to do in mass-market cinema, since most people will not pay to have their beliefs questioned. All of Yousry Nasrallah's films have some of these characteristics of art cinema.

However, since film is an expensive medium (compared to literature, for example, in which a writer can produce a novel for the cost of survival plus pen and paper), autonomy in cinema is always relative at best, and must rely on a variety of strategies in order to exist. In Europe, one strategy has been state subsidies. France has the most comprehensive system in Europe for the public funding of cinema (Jäckel 2003, 49), having made major investments in the film industry since the 1980s (Jäckel 1999, 178). This system relies partly on the use of television. The Franco-German public television channel Arte,[4] launched in 1992, is a prestigious producer of autonomous cinema (Jäckel 2003, 55–57; Emanuel 1999, 85), whose audience is "endowed with cultural capital" (Jäckel 1999, 184). French film policy not only supports French filmmakers; it has also benefited many filmmakers from elsewhere "who, for various reasons, have found it difficult to make films in their own country" (Jäckel 1996, 85). Nasrallah has relied on French state funding since his first film, and nearly all his films were co-produced by Arte. We will consider his use of this strategy below.

THE FORMATION OF AN AUTONOMOUS DISPOSITION

Nasrallah wanted to make films from adolescence, but when he graduated from high school, he could not enroll in the Film Institute (Ma'had al-Sinima), because applicants were then required to have a bachelor's degree.[5] So he enrolled in the economics and political science program at Cairo University. There he became involved in the emerging student protest movement, and participated in pro-democracy demonstrations in 1972. During this period, he joined the Egyptian Communist Workers Party,[6] which in his view had the best analysis of the policies of the military regime that had taken power in 1952; it argued that president Gamal Abdel Nasser's claim to have established socialism was "simply a cover for the militarization of the state."

While he was still at the university, the Film Institute changed its admission policy; he enrolled, but found it "boring and reactionary." In 1978, after finishing his university education, he went to Beirut, hoping to make a film on young Palestinians in Lebanon and Jordan, but could not obtain funding. Instead, he stayed in Beirut for four years, working as a film critic for the Lebanese leftist newspaper *Al-Safir*. Meanwhile, he withdrew from all political parties and organizations. Egyptian communist groups had already begun to disintegrate under state pressure before he left Egypt. In any case, he felt that "if you want to make art, you shouldn't do it within a centralized, dogmatic party." Though he liked communists' ideas, he was uncomfortable with their organizational structures, especially once he learned about the oppressive character of Soviet communism, an issue Egyptian communists avoided discussing. Nevertheless, he has remained strongly influenced by leftist ideas, which are reflected in his films, as we will see.

Being alone in Lebanon during the civil war made him focus on survival and self-reliance, and freed him from certain social constraints that he experienced in Egypt. As he put it: "There was something very decisive in the experience in Beirut. . . . I was living in the way that best accorded with my nature . . . far from all the institutional structures in Egypt, structures of family, sect, or party. . . . I was alone. . . . I think this was the kind of moment that shapes a person as an artist."

SUMMER THEFTS

In Beirut he met the Egyptian filmmaker Youssef Chahine, who invited him to return to Egypt to work as an assistant on his film *Adieu Bonaparte* (1985), a French-Egyptian co-production. After this experience, he made his first film, *Summer Thefts* (*Vols d'été / Sariqat Sayfiya*, 1988). The film is largely autobiographical. Born in the Cairo suburb of Giza and raised in the affluent neighborhood of Zamalek in central Cairo, Nasrallah grew up in a Christian landowning family that was terrified of Nasser and lost a great deal as a result of his policies. As a child, he spent summer vacations on his family's farm in the village of Akyad in the Nile Delta. The film begins in July 1961. Yasser, a young boy from a wealthy landowning family, is on his family's farm for summer vacation when president Nasser announces a set of "socialist" reforms. Most of the family is furious. Yasser's aunt Mona considers getting a divorce and marrying an opportunist who is close to the regime, in the hope of holding onto more of her land.

Yasser makes friends with a peasant boy, Leil, but his mother, Reema, forbids him to associate with peasants ("those scum"). Hence when his Nasserist cousin Dahlia arrives after a long absence, he tells her not to greet her servant Khadra with a kiss, "because she's a peasant." Yet he longs to swim in the canal "like the peasants." He is forbidden to do so, ostensibly for fear he will catch bilharzia, a disease that affects the urinary tract. The implied sexual attraction between Yasser and Leil is prohibited by both sexual and class taboos. The two boys swim in the canal together anyway, and he does catch bilharzia.

And Yasser begins to embrace socialism. When his parents get divorced, he fears he will have to go live with his father because Reema will be unable to support him and his sister, so he imitates Robin Hood, stealing valuables from rich people's houses, with Leil's help. The theft is discovered and Leil is arrested. The film then skips to 1982. Yasser has spent several years in Beirut, and returns to find the house demolished. Reema has sold her land because there are no longer any peasants to farm it; Mona has married her opportunist and kept her land for purely sentimental reasons. No longer able to live by farming, Leil is about to emigrate to Iraq. Yasser tells him that he was glad to have caught bilharzia by swimming in the canal. He adds, "I've never loved anyone as much as I loved you," and they swim in the canal again.

Nasrallah's interest in taboos, which runs through all his films, follows from the deeper question of how to cope with a frightening world. He explained:

If you look at all my films from that point of view, you'll find that they're all about . . . going somewhere that people try to frighten you away from. They're all films about characters . . . who don't accept being victims. There's a sort of Arab broken record that says, America is beating us up, Israel is occupying us, our governments oppress us, Mommy and Daddy are horrible and made me into a criminal. This gives our cinema something, and fosters something in us, that's opposed to modernity. To me, modernity means that yes, the world is frightening, but you're not afraid, you can cope with it. . . . What made me aware of this is the four years I spent in Beirut.

Nasrallah's view of Nasser's "socialism" was influenced by a book (Amir 1958) that critiqued Nasser's land reforms from a communist perspective: land was redistributed to peasants, but they were only allowed to plant certain crops, such as cotton or rice, which were grown for export and whose only buyer was the state, which bought them at low prices in order to compete in global markets. Meanwhile, affluent landowners still had sizeable estates, and were free to plant orchards, whose fruit could be sold at higher prices. In reality, "the poor were made to carry the burdens of development." State agricultural policies in the 1970s made survival more difficult for peasants, and by the end of the decade, many were emigrating to become manual laborers in Arab oil-producing countries.

Summer Thefts was not an easy film to produce. In the 1980s, Nasrallah realized that the Saudi video market had become the major source of funding for Egyptian cinema. Saudi consumers had started to buy large quantities of videocassettes, and the price of a videocassette was high. Moreover, advertisements were not permitted on Saudi television, but they could be seen on videocassettes, and this produced considerable revenue for distributors. However, with this new market came new restrictions: censorship was stricter than in Egypt, and Saudi distributors valued a film mainly according to the popularity of its stars. Stars place huge burdens on a film's budget, as we will see below, and the need to pay for them can restrict a filmmaker's autonomy. Nasrallah tried to cast Yousra, a major star, but she declined; the film's controversial political stance, and his status as an unknown, made working with him a risky proposition for a star. A wealthy cousin contributed US $50,000 to finance the film, and Youssef Chahine suggested that with that sum, he could make the film with amateur actors: "You'll be able to do what you want." Further assistance came in the form of a prize for the screenplay from the French Cultural Center in Cairo (Salih 1988), which covered the cost of film stock and processing using the recently invented, low-cost Super 16 format.

In short, Nasrallah's participation in the 1972 student movement, followed by his experience of self-reliance and distance from social constraints in Beirut, helped shape a disposition toward autonomy. He was able to follow this disposition when making *Summer Thefts* thanks to his family's economic capital, the technical advance of Super 16, and state funding from Europe. This last factor would be decisive in his subsequent career. The initial results were encouraging: the film was shown at Cannes and distributed in France. Samir Farid (1988) described its critique of Nasserism as one-sided, but it otherwise received enthusiastic reviews in the Egyptian and French press,[7] and won a prize for best first film from the Egyptian Association of Film Writers and Critics, as well as second prize at the Bergamo Film Meeting. Nasrallah recalls: "Suddenly I tasted something I think is very precious . . . the freedom to make a film without any restrictions. No one told me I had to use a certain actor, or that the screenplay had to include this and not that. . . . From then on, that was the crucial thing I looked for when writing a film, when setting up the production: to what extent could I maintain the freedom that I experienced in my first film?"

MERCEDES

Nasrallah's next film, *Mercedes* (Mirsidis, 1993), follows Noubi, a communist from an upper-class family, who struggles to figure out how to live in an Egypt that seems to have completely rejected his ideals. In the 1970s, Noubi's mother has him confined to a mental hospital to cure him of communism. He is released with the fall of the Berlin Wall, and emerges to find his family consumed by greed, ostentation, and snobbery. His aunt seems to deal in drugs, smuggling them in the corpses of murdered children. Former leftists have sworn allegiance to capitalism and integrated themselves into Egypt's business elites and authoritarian regime. Migrant workers are leaving for Iraq and returning in coffins, but the media are preoccupied with the Egyptian soccer team's 1990 World Cup match against England, Egypt's former colonizer, portraying the Egyptian team's loss as a national disaster.

Rather than narrating a story that enables the audience to form and test hypotheses about what will happen, the film follows Noubi as he struggles to make sense of a series of disparate social realities, whose relations to one another remain ambiguous. He searches for his gay half-brother, Gamal, and finds him in a cheap cinema, which an all-male audience uses as a space for carnivalesque social rebellion based on drug use, gang loyalties, and homosexual encounters (see Armbrust 1998a, 426; Armbrust 2001, 37–38). Allusions to the biblical story of the Flood abound. Downtown Cairo is in flames as the police battle Islamist militants. Finally, Noubi, his girlfriend, and Gamal escape to the wilderness at the edge of the desert, surrounded by animals, as if they have just disembarked from Noah's Ark, ready to rebuild humanity. Nasrallah explained:

> I began writing it in 1989. The whole socialist bloc was collapsing. . . . Terrorism was starting to appear. Sadat had been assassinated. . . . Bombs were being thrown in Cairo, people were being shot in the street. . . . The atmosphere was like the end of the world. We started to hear about very strange crimes. . . . And you're someone who always dreamed of a just world and so on, and when you talk about that, people . . . tell you you're an idiot or crazy. . . . At the time, there were a lot of Mercedes cars. . . . Their owners would drive them in the most outrageous way, as if they owned the country.[8] . . . I wanted to tell a story about a socialist in a world where socialism is collapsing.

Mercedes was the first film Nasrallah made for Arte. The film received positive reviews in France and in Egypt, but did poorly at the box office, no doubt partly because it lacks a conventional storyline (al-Shinnawi 1993). The widespread rejection of leftist ideas, which inspired the film, probably also made audiences unlikely to be receptive to it. Many viewers must also have disapproved of the sympathetic portrayal of gay characters. When the film was shown at the National Festival for Egyptian Cinema in Cairo in 1994, some journalists attacked it "as perversity made for the sake of hostile foreigners," particularly because of its French funding, "which they took as an indication of a sinister cultural agenda" (Armbrust 2002, 926). In their view, Nasrallah had "sullied Egypt's national reputation by showing foreigners an unflattering view of Egyptian society" (Armbrust 1998b, 385). I have argued elsewhere (Geer 2009) that nationalism favors heteronomy among cultural producers; it is not surprising that nationalist concepts were used as symbolic weapons to attack a film for exposing social ills.

Nasrallah's reply to these accusations is that with funding from European public television, "you're free to make your film as you like. . . . It's not . . . like what people usually imagine, that the West is conspiring against us, imposing conditions on us." When Arab producers refused to finance *The Gate of the Sun* (2004), his film about the Palestinian cause (discussed below), and Arte financed it instead, conspiracy theorists were confused. "Because they don't interact with the rest of the world. . . . People here have been cut off from the world for sixty years, not understanding how it works, and not wanting to understand."

Moreover, there are few other funding options: "Egyptian cinema is in an awful crisis." Its traditional market, the Arab world, has collapsed because of poverty, wars, protectionist measures, and competition with American and Indian films. The domestic market "can cover only a few comedies and so on, which I have nothing against." Censorship in Saudi Arabia is so strict that when *Mercedes* was distributed there, forty minutes of the film were cut, including everything to do with Christianity (a church, a wedding, a funeral), along with the dancing, the kisses, and the drugs. "So obviously, if you want to make the films you want to make, the way you want to make them, you have to find other markets. . . . I worked for a long time with Arte. . . . They want a film that's an hour and a half or two hours long, or four hours long, that they can put on television, and that's it. . . . Their only condition is that they like the screenplay."

Arguably, for Arte, "they like the screenplay" means that, in their view, it responds to the aesthetic standards of art cinema. This was the beginning of a long relationship with European television channels, with which all his subsequent films until *Scheherazade Tell Me a Story* (*Femmes du Caire / Ihki Ya Shahrazad,* 2009) were co-produced. One aspect of Nasrallah's cultural capital—his multilingualism—must have facilitated this; he obtained all his primary and secondary education in a German school in Cairo, learned impeccable French at home (Godard 1988), and is fluent in English.

ON BOYS, GIRLS, AND THE VEIL

The interest in working-class lives that is apparent in Nasrallah's first two films is developed into a sophisticated ethnography in his documentary, *On Boys, Girls, and the Veil* (*A propos des garçons, des filles et du voile / Subyan wa-Banat,* 1995). It explores the social world of actor Bassem Samra (who had a minor role in *Mercedes*), through his daily life at home with his family, his job as a teacher in a vocational school, his friendships, and his attempts to get acting jobs, focusing on the social norms that structure contacts between young men and women, and particularly on the significance of the *hijab,* or Islamic headscarf, which by then had become a standard part of the attire of most Egyptian Muslim women. As Walter Armbrust (1998b, 383–384) notes: "Nasrallah's goal

Leil and Yasser in *Summer Thefts*.

is to suggest that the matter of the *hijab* is not exclusively linked to religion. . . . People in the film talk about the *hijab* as a matter of modesty, a fashion statement, a phenomenon of peer pressure, and as a practical response to the modern imperative of female work in the public domain."

On Boys, Girls, and the Veil was another co-production with Arte, and it received very positive reviews in France. It was cleared by the Egyptian censors but never had a commercial release in Egyptian cinemas; the authorities apparently preferred to avoid controversy on a sensitive topic. Armbrust (1998b) explores the film in detail, but one additional aspect of it merits further consideration: the complex involvement of Bassem Samra, an actor playing himself in a documentary, whose role overlaps with that of the director. This collaboration between Samra and Nasrallah, which would reappear and develop in subsequent films, can be interpreted as a way of transcending the limitations of the way in which Nasrallah's first two films dealt with the working class, from the point of view of an outsider. As Nasrallah observed: "I filmed it with his real family. But . . . it's not really him. It's the image of himself that he wants to give you. . . . He plays two roles at once: he's there as a character, and at the same time he's introducing me to the others. In a sense he plays the role of the director."

During the 1948 Arab-Israeli war, stunned Palestinian villagers
look on as an Arab Liberation Army commander tells them
that the situation is hopeless in *The Gate of the Sun*.

Hebba faces down her husband in *Scheherazade Tell Me a Story*.

THE CITY

Nasrallah got the idea for *The City* (*La ville* / *Al-Madina,* 1999) from observing the destruction of parts of the working-class Cairo neighborhoods of Rod al-Farag and Bulaq, which are located on the opposite bank of the Nile from his apartment in the upscale area of Zamalek. Some of the inhabitants of these areas were moved to suburbs; their old neighborhoods, including the market of Rod al-Farag, were replaced with commercial and residential buildings for the wealthy. Nasrallah recalled that this had also happened to Les Halles, the old market in central Paris (starting in 1969). He therefore planned a film focusing on these two neighborhoods and their similar fates. Lacking familiarity with both places, he enlisted Nasir Abd al-Rahman, a scriptwriter from Rod al-Farag, and Claire Denis, a French director, to help him write the script (Farid 2000).

The film deviates from this plan in ways that make it less about working-class neighborhoods and more about the individual's liberation from oppressive social structures. Bassem Samra plays Ali, who works as an accountant in a butcher shop in Rod al-Farag and is determined to become an actor. His father, who is among the vendors moved out of the old market, disparages his ambitions and pressures him to join him in business in the new market. In a screen test, an Egyptian director berates him for fancying himself an actor, implicitly because he is from the wrong social class. Nasrallah observed that the same class prejudice was reflected in complaints about the film in Egypt, expressed once again in nationalist terms: "You could hear people say, Oh, my, couldn't you have filmed *The City* in Zamalek? Did you have to go to Rod al-Farag and make Egypt look ugly? . . . I don't find Rod al-Farag ugly, I find it beautiful. . . . The taboo is against seeing. . . . Anything that has to do with the world as it is, with what really happens, with what the country actually looks like . . . you're not supposed to talk about it. . . ."

Like Nasrallah, Ali escapes restrictive social ties by emigrating; he goes to Paris with an acting troupe. Two years later, he is an illegal immigrant, boxing in rigged matches. Claire Denis was then playing a major role in the mobilization of French filmmakers in support of undocumented immigrants (Ayad 1998). Instead of focusing on Les Halles, the middle section of the film explores the world of clandestine Arab workers in Paris. When Ali rebels against the organizers of the rigged boxing matches, they try to kill him, and he wakes up from a coma with amnesia. An Egyptian consular official accuses him of being a swindler and tarnishing Egypt's reputation. Ali returns to his family, but they are strangers to him. Nasrallah explained: "Ali does what he wants to do, and comes back an actor. Losing his memory is the best thing that ever happened to him, because he can now separate people he can't stand from people he likes, without the baggage of saying, That's my father, that's my grandmother, and so on. He says, I like this person right now. He becomes a free human being."

Once again, Samra's role blurs the distinction between acting and living. He and his character share ambitions, a social background, and the obstacles that result. Ali tells the director that he wants to be an actor because, when he goes about his daily life, he does not really see anything, but when he pretends he is acting, he sees every detail, feels as if he is embracing the whole world, and stops feeling lonely.

Nasrallah's application for a grant from the Fonds Sud, a French state subsidy for the production of films from the global South, was rejected on the grounds that more than 25 per cent of *The City* takes place in France, and that this deprived the film of "cultural specificity" (Ayad 1998). Fortunately, Arte and the other European institutions that funded the film did not share this culturalist perspective, and Nasrallah managed to make the film for about EGP £2 million (about US $600,000 in 1998 dollars). To reduce costs, it was shot in video and transferred to 35mm film. With that budget, Nasrallah could not have afforded an Egyptian star, whose salary would have been at least EGP £1 million (about US $300,000); hence, once again, he worked with non-professional actors. This choice had other advantages; in his view, the habits that professional actors acquire from working on TV dramas make them less adaptable to his preferred approach of shooting the same scenes many times, in different ways (Farid 2000). The film won the Special Jury Prize at the 1999 Locarno Film Festival, Samra won the prize for best actor at the 2000 Carthage Film Festival, and the French press gave the film high praise on the whole. Egyptian critics described it as a great work of art, which honored Egypt in international festivals, and they lamented the fact that it was shown only in one cinema in Cairo, with little publicity.

THE GATE OF THE SUN

The Gate of the Sun (*La porte du soleil / Bab al-Shams,* 2004) is a two-part, four-and-a-half-hour film about the Palestinian predicament, based on Lebanese writer Elias Khoury's celebrated Arabic novel of the same title (Khoury 1998; English translation, Khoury 2006). Nasrallah wanted to make a film about

Palestine as a reply to the ostensibly pro-Palestinian discourses of Arab governments, aimed at silencing internal dissent rather than promoting solidarity with Palestinians.

> I'm not Palestinian, but I've been paying for Palestine all my life. . . . For sixty years, I've been told, Shut up, don't open your mouth, and the only narrative that's been allowed on Palestine is the narrative of Nasser, Saddam Hussein, and Hafez al-Assad. . . . That's what gives the novel its legitimacy: taking a narrative that was monopolized by governments and bizarre organizations, and telling them, You don't understand anything. . . . You don't know how to talk about Palestine. I know how to talk about Palestine.

Khoury, who fought on the side of the Palestinian Liberation Organization (PLO) in the Lebanese civil war of 1975–1990, is a major literary figure in Lebanon (Hoffman 2006, 52–53; Douin 2004). The novel is based partly on stories he collected from Palestinian refugees. It deals with the lives of Palestinian peasants in the 1940s, the ethnic cleansing they experienced at the hands of Zionist militias in 1948 (see Pappe 2006), the resulting exodus of hundreds of thousands of Palestinians, and the lives of Palestinian refugees and resistance fighters in Lebanon until the 1990s. This multitude of stories is encompassed within a frame story, as in the *Thousand and One Nights* (see Jarrar 2008, 308–310). The main narrator is Khalil, an orphan in his forties, who was born in a refugee camp in Beirut and fought as part of the PLO during the civil war. Working as a nurse in the hospital of the Shatila refugee camp, he looks after a dying, comatose patient: Yunes, a hero of the 1948 war and the Palestinian resistance, who has been like a father to him. From 1948 until 1968, Yunes went back and forth between Lebanon and Galilee, where his wife, Nahilah, raised their children in what was now Israel. Their secret meeting place was a cave called Bab al-Shams (the Gate of the Sun). Khalil's lover, Shams, a self-reliant woman who led a combat unit, has killed one of her other lovers and been killed in retaliation. Khalil has taken refuge in the hospital, fearing her family will blame him and take revenge. He sits by Yunes's bedside, telling him these stories and many others, to coax him back to consciousness.

The novel critiques the heroic, conventionally masculine nationalist discourse of Palestinian resistance fighters of Yunes's generation (see Kanafani 2008; Head 2011). In 1968, Nahilah tells Yunes that he understands nothing: while he has been living the life of a revolutionary, she has been struggling with mundane reality for twenty years, raising their children in poverty and living on charity. She is tired of his stories about how some hero, such as Nasser, will liberate Palestine; she needs money to help their eldest son open a garage. She supports the struggle for Palestinians' rights, but believes that things can no longer be put back the way they were (Khoury 1998, 391–410).

Nasrallah wrote the script with Khoury and Lebanese director and film critic Mohamed Soueid. The film expresses the novel's main points by completely reworking its structure. While the novel proceeds by chains of associations between memories, skipping back and forth in time, the film uses fewer flashbacks, because, as Nasrallah said, film narrative cannot sustain such a large number of digressions. Lacking space for all the novel's events, the film focuses more on the central characters. Details are simplified and related stories are merged. But like the novel, the film makes room for contradictory versions of stories, told by different, unreliable narrators (see Caiani 2007, 141–142).

Through rearrangement of events into a more chronological sequence, the two parts of the film roughly correspond to two conceptions of history. The first part presents idyllic images of Palestine before 1948, followed by the horror of what Zionists did to it. Its lyrical style is comforting, as Nasrallah explained, "because you see yourself as a victim." The second part, which deals mainly with events from the 1950s onward and largely abandons this lyricism, is "basically about what we did to ourselves . . . what it's like to live in a refugee camp, in exile, what it's like to live through a civil war. That's an Arab reality." Thus the film escapes "the dualism of executioners and victims" (Frodon 2004). Nasrallah wanted Yunes in the film to look like the traditional Arab leaders of the 1950s and '60s, father figures whose stifling hegemony must be shaken off. A character says, referring to Khalil: "This man has too many fathers."

Nasrallah sought funding for the film from Egyptian and other Arab television channels, but they refused, seeing the topic as a thorny issue (Nasr 2005). Only one Arab production company, the Moroccan company 2M, supported the film (Frodon 2004). So once again, *The Gate of the Sun* was produced mainly by Arte, along with other European institutions.

Both French and Egyptian critics lavished praise on the film; *Cahiers du cinéma,* the canonical French art-cinema magazine, gave it a glowing review (Hansen-Løve 2004). In Egypt, however, only three copies were shown in cinemas, and there was very little publicity; an Egyptian critic described this as a great injustice (al-Shafii 2005). I will suggest a different interpretation of this distribution and marketing strategy below.

THE AQUARIUM

In *The Aquarium* (*L'aquarium / Junainat al-Asmak*, 2008), the two main characters are affluent professionals in their thirties who live in Zamalek. Laila (Hend Sabry) is the ambitious host of a late-night radio call-in show on which listeners reveal personal secrets.[9] Youssef is an anesthetist who enjoys listening to his sedated patients talk. Both are terrified of acknowledging their own feelings or indeed taking any risks.

The title refers to a public park in Zamalek; it contains an underground aquarium in an artificial cave, and is known as a meeting place for lovers. The fish in the tanks, like the characters, are trapped behind glass walls (Salim 2008), while the cave evokes an inner world of frightening desires (El-Shakry 2008). The film's slow visual rhythm often gives the impression that the camera is under water. Laila's sound engineer Zakki (Bassem Samra) is in love with her, but she remains in a safer arrangement, living with her mother and having a relationship with a wealthy and powerful older man, who requires no emotional involvement. Youssef is in a relationship with a divorcee, but cannot communicate with her. Egypt's social ills continually intrude on the lives of the protagonists, but they refuse to get involved. After Laila takes a call from an HIV-positive listener, a friend invites her to visit an HIV-AIDS support group, but she refuses. Youssef drives through a silent demonstration organized by Kefaya, a movement against one-party rule in Egypt (see El-Mahdi 2009) but appears completely indifferent.

The Aquarium adopts stylistic traits of avant-garde cinema, as Tartoussieh (2012) observes; it does this more than any of Nasrallah's other films that I have seen. Actors deliver monologues about their characters, speaking directly to the camera about things that the characters cannot say to one another; thus, like *The City*, the film presents acting as a way to get closer to reality. Sometimes the actors switch between the first and third persons when talking about their characters. In his monologue, Bassem Samra says "I" instead of "Zakki," corrects himself twice, and finally says bitterly, "Yes, I love Laila," without correcting himself. Moreover, he behaves like a film director: he asks an apparition of Hend Sabry to repeat one of her lines from an earlier scene, and corrects her delivery.

The French newspaper *Le Monde* gave the film a positive review. Egyptian reviews were mixed; some described it as great art, while others found it incomprehensible. Very few copies were shown in Egyptian cinemas. Nasrallah explained that the marketing and distribution strategy was intended to meet the expectations of the audience that wants to see a "different" film (Nasr 2008). This suggests that limited distribution and publicity is a way of signaling that the film is meant for a restricted audience, which gains symbolic profits from this exclusivity.

SCHEHERAZADE TELL ME A STORY

Scheherazade Tell Me a Story (*Femmes du Caire / Ihki Ya Shahrazad*, 2009) is about women. Wahid Hamid, who had written the blockbuster film adaptation of Alaa al-Aswany's novel *The Yacoubian Building* (2006), wrote the script and proposed it to Nasrallah. The protagonist, Hebba (Mona Zaki, a major star), hosts a popular T v talk show that bravely challenges the government on political issues. Her husband, Karim, is an unprincipled deputy newspaper editor, who hopes to replace the current editor when the latter moves on. A high official tells Karim he has a shot at the promotion if he persuades his wife to avoid political issues on her show. Under pressure from Karim, she does three episodes about women's issues. First, an upper-class woman in a private mental hospital explains that she never married, and has remained a virgin, because she never found a man who saw her as anything but a sex object. Next is the story of three working-class sisters who became secretly engaged to their shop assistant, without telling one another; when they found out, one of them killed him. After seeing this episode, Karim accuses Hebba of tarnishing Egypt's reputation. Finally, a dentist tells how she was the victim of a rich, powerful man who married a series of wealthy women to extort money from them. He was then appointed as a minister in government, and she responded by staging a one-woman protest in front of Parliament, surrounded by riot police. Karim is passed over for the promotion, and beats Hebba, who then appears on her show covered in bruises, to tell her own story.

Scheherazade was an entirely Egyptian, commercial production, and it was Nasrallah's most successful film at the box office; it sold half a million tickets (Fabre 2010). Hence it is not surprising that it is largely a melodrama, like many of the most profitable Egyptian films. For the most part, the female characters are innocent victims of thoroughly repulsive men.[10] But they are not helpless victims; they resist intimidation, and in Nasrallah's view, telling their stories in public is a kind of rebellion (Abu al-Suud 2009). Like Scheherazade in the *Thousand and One Nights,* Hebba talks in order to not to be crushed. The film was also a way for Nasrallah to overcome his own fears about his ability to reach a wide audience.

The Egyptian press praised the social critique implicit in the story, despite reservations about the use of stereotypes. Reviews in France approved of the film's exploration of the political aspects of love, while lamenting the flatness of the characters, and characterized the film as a compromise between art cinema and soap opera. While the film is not as autonomous as Nasrallah's earlier films, it is clearly more autonomous than most mainstream cinema.

AFTER THE BATTLE

In the midst of the revolutionary uprising that began in Egypt on January 25, 2011, Nasrallah filmed *After the Battle* (*Après la bataille / Bad al-Mawqia,* 2012), which returns to the topic of the challenge to social norms represented by emotional bonds and solidarities that cross class boundaries. Blending fiction with documentary, it begins with an incident that took place on February 2 of that year: a group of horse and camel riders attacked anti-regime demonstrators in Cairo's Tahrir Square, before being chased out by protesters. Like Rossellini's neorealist cinema, which Nasrallah had in mind, *After the Battle* deals with major historical events that were unfolding during the filming, through the exploration of the subjective experiences of fictional characters (Nasrallah et al. 2013). Reem (Minna Shalaby), an affluent woman, has a chance encounter with Mahmoud (Bassem Samra), a rider who participated in the attack on Tahrir Square. Like the heroine of Rossellini's *Europe '51,* she faces the incomprehension and hostility of her social circle as she becomes involved in the lives of poor people. In Nazlet el-Samman, a village near the Pyramids where Nasrallah had filmed *On Boys, Girls, and the Veil,* men like Mahmoud earned their living by selling rides to tourists, until the regime and the uprising undermined their business. Tricked into riding into Tahrir Square to defend the regime in exchange for empty promises, Mahmoud was publicly humiliated as videos on the Internet showed him taking a beating at the hands of protesters, and his children were bullied by their classmates at school.

Reem prods Mahmoud, his wife, and other inhabitants of Nazlet el-Samman into challenging certain kinds of domination—for example, by attempting to form a labor union for riders. Yet the villagers are not mere ignorant bumpkins in need of enlightenment: they push back against Reem's "paternalistic developmentalism," an attitude that has tended to characterize the Cairo intelligentsia's perceptions of the rural poor in Egypt (Abu-Lughod 2005). The village's real inhabitants participated in writing the screenplay as the film was being shot, and this collaboration is mirrored in scenes suggesting that Reem can contribute to the life of the village only through dialogue with its inhabitants, rather than by giving them a lecture. At the same time, she pushes back against the deep class prejudices of her upper-class revolutionary friends, who pay lip service to the idea of talking to ordinary people in the street, but in reality are terrified of the breakdown of class divisions.

Though actors Samra and Shalaby are major stars, Nasrallah returned to the strategy of co-production with French television; his insistence on working without a script written in advance, and shooting for as long as necessary, would no doubt have seemed risky to commercial film producers. The state-run newspaper *Al-Ahram* made much of the fact that one of the French producers is Jewish, accusing the film of being part of a Zionist conspiracy; a director named Ahmad Atif played a prominent role in this attack, whose main motivation could thus be professional rivalry. Still, *After the Battle* received very positive reviews in the Egyptian and French press and was shown at the Cannes film festival.

Nasrallah's social background and biography, combined with the emergence of new types of European public funding for cinema just as he was starting his career, have enabled him to maintain a relatively autonomous trajectory for thirty years, and to gradually achieve consecration as a filmmaker, with the support of critics in both Egypt and France. This slow process is in keeping with the long production cycle characteristic of autonomous cultural production, in which "the most innovative works tend, *with time,* to produce their own audience" (Bourdieu 1996, 253). It is this gradual consecration that made it possible for him to direct a film like *Scheherazade Tell Me a Story* and have it financed entirely by an Egyptian production company. Nasrallah's budgets are now much bigger than before, though still less than those of such Egyptian blockbusters as *The Yacoubian Building.* And in recent years, some of his films have appeared repeatedly on television in Egypt. As he put it: "In 1988, nobody wanted to work with me. Nobody knew who I was. . . . I started making films, and . . . actors realized that the actors who worked with me acted very well, and this made them want to work with me, too. . . . My films have started to create their own audience . . . my friends' children and their friends. . . . Another generation. . . . They're the ones who brought my generation to see my films."

NOTES

1. I would like to thank the Middle East Institute at the National University of Singapore, which generously funded this research.

2. For a fuller explanation of the concept of field, see Bourdieu (1996). For a discussion of the application of this theory to cinema, see Duval (2006) and Nakajima (2010).

3. The classical Hollywood style has "dominated the world's screens" since the 1920s, both in American films and in films made elsewhere (Bordwell, Staiger, and Thompson 1988, 619–626). Meanwhile, a variety of mass-market styles have emerged, some of which are conventionally associated with particular countries. Arguably, these styles share key characteristics with the classical Hollywood style, and these similarities distinguish all of them from art cinema. Like Higson (2000), I question the usefulness of the concept of "national cinema." I would argue that cinematic tastes have more to do with cultural capital than with geography.

4. Arte gets 95 percent of its budget from state funding, which is paid for by a tax on TV ownership. It is not allowed to show advertising, and it manages its budget autonomously.

5. Unless otherwise indicated, Nasrallah's biographical information and quotes are taken from a four-hour interview conducted by the author with the director in Arabic, at the director's home in Cairo, on May 7, 2012.

6. For an overview of this party, see Ismael and El-Sa'id (1990, 129–147). On the 1972 student protests, see Abdalla (1985, 176–211).

7. The film reviews consulted for this chapter were taken from the Egyptian periodicals *Akhir Saa, Al-Ahram, Al-Ahram al-Masai, Al-Ahram Weekly, Al-Akhbar, Al-Arabi, Al-Badil, Al-Dustur, Al-Jumhuriya, Al-Masa, Al-Misri al-Yawm, Al-Qahira, Al-Shuruq, Ruz al-Yusif,* and *Shashati,* and the French periodicals *Cahiers du cinéma, Le Monde,* and *Libération,* from 1988 to 2010.

8. "The expensive imported automobile (especially the Mercedes in later years) as symbol of decadence is . . . a familiar device in Egyptian cinema" (Armbrust 1995, 108).

9. The idea for Laila's program was inspired by a real Egyptian radio show, called "Itirafat Layliya" (Night Confessions), that was hosted by Buthayna Kamel. However, Laila's character is clearly not based on Kamel, a well-known political activist.

10. The exception is the story about the three sisters and the shop assistant, which intrigued Nasrallah because of its reversal of conventional roles: here, the man is dominated by women.

FILMOGRAPHY OF YOUSRY NASRALLAH

Summer Thefts / Vols d'été / Sariqat Sayfiya. 1988. Distributed by Misr International Films. 102 minutes.

Mercedes / Mirsidis. 1993. Distributed by Misr International Films. 105 minutes.

One Day with Youssef Chahine / Une journée avec Youssef Chahine. 1994. Distributed by Canal+. Short film.

The Extra / Le figurant. 1994. Distributed by Canal+. Short film.

On Boys, Girls, and the Veil / A propos des garçons, des filles et du voile / Jugend, Liebe und Koran / Subyan wa-Banat. 1995. Distributed in the United States by Arab Film Distribution. 72 minutes. Documentary.

The City / La ville / Die Stadt / Al-Madina. 1999. Distributed by Misr International Films. 108 minutes.

The Gate of the Sun / La porte du soleil / Das Tor zur Sonne / Bab al-Shams. 2004. Distributed by Misr International Films. 278 minutes.

The Aquarium / L'aquarium / Das Aquarium / Junainat al-Asmak. 2008. Distributed by Misr International Films. 90 minutes.

Scheherazade Tell Me a Story / Femmes du Caire / Ihki Ya Shahrazad. 2009. Distributed in the United States by ArtMattan Productions. 134 minutes.

Interior/Exterior / Dakhili/Khariji. 2011. Short film included in *18 Days / 18 Yawm*. Distributed by Eurozoom.

After the Battle / Après la bataille / Nach der Revolution / Bad al-Mawqia. 2012. Distributed by MK2 Diffusion. 116 minutes.

REFERENCES

Abdalla, Ahmed. 1985. *The Student Movement and National Politics in Egypt, 1923–1973*. London: Al Saqi Books.

Abu al-Suud, Walid. 2009. "Yusri Nasrallah: Al-Fann Huwa al-Iktishaf wa-Laysa Taqdim al-Mawaiz." *Al-Shuruq*, July 1.

Abu-Lughod, Lila. 2005. *Dramas of Nationhood: The Politics of Television in Egypt*. Chicago: University of Chicago Press.

Amir, Ibrahim. 1958. *Al-Ard wa-l-Fallah: Al-Masala al-Ziraiya Fi Misr*. Cairo: Matbaat al-Durr al-Misriya li-l-Tibaa wa-l-Nashr.

Armbrust, Walter. 1995. "New Cinema, Commercial Cinema, and the Modernist Tradition in Egypt." *Alif: Journal of Comparative Poetics* (15): 81.

———. 1998a. "When the Lights Go Down in Cairo: Cinema as Secular Ritual." *Visual Anthropology* 10 (2–4): 413–442.

———. 1998b. "Veiled Cinema: A Conversation with Yousry Nasrallah." *Visual Anthropology* 10 (2–4): 381–399.

———. 2001. "Colonizing Popular Culture or Creating Modernity? Architectural Metaphors and Egyptian Media." In *Middle Eastern Cities 1900–1950: Public Places and Public Spheres in Transformation*, edited by Hans Chr. Korsholm Nielsen and Jakob Skovgaard-Petersen, 20–43. Aarhus: Aarhus University Press.

———. 2002. "Islamists in Egyptian Cinema." *American Anthropologist* 104 (3): 922–931.

Ayad, Christophe. 1998. "Dans *la Ville*, entre Le Caire et Paris." *Libération*, December 16.

Bordwell, David, Janet Staiger, and Kristin Thompson. 1988. *The Classical Hollywood Cinema: Film Style and Mode of Production to 1960*. London: Routledge.

Bourdieu, Pierre. 1996. *The Rules of Art*. Translated by Susan Emanuel. Cambridge: Polity Press.

Caiani, Fabio. 2007. "'My Name Is Yālū'. The Development of Metafiction in Ilyās Khūrī's Work." *Middle Eastern Literatures* 10 (2): 137–155.

Douin, Jean-Luc. 2004. "Le conte tragique de l'épopée de la Palestine." *Le Monde*, October 6.

Duval, Julien. 2006. "L'art du réalisme: Le champ du cinéma français au début des années 2000." *Actes de la recherche en sciences sociales* (161–162): 96–115.

El-Mahdi, Rabab. 2009. "Enough! Egypt's Quest for Democracy." *Comparative Political Studies* 42 (8) (August 1): 1011–1039.

El-Shakry, Omnia. 2008. "'A Radioscopy of the Egyptian Soul': Yousry Nasrallah's *The Aquarium*." *Middle East Journal of Culture & Communication* 1 (2) (July): 216–218.

Emanuel, Susan. 1999. "Quality, Culture and Education." In *Television Broadcasting in Contemporary France and Britain*, edited by Michael Scriven and Monia Lecomte, 83–93. New York: Berghahn Books.

Fabre, Clarisse. 2010. "Yousry Nasrallah: 'La femme en Egypte est devenue un genre de servante de l'homme.'" *Le Monde*, May 5.

Farid, Samir. 1988. "Sariqat Sayfiya: Nisf al-Haqiqa an Kull Shay." *Al-Jumhuriya*, October 31.

———. 2000. "La Ataamal maa al-Nujum, Li-annani Atahaddath an al-Shabab." *Al-Jumhuriya*, November 22.

Frodon, Jean-Michel. 2004. "Construire un imaginaire." *Cahiers du cinéma*, October: 48–49.

Geer, Benjamin. 2009. "Prophets and Priests of the Nation: Naguib Mahfouz's *Karnak Café* and the 1967 Crisis in Egypt." *International Journal of Middle East Studies* 41 (4) (November): 653–669.

Godard, Colette. 1988. "*Vols d'été*, de Yousry Nasrallah." *Le Monde*, May 15.

Hansen-Løve, Mia. 2004. "Le rêve éveillé." *Cahiers du cinéma*, October: 48–50.

Head, Gretchen. 2011. "The Performative in Ilyās Khūrī's *Bāb al-Shams*." *Journal of Arabic Literature* 42 (2–3) (January 1): 148–182.

Higson, Andrew. 2000. "The Limiting Imagination of National Cinema." In *Cinema and Nation*, edited by Mette Hjort and Scott MacKenzie, 57–68. London: Routledge.

Hoffman, Adina. 2006. "Recollecting the Palestinian Past." *Raritan* 26 (2): 52–61.

Ismael, Tareq Y., and Rif'at El-Sa'id. 1990. *The Communist Movement in Egypt, 1920–1988*. Contemporary Issues in the Middle East. Syracuse, N.Y.: Syracuse University Press.

Jäckel, Anne. 1996. "European Co-production Strategies: The Case of France and Britain." In *Film Policy: International, National, and Regional Perspectives*, edited by Albert Moran, 85–96. London: Routledge.

———. 1999. "Broadcasters' Involvement in Cinematic Co-Productions." In *Television Broadcasting in Contemporary France and Britain,* edited by Michael Scriven and Monia Lecomte, 175–197. New York: Berghahn Books.

———. 2003. *European Film Industries.* London: British Film Institute.

Jarrar, Maher. 2008. "The Arabian Nights and the Contemporary Arabic Novel." In *The Arabian Nights in Historical Context: Between East and West,* edited by Saree Makdisi and Felicity Nussbaum, 297–316. Oxford: Oxford University Press.

Kanafani, Samar. 2008. "Leaving Mother-Land: The Anti-Feminine in Fida'i Narratives." *Identities* 15 (3): 297–316.

Khoury, Elias. 1998. *Bab al-Shams.* Beirut: Dar al-Adab.

———. 2006. *Gate of the Sun.* Translated by Humphrey Davies. New York: Picador.

Nakajima, Seio. 2010. "Film as Cultural Politics." In *Reclaiming Chinese Society: The New Social Activism,* edited by You-Tien Hsing and Ching Kwan Lee, 159–183. Abingdon, Oxon, UK: Routledge.

Nasr, Muhammad. 2005. "Al-Mukhrij Yusri Nasrallah: Bab al-Shams an al-Insan al-Filastini, wa-50 Sana min Umr al-Qadiya." *Al-Ahram,* January 19.

———. 2008. "Al-Mukhrij Yusri Nasrallah: Junaynat al-Asmak Yadu Ila Adam al-Khawf aw al-Ikhtiba." *Al-Ahram,* April 2.

Nasrallah, Yousry, Georges-Marc Benamou, Jérôme Clément, and Jean-Michel Frodon. 2013. Après la bateille: *Un film de Yousry Nasrallah.* Paris: MK2.

Pappe, Ilan. 2006. *The Ethnic Cleansing of Palestine.* London: Oneworld Publications.

Salih, Ahmad. 1988. "Sariqat Sayfiya Anqadh Sumat Misr." *Al-Akhbar,* June 6.

Salim, Shayma'. 2008. "Junaynat al-Asmak: Hal Tajru' 'ala al-Khuruj Minha?" *Al-Badil,* July 9.

al-Shafii, Ula. 2005. "Dirama Malhamiya Shadidat al-Shairiya an al-Wujud al-Filastini." *Al-Arabi,* January 8.

al-Shinnawi, Tariq. 1993. "Mirsidis Alladhi Lam Yushahidhu Ahad." *Ruz al-Yusif,* December 20.

Tartoussieh, Karim. 2012. "Life Is Like a Bowl of Fish: The Aquarium, the French New Wave and the Urban Reflection of the Cairene Self." *Journal for Cultural Research* 16 (2–3): 283–296.

Mohamed Chouikh at the International Festival
of Francophone Film, Namur 2005.

8

Mohamed Chouikh

FROM ANTICOLONIAL COMMEMORATION
TO A CINEMA OF CONTESTATION
(ALGERIA)

Guy Austin

Mohamed Chouikh occupies a key position as a kind of relay between the post-colonial, idealized Algeria of the 1960s and what one might call the contested, dysfunctional Algeria of the 1980s and since. As an actor, he played a part in the pioneering Algerian films of the sixties and early seventies, sometimes known as *cinéma moudjahid* or what we might call freedom-fighter cinema, predominantly state-sponsored, nationalist commemorations of the liberation struggle against French colonial rule. But his work as director, especially his mature work from *The Citadel* (1988) onward, interrogates the social, cultural, and political power of the Algerian state. Chouikh in this way embodies a general shift within Algerian cinema from the nationalist and anticolonial confidence of the presidency of Boumediene (1965–1978) to the disjuncture between the state and the people, the contestation of the one-party system of the FLN (Front de libération nationale), and the search for emancipation from traditional conceptions of gender, history, and power of the 1980s and since (see Austin 2012). His work can in this way be related to current forms of Algerian protest and can be read as mirroring the disillusionment of the Algerian people with state power. This cinema of contestation has focused in particular on women's rights, and on the codes of violence (both literal and symbolic) that are imposed upon women in the Arab world. In terms of aesthetics, Chouikh's cinema makes sustained use of allegory, metaphor, and symbol, but rather than instrumentalizing these as means to perpetuate a nationalist discourse based on realism, Chouikh effectively uses them as forms of critique, as well as—less obviously—in order to celebrate the possibilities that he still locates in values such as pluralism and tolerance, and in formal terms in the visual construction of space.

This account of Chouikh's work will establish 1984 as a key turning point in his career, marked by his short film *Maqam Echahid* (about the martyrs' monument in Algiers—hence the culmination of a discourse of commemoration around the official history of the Algerian Revolution), but also the year of the infamous Family Code, which Chouikh opposed. The subsequent years saw an increasing politicization of Chouikh's cinema as he positioned himself more openly against state policy, initially in the realm of gender. The social critique in Chouikh's cinema will be contextualized in relation to the key moments and policies of the FLN-run Algerian state from the 1980s onward: the introduction of the Family Code in 1984—to which Chouikh responded with *The Citadel;* Black October, when the army fired on protestors—Chouikh's response was the film *Youcef: The Legend of the Seventh Sleeper;* and the terror and counter-terror of the so-called civil war or "black decade" of the nineties, which Chouikh reinterpreted in the films *The Desert Ark* and *Hamlet of Women.* Throughout Chouikh's films, a concern is apparent with the disempowerment (and possibilities for reempowerment) of the individual—women in a patriarchal tradition (*The Citadel, Hamlet of Women*); the anticolonial fighter on the margins of official history (*Youcef*); and the victims of collective intolerance and violence (*The Desert Ark*). But initially Chouikh's contribution to Algerian cinema was in fact as part of the nationalist mythologizing of the anticolonial struggle.

ANTICOLONIAL COMMEMORATION

Mohamed Chouikh was born at Mostaganem, on the Mediterranean coast of western Algeria, in 1943. He thus passed formative and teenage years during the time of the anticolonial war against the French occupation of Algeria, which took place between 1954 and 1962. The young Chouikh was a member of the subtly nationalist scouting movement, and also a keen actor in his local theater group. It was in his twenties, after Algeria gained independence in 1962, that he made the transition from theater to cinema. To some degree one can identify his early career in film with the development of an Algerian cinema in the early years of the independent Algeria. The primary aim of the embryonic national cinema was to represent the liberation struggle against the French. Certainly in the first decade of its existence, Algerian cinema was instrumentalized by the FLN, which sought to legitimize its one-party system by reference to the "million martyrs" of the revolutionary struggle. To facilitate this, the film industry had been nationalized as early as 1964, two years after independence. This was the context for Chouikh's first steps in cinema—as an actor. He appeared in the first full-length fiction film that can be considered 100 percent Algerian, *The Wind from the Aurès* (*Le Vent des Aurès / Rih al-awras*, Mohamed Lakhdar-Hamina, 1966). At the end of the decade, Chouikh also starred in the action film *The Outlaws* (*Les Hors-la-loi / Al-kharijoun an-alkanoun*, Tewfik Fares, 1969). Although diverse in style—*The Wind from the Aurès* is a tragic portrayal of national suffering, *The Outlaws* as close as Algerian cinema has come to the genre of the Western—both films can be classified as belonging to the state-supported cinema of anticolonial mythology. In the terminology of the time, they were examples of *cinéma moudjahid*. A variant, but nonetheless still a form of hegemonic, state-sanctioned discourse, was to emerge in the early seventies with the so-called *cinéma djidid* or "young cinema." Chouikh again featured as an actor in this socialist-realist genre, appearing in *The Nomads* (*Les Nomades /Masirat al-ruhhal*, Sid Ali Mazif, 1975). *The Nomads* included a positive portrayal of the Soviet-inspired Agrarian Revolution that had recently taken place, and in 1976 the film was welcomed by the Algerian newspaper *La République* as an important contribution to the national project whereby "toutes les forces vives de la nation s'emploient à mener à bien cette tâche commune" [the lifeblood of the nation is being focused on achieving this common task] (see Aissaoui 1984, 170). It is possible therefore to characterize Chouikh's acting career in Algeria as largely at the service of dominant discourses within state-sponsored cinema. This was to change dramatically—although not immediately—after his move into directing.

A measure of the growing disjuncture between Chouikh and the censor was the fate of an early documentary short he worked on about the Agrarian Revolution; despite using commentary taken from a montage of President Boumediene's speeches, the film was judged to be dissenting from the party line, and was denied distribution (see Taboulay 1997, 31). Interviewed in the nineties, Chouikh observed that when he began to work as a director, the authorization and financing of film projects was entirely controlled by the Algerian state. Moreover, production was often patterned according to a calendar of key anniversaries, notably commemorations of the start of the liberation struggle in 1954 and its successful conclusion in 1962. The budget for films celebrating the war against the French remained larger than for other topics, a situation that continued into the eighties. For the twentieth anniversary of independence, in his feature film debut *Breakdown* (*Rupture / al-Inquita'*,1982), Chouikh made use of such a budget while also attempting to transcend official discourse on the war: "I wanted to escape the simplified discourse. But in reality I was caught in the system like the others" (cited in Taboulay 1997, 30, my own translation). Unlike Okacha Touita's *The Sacrificed* (*Les Sacrifiés*)—made the same year but seized by the censor because it portrayed violent divisions within the resistance struggle—*Breakdown* was absorbed into state discourse. Chouikh's narrative of a young man fighting against colonial oppression prior to World War II was deemed acceptable, if unoriginal; one reviewer noted that the film often quoted from others that Chouikh had already worked on as assistant director, notably Lakhdar-Hamina's *Sandstorm* (*Vent de Sable /Rih al'rimâl*) of a year before (see Aissaoui 1984, 264).

The watershed year for Chouikh's relationship with the state came in 1984. The primary reason was the official status granted to the Family Code, a patriarchal abrogation of women's rights, which motivated Chouikh's engagement with the issue of gender in his subsequent films. This was also the year of what we might call his last attempt to undermine hegemonic state mythologizing from the inside, with his short documentary *Maqam Echahid*. Erected two years earlier to mark twenty years of independence, the martyrs' monument in Algiers was the focal point of the FLN's commemoration of the anticolonial struggle. But the monument can be read as denying rather than celebrating the sovereignty of the Algerian people. As Ranjana Khanna writes, Maqam Echahid functioned as "a single location through which to channel a process of mourning, loss, and victory," but it ultimately revealed the state's disregard for the "disposable bodies" of its subjects (Khanna 2008, 18, 20). Although Khanna does not mention Chouikh, her comments here can be fruitfully applied to his work after 1984. In contrast to the symbolism of the martyrs' monument—a monolith within which Chouikh had attempted to find plural meanings in his documentary, as he had tried to find plural meanings within the monolith of official history in his feature *Breakdown*—we might say that Chouikh's later cinema concerns the Algerians who are "much more transitional and disposable than the monument." His later films represent these subaltern figures who, despite being "the leavings, the uncounted, the utterly disposable" of Algeria (ibid., 21, 20), are also its survivors. Hence the women, the children, the old men, in summary the dispossessed, who recur in Chouikh's mature filmography against a background of violence and disempowerment imposed by patriarchy (*The Citadel*, *The Desert Ark*), by the state (*Youcef*), or by terrorism (*Hamlet of Women*).

ONCIC (Office national pour le commerce et l'industrie cinématographiques), the state body that controlled the film industry, had both produced and distributed *Breakdown*. Chouikh had joined ONCIC with the aim of using it for his own purposes: "We liked to say we were entering the system like a Trojan horse, to fight from the inside" (in Taboulay 1997, 31). The risk of such a position is perhaps best reflected in Pierre Bourdieu's inverted use of the term, whereby "Trojan horse" applies not to dissident directors trying to smuggle their messages past the state censor, but those artists whose submission to state orthodoxy undermines the resistant possibilities of art itself (conceived of by Bourdieu as a potentially autonomous field): "Producers who are the most devoted to internal truths and values are considerably weakened by that sort of 'Trojan horse' represented by writers and artists who accept and bend to external demand" (Bourdieu 1996, 221).

How was Chouikh to make films that avoided "bending" to the "external demands" of the state? His key strategy in his mature work was to use symbolism and allegory. By eschewing the socialist-realist style of the seventies he nonetheless risked falling into the heavy-handed political symbolism and the "langue de bois" or political cant that he saw in state-sanctioned cinema. Indeed, Viola Shafik has noted how, historically, postcolonial Arab regimes have often required their own domestic cinema to rely on the instrumentalization of metaphor and symbolism: "Political metaphorism prevailing in the rhetorics of nationalist and socialist leaderships is a clear characteristic of some mainstream and most realist anticolonial cinema" (Shafik 2007, 63). In Algeria this can be seen in the *cinéma moudjahid* (with its schematic symbolism illustrating the liberation struggle against the French) as well as in the *cinéma djidid* that followed (a socialist-realist cinema celebrating work). But Chouikh's use of allegory is different, as we shall see. He tends to build convincing localized narratives that can also function as allegories of the state of the nation. That his films are not always immediately identifiable as allegorical is no hindrance to their functioning on two levels. As Angus Fletcher reminds us, allegory represents an important means of conveying meanings that are not literal and therefore may escape censorship, but this level of meaning is not always discernible to all viewers: "We must avoid the notion that all people must see a double meaning for the work to be rightly called allegory. At least one branch of allegory . . . serves political and social purposes by the very fact that a reigning authority (as in a police state) does not see the secondary meaning" (Fletcher 1964, 8). Chouikh's cinema functions in such a way in postcolonial Algeria, where, despite the official ending of the one-party state, the military-political elite known as *le pouvoir* still exists and the state still has a powerful role in censorship of the media—a role that was increased in the twenty-year state of emergency that ran from 1992 to 2011 (see for example Stora 2001). The importance of allegory in such circumstances is one key characteristic of Chouikh's cinema in the context of a country where the political reforms of 1989–1990 were short-lived and which has, more recently, been largely untouched by the so-called Arab Spring. Moreover, Chouikh's use of allegory offers a potential strategy for cinema in the Arab world, certainly in those Arab societies where autocratic regimes remain: the possibility of filmmaking that is contestatory yet viable, dissenting yet visible.

CONTESTATION: BLACK OCTOBER 1988

Black October 1988 is for modern Algeria an important, climactic moment, when the disjuncture between the Algerian people and the state became explicit. Assia Djebar has called this "the autumn of the six hundred dead" (Djebar 2000, 140), when the state shot, imprisoned and allegedly tortured hundreds of protestors. The mythologizing of the Algerian revolution in FLN ideology, with its parade of martyrs, was in effect destroyed by the state's own creation of hundreds of young martyrs to dissent in Black October: "La jeunesse algérienne ... neutralise, en octobre 1988, par equivalence, le signe fondateur et légitimant du pouvoir nationaliste, 'le sang des martyrs,' sa rente symbolique, en versant son propre sang, en subissant la torture et les prisons" [In October 1988 Algerian youth neutralized the founding, legitimizing sign of nationalist power, the symbolic payment made with 'the blood of the martyrs,' by in turn shedding its own blood, by suffering torture and imprisonment] (Mediene 1992, 72). According to Chouikh himself, Black October was a revolt of the young generation against their symbolic fathers, against thirty years of lies built around a utopian and disempowering discourse that celebrated the martyrs of the liberation struggle while ignoring pressing everyday issues, such as devastating unemployment and a chronic housing shortage (see Taboulay 1997, 49). The short-term result of the protests was in fact a relaxation of state control over the media and a brief opening up of the political and civic system, with the official end of the one-party state (reforms that were not to last beyond the early nineties). If 1988 was thus a watershed in the relations between the people and the state, and in the representation of what it was to be Algerian, it was also for Chouikh the year that saw the release of his first successful allegory, his anti-patriarchal parable *The Citadel*.

THE CITADEL: A PROTEST AGAINST PATRIARCHY

The Citadel (*La Citadelle / Al-qal'a*, 1988) had been written in 1984 but was ignored by the authorities for four years. (There was a similar delay with his subsequent film, *Youcef.*) When Chouikh's script was finally approved, it was assumed to be a folkloric and inoffensive portrayal of a traditional Algerian village. As Chouikh noted drily, "Those who let me make this film had no idea of its impact." The release of *The Citadel* contributed to the contestatory spirit of 1988: "The people, intellectuals, women, adopted it as their standard-bearer" (cited in Taboulay 1997, 41–42). The target of Chouikh's critique was the Family Code of 1984. Rather as 1988 marked a crux in political relations, 1984 has been described as "the year of the rupture between women and their government, and [of] women's radical questioning of the state's legitimacy" (Lazreg 1994, 197). Protest groups were set up demanding the abolition of the code, of polygamy (which it sanctioned), and of inequity in property and divorce rights. For his part, Chouikh saw the Family Code as "contrary to all the slogans, the rights, the supposed freedoms of women. This code makes a woman an eternal child, forced to obey her husband and parents, destined only for procreation" (cited in Taboulay 1997, 43).

Women are depicted in *The Citadel* as entirely subordinated to men, subservient to their husbands, limited to certain private spaces (the house and the yard), and burdened by domestic tasks. The multiple wedding ceremony at the start of the film—a potential example of the picturesque folklore that the authorities mistakenly discerned in Chouikh's script—is in fact an induction into a world of patriarchal violence, both literal and symbolic, ringing with gunshots and a demand for the immediate consummation of the weddings. From this point on, throughout the film, Chouikh excavates the figure of woman in Algerian culture, depicting the denial of rights enshrined by the Family Code and by the *sharia*. This is most effectively realized in the allegorical figure of the female mannequin, literally a woman without the ability to move or speak. The film ends with a mock wedding between Kaddour, a man without status or symbolic capital in the community, and the mannequin. Kaddour, the women, and the children of the community—most poignantly, the little girl who observes the mock wedding and Kaddour's subsequent death, and whose frozen image is the last shot of the film—are the subaltern elements of Algerian society, what Khanna would call the "leavings" or the "disposable." As we shall see below, Chouikh positions these subaltern discontents as the basis of an alternative society in his later films *The Desert Ark* and *Hamlet of Women*.

The Citadel demonstrates Chouikh's acute awareness of the ambivalent status of women in Algerian—and Arab—culture. As he himself notes, "woman has always been considered the guardian of the values of Arab society" (in Taboulay 1997, 42). But this role is dependent on confining women to a maternal function: "The representation of women in Algerian cinema is no different from that of women in the Arab world. Women are only regarded as sacred in their role as mothers" (ibid., 43).The Tunisian filmmaker and critic Férid Boughedir agrees: "Pour les Arabes, totalement méditerranéens en cela, la mère signifie toujours CE QU'IL YA DE PLUS IMPORTANT" [for the Arabs, entirely Mediterranean in this respect, the mother always signifies WHAT IS MOST IMPORTANT] (Boughedir 2004, 105; capitals in the original). *The Citadel* hollows out this convention by showing that it is men who wield power: the four wives of Sidi the village elder, for example, despite having borne him children, are almost entirely without status. When the family eats a meal, Sidi sits apart, consuming the meat that his wives and children are denied. When he throws scraps of meat to the dogs, one of his wives cries in fury and despair at her situation, screaming "C'est une vie de chien." The equation of women with animals recurs in *The Desert Ark* when Myriam's mother declares that the status of women in the community is lower than that of a grasshopper or a frog.

The Citadel thus functions as a powerful indictment of regressive customs which are legitimized by a set of patriarchal conceptions derived from the Family Code and from sharia law. But there is a possible allegorical reading here too, since the citadel can be construed not just as an isolated mountain community, but as Algeria. Notably, power within both the citadel and the state is in the hands of a small number of elderly men. Chouikh has suggested the similarity between the exercise of patriarchal power in the citadel and in the state more widely: "I show that the power to make decisions is in the hands of the old men of the community. Their seniority gives them power over life and death. Their legitimacy is not very far from the 'historical' legitimacy of the system" (in Taboulay 1997, 42). (The same comparison could also be applied to the village in *Hamlet of Women*.) Both communities, moreover—the citadel and Algeria—are for Chouikh characterized by stasis and a rejection of change. Although the setting is very different, the cyclical narrative and the atmosphere of claustrophobic enclosure generated in *The Citadel* are precursors for the more recent, urban depictions of Algeria as a site from which there is no escape in films such as Tariq Teguia's *Rome Rather Than You* (*Rome plutôt que vous / Roma wa la n'touma,* 2006) and Nadir Moknèche's *Délice Paloma* (2007).

YOUCEF: THE LEGEND OF THE SEVENTH SLEEPER:
EXCAVATING ALGERIAN INDEPENDENCE

If *The Citadel* critiques the disempowerment of women in Algeria, Chouikh's subsequent film, *Youcef (Youcef: La légende du septième dormant / Youcef kesat dekra sabera,* 1993), concerns the legitimizing of the Algerian state via the re-cuperation of the revolutionary anticolonial struggle. One might say that just as women are the property of the patriarchal elders in *The Citadel,* so history becomes the property of the FLN authorities in *Youcef.* Ranjana Khanna has written that "Algeria set itself up as the avant-garde third world nation that had effectively rid itself of the imperialist machine and was working on an Islamist socialist model," suggesting that it would "value the work done by men and women alike during the war of independence" (Khanna 2008, xiii). In effect, argues Khanna, the independent Algeria betrayed these ideals. The realization of this betrayal is the context for *Youcef.* The full title of the film is *Youcef: The Legend of the Seventh Sleeper,* and the narrative derives from a myth according to which seven young men, persecuted for their religion, fall asleep in a cave and awake 372 years later to find the world changed for the better. In Chouikh's version, the premise is twisted so that when the sleeper awakes he finds himself in an alien world, but one where corruption reigns, and where the ideals of the revolution have been betrayed. The anticolonial struggle has been replaced by a new regime no better than that of the French. In Chouikh's words, between independence in 1962 and the early nineties, Algeria has been trapped in a thirty-year-long coma (see Taboulay 1997, 58).

Awakening from his own symbolic sleep (he has been in an asylum since the last days of the war), Youcef escapes from incarceration in the desert and crosses Algeria, encountering the dispossessed wherever he goes, and witness-ing suffering and abuse, including the burning of an "impure" woman's house and her child—an atrocity he associates with the French occupiers but which it transpires is perpetrated by Islamists. He is ultimately presented with a list of grievances by the suffering Algerian people, who see him as their only represen-tative, before being co-opted by the local authorities into a nationalist parade, where his return to the fold is celebrated. Ultimately Youcef is shot dead as part of a conspiracy to silence his grievances, and also to silence the dissent of those for whom he speaks. The state thus disposes of Youcef, while its celebration of his return—replete with nationalist rhetoric and iconography—also turns him into one of the anonymous martyred bodies that Khanna has suggested feed nation-alist monuments like Maqam Echahid, and continue to legitimize authoritarian

Youcef trying to contact rebel command in *Youcef.*

state power. In his return from exile and in his death Youcef can also function as an allusion to the fate of Mohamed Boudiaf, another war veteran who was exiled at the end of the war and returned to Algeria in the early nineties. Boudiaf was in fact welcomed as a reformist president in 1992, when the state had criminalized many Islamist groups and declared a state of emergency. Widely perceived as a man willing to weed out corruption within the state, Boudiaf was assassinated in suspicious circumstances after less than six months in office. Although Chouikh had written the film years before this event, and indeed finished shooting before Boudiaf's return, the parallels were resonant enough for him to be approached by the authorities to explain the apparent similarity to real life.

If the role of the state in *Youcef* is largely sinister, and the tenor of the film largely tragic, the state has become distant, farcical and irrelevant a decade or so later in *Hamlet of Women*: the women of the village defend themselves against terrorism while the government and male leaders abdicate responsibility during most of the narrative. Where the state organizes a legitimizing ritual in *Youcef,* in *Hamlet of Women* it cancels an election and a mayoral visit, even sending a minor official to collect back the posters and national flags he had distributed, symbolizing the state's withdrawal from the lives of its own citizens during the civil conflict of the black decade.

Of all the evocative spaces depicted in *Youcef*—from the desert to the market to the streets where demonstrations are shown—the cave is a privileged setting.

The desert as an open, quasi-ornamental space at the end of *The Desert Ark*.

Defending the village in *Hamlet of Women*.

It is here that Youcef shelters at the margins of society, and here that he finds his old comrades' skeletons—the relics of the war of liberation whose ideals the state has long since abandoned, along with these forgotten corpses. The cave is an ambivalent space, both refuge and prison, represented in various Algerian films from Mohamed Zinet's *Alger Insolite* (*Tahia ya didou!* 1971) to Chouikh's own *Desert Ark,* where the separated lovers Myriam and Amin are reunited in a cave. The historical associations of the cave situate it as a site of terror—of French colonial atrocities such as the nineteenth-century *enfumades,* which saw villagers immured in caves and asphyxiated by smoke—as well as a place of shelter and escape, as in the cave of Dahra from Assia Djebar's film of female resistance, *The Nouba of the Women of Mount Chenoua* (*La Nouba des femmes du Mont Chenoua,* 1978). It is thus a microcosm of the nation, a place of both suffering and resistance. The cave is also a Platonic trope, and clearly functions as such in *Youcef.* This is a space of inquiry and truth-telling, where myths will be debunked as merely the shadows of an illusory, enclosed world with no relation to reality. This is made explicit when, asking why he cannot see any evidence of independence and freedom in the world around him, Youcef is told by an old colleague that independence is real, and that cinema can prove this. He proceeds to screen the anticolonial classic *The Battle of Algiers* for Youcef on the wall of the cave—to prove that independence actually happened. But the Platonic allegory at work here repositions *The Battle of Algiers* not as a historical document, nor a militant masterpiece of cinema, but simply as a fiction, part of the mythologizing of the struggle that has allowed the postcolonial state to maintain its regime. *The Battle of Algiers* has become a fiction of liberation, not an index of it. Youcef himself, who has seen the reality of the independent Algeria, is Plato's lone philosopher, whose message from the real world is unlikely to be welcomed by those mesmerized by the glowing images on the cave wall. The final irony in this brilliant sequence is when Lyes, the former comrade who screens the film, urges Youcef to exploit resistance connections and his training as an architect to design monuments for the martyrs of the revolution. What the Algerian state requires, it seems, is not a revelation of how it treats its own people, but another monument like Maqam Echahid.

THE DESERT ARK: AN ALLEGORY OF CIVIL CONFLICT

After President Boudiaf's return and assassination, predicted in the narrative of *Youcef,* Algeria slid into a traumatizing conflict. The so-called civil war of the 1990s saw up to 200,000 killed in a struggle between state autocracy and Islamic fundamentalism (see Stora 2001). *The Desert Ark* (*L'Arche du désert*, 1997) figures the violent disputes over Algerian identity at this time—and beyond that, competing conceptions of Arab identity—as a series of spatial compositions. By setting the film in the desert, in a village served by an oasis, Chouikh maximizes the tensions around the possession of habitable space. But there is also a political resonance here since the desert (known in Algeria simply as "the South") is also a place of exile and escape. It is here that certain resistance leaders who had participated in the war against the French were imprisoned, and subsequently after independence it was again in the desert that resistance fighters from other factions were imprisoned by the victorious FLN. More recently, in the nineties, the desert had become a place of asylum since it offered a potential escape from the violence that surrounded Algiers and much of northern Algeria. Without reducing the representation of space to the schematic, Chouikh manages in *The Desert Ark* to present the desert village as a series of interrelated spaces where different levels of codified behavior (and different levels of freedom from such strictures) are situated.

We might compare the tension established in the film between such spatial restrictions and the open spaces of the desert beyond with Deleuze and Guattari's description of the desert as a smooth, "horizonless" space of nomadic possibilities (see Deleuze and Guattari, 2004, 418). Throughout the film, from the opening shot onward, the desert is presented as an infinite space, a reflection of the sky, often shown at sunset or sunrise. The village beside the oasis is an enclave within this vast almost abstract space where a community of two tribes (signified by green and blue flags) has been established. Social hierarchies and functions (each villager has a specific role, each tribe has its elder and its priest, one tribe dominates the other but coexistence is guaranteed, as in a caste system) ensure the continued survival of this community. But it is significant that certain freer forms of identity are not accommodated by this social structure. This is particularly a question of desire and of the breaking of taboos. Hence the early scene that motivates the entire narrative takes place, importantly, outside the palisade, on the edge of the desert, where two unmarried lovers from opposing tribes (Myriam and Amin) are discovered embracing.

Immediately separated, the couple are kept apart by the village and by their own tribes. While Amin is beaten and later escapes to a ruined citadel outside the village, Myriam is incarcerated in a series of enclosed spaces. These include: the tower of the *marabout* where she runs to seek asylum; the family home where she is chained to prevent escape; the temple where she is tied up to have the "devil" inside her driven out; the cell where she is imprisoned prior to her wedding; and finally the tent where she is required to consummate an arranged marriage with a member of her uncle's tribe (they arrive to take possession of the village and of Myriam herself). Tribal segregation is moreover enforced by a series of barriers erected within the village, dividing it up into green and blue zones. This attempt to police space, in Deleuze and Guattari's terms to establish "fixed paths in well-defined directions, which restrict speed, regulate circulation" (Deleuze and Guattari 2004, 425), is ridiculed when a herd of goats pushes past the barriers and carries on, oblivious.

The theme of exile here is less a political commentary on the discontents of the FLN, or a reflection on the fate of returning leader Mohamed Boudiaf, than a means of visualizing in space the exclusion of certain ways of being in Arab culture. Halfway through the film the site of an alternative community is revealed when the independent, unmarried Houria and her followers (predominantly but not exclusively unmarried women) are shown as a series of black-clad silhouettes watching the action from outside the village. These exiles congregate around Houria, who is described by the old man El Moutanabi as "the mother of the citadel"; they live in a ruin that has been abandoned by the current community. Thus in both space and time this group is othered, beyond the pale and yet also in touch with long-standing forms of existence that have been rejected by the villagers. This is not a question of religion (notably, the village in this regard is spatially dominated by the *marabout*'s tower rather than by any mosque, and practices pre-Islamic folk beliefs), but an openness that accommodates plurality, desire, pleasure, and excess outside of social structures and strictures. Hence Myriam and Amin are welcomed but marriage is shunned. The exiles, especially Houria, dance and sing, not in a formalized group but as individuals. There is thus a clear distinction between their self-expression in dance and the more structured ritual performances of the villagers celebrating Myriam's hastily arranged wedding. For the latter sequence, Chouikh pans slowly along a group of women singing and making rhythmic gestures, but all seated and in a sense homogenous. There is a binding sense of conformity here, as in the many wedding scenes that regularly punctuate Arab cinema and that characteristically show the genders as segregated: to take just two examples among many, this is evident in the Algerian comedy *Omar Gatlato* (Allouache, 1976) and the Tunisian coming-of-age film *Halfaouine* (Boughedir, 1990). But in *The Desert Ark* when the exiles dance in a cave-like space within their ruined citadel, they do so as individuals, men and women alike, and the camera circles back and forth without any sense of linearity or division. The exiles are also free from the taboos and customs that regulate female dress and comportment. Houria embodies this freedom: her hair is always free, her arms bare, and as well as singing and dancing she also curses, spits, and even at one point begins shaking and having a fit as Myriam is recuperated by her own tribe and taken away to be forcibly married.

Chouikh's use of symbolism at the end of the film involves a young boy, Salim, escaping a massacre that engulfs the village to set off in search of a place where "they don't kill children and burn houses." The allusion to the atrocities of the black decade is clear. As the screenplay (reproduced in full in Taboulay 1997) notes, the desert is the only solution. Notably, Houria and most of her colleagues have left too, walking into the desert, seemingly to form another alternative, women-dominated community where taboos are again challenged as in *Hamlet of Women* (2005). Chouikh's final sequence here can be compared to the ending of *Rachida* (2002) by his wife—and the editor of most of his films—Yamina Bachir-Chouikh. *Rachida* ends demonstratively with the gaze of the eponymous young schoolteacher straight at the spectator in the aftermath of a massacre. This gaze signifies Rachida's defiant survival despite the atrocities she has experienced, and despite being one of the principal targets of fundamentalist violence, namely a "modern" woman. At the end of *The Desert Ark* the symbolic survivor of the massacre is Salim, and he too glances at the camera before setting off into the desert. The look at the camera in Chouikh's film is only a brief glance, but nonetheless breaks down the so-called "fourth wall" of film spectatorship. The fleeting nature of this glance makes it all the more startling, a challenge to the adults, the (male) elders, the patriarchal leaders of the state who, as in Chouikh's other mature films, have failed to protect the dispossessed, the subaltern and the children of the community.

HAMLET OF WOMEN: AN ESCAPE FROM TRADITION

In Chouikh's *Hamlet of Women* (*Douar de femmes / Douar nisaa'*, 2005), the adult men of the community abandon a remote village in the woods to the women and children and set off to work in a distant factory (see Brahimi 2011). The disappearance of the men is in part a reference to the withdrawal of the state and its failure to protect the Algerian populace during the terror of the nineties, but this is also a moment of liberation: it facilitates a temporary overthrow of patriarchal control after which the women, easily evading the feeble strictures of the village elder, now carry arms to protect the community from the threat of terrorism, and (literally in the case of Sabrina, the protagonist), wear the trousers. Another symbolic representation of this new freedom is the healing of Sabrina's younger sister, who had her throat partially cut by Islamist terrorists (an action that, as well as recalling the atrocities of the black decade, also symbolizes an attempt to silence women's voices) but gradually recovers her voice to speak and sing. However, unlike *Rachida,* which also concerns a young woman in an isolated village threatened by terrorism, in *Hamlet of Women* the enduring threat is less from the terrorists (who are caricatures, pantomime villains) than from the men of the village themselves. Hence the film both begins and ends with a threat of male violence against disobedient women. The state too is seen as a guarantor of patriarchal power; when a rumor spreads that politicians are about to visit the village, the women assume their traditional positions inside the home. The women's taking over the village is revealed as transient when the men return to reestablish patriarchal control at the pessimistic close of the film. Just as *The Desert Ark* ends with young Salim walking alone into the desert, so *Hamlet of Women* pictures Sabrina alone, walking disconsolately back to the village through the darkening woods. The return of the menfolk has not only reestablished patriarchy; it has seemingly separated Sabrina (the most militant woman of the group) from the other women of the village, as well as bringing about a symbolic nightfall after the thrilling dawn of the women's assumption of power in the community.

Nonetheless, throughout the film Chouikh celebrates the women's contestation of traditional restrictions on their bodies, their dress, and their actions. They talk openly of desire (notably for Amin, the handsome visitor from Algiers), they refuse to wear the veil when he enters the community, and in the climactic shootout with the terrorists, they cross the demarcation line that prohibits them from going beyond the limits of the village. If Sabrina is the most active and vociferous of the women, the first to throw off patriarchal and Islamic expectations—she even refuses to pray, since this will make her vulnerable to attack—she is also presented as a young avatar of the mysterious woman in black, Khadidja, a vengeful mother who walks the mountains nearby in search of the terrorists who killed her son. A modern-day version of the female resistance leaders of ancient Algerian history and of the liberation struggle against French colonialism, Khadidja is the first to open fire on the terrorists, thus safeguarding the village. Moreover, in a resonant piece of casting, she is played by Messaouda Adami, who also plays Houria, the leader of a prototype hamlet of women in *The Desert Ark.* There is thus a sense of continuity here, of an ongoing struggle for women to be heard, evoked also in Assia Djebar's *The Nouba of the Women of Mount Chenoua.*

SYMBOLIC VIOLENCE, SPACE, AND AESTHETICS

It is through his construction of space that Chouikh depicts the violence (literal and symbolic) that builds within the microcosmic communities of his films, as well as the possibility of survival in alternative sites. In Chouikh's contestatory cinema, violence is visited upon the bodies of the dispossessed—bodies that Khanna has read as "disposable" in the actions of the Algerian state. But although there are moments of physical violence in his films—the assaults on women in *The Citadel, Youcef,* and *Hamlet of Women,* the massacre in *The Desert Ark*—it is principally symbolic violence that is evoked by Chouikh's on-screen construction of space. As Bourdieu has noted, "space is one of the sites where power is asserted and exercised . . . as symbolic violence that goes unperceived as violence" (Bourdieu et al. 1999, 126). It is by means of spatial compositions that Chouikh's filmmaking renders visible the invisible patterns of domination and submission, the symbolic violence that is otherwise naturalized, authorized, and thus effectively hidden by patriarchal structures such as the Family Code. Power over space, power *as* space, is crucial in his films.

The primary construction of space in Chouikh's work is as a series of private enclaves where patriarchal power is expressed. At its most extreme, this is a question of the privatization of space—and of the Algerian woman (by extension, the Algerian state, or the Arab state) as the private property of the male elite. Colonial history has played a part in entrenching such symbolic violence: certainly, for Assia Djebar, the Algerian woman under colonialism was "doublement emprisonnée dans cette immense prison" [doubly imprisoned in this immense prison] (Djebar 1980, 159). But outside colonial oppression, Chouikh has declared that in Arab culture "the woman's body is the sole property of the man who owns her, and any gaze from outside is considered an intrusion on private property" (in Taboulay 1997, 46–47). Similarly, a number of writers and intellectuals have observed that after independence, the state in Algeria instrumentalized the anticolonial struggle, turning it into a commodity that legitimized the one-party system, and into a property that no longer belonged to the nation but to the FLN alone. There was a prescient warning from Fanon that after independence, "the party, which during the battle had drawn to itself the whole nation . . . is becoming a means of private advancement" (Fanon 2001, 137–138). In the nineties it became clear that the struggle itself had been appropriated: "La lutte du peuple algérien pour son indépendance a été privatisée . . . elle est devenue la propriété exclusive du FLN" [The struggle of the Algerian people for their independence has been privatized, it has become the exclusive property of the FLN] (Sansal 2006, 43). Chouikh makes frequent use in his films of settings that represent Algeria as an enclosure, a private space, even a prison. The recurrent tropes of incarceration in his cinema include the asylum and the cave in *Youcef*; the citadel itself in *The Citadel* (shut off from the outside world by huge boulders that block our first view of the community), the numerous enclosures where Myriam is imprisoned in *The Desert Ark*, and to some extent the isolated village in *Hamlet of Women*. This often overlaps with restrictions on women's free circulation, particularly in *The Citadel*.

Positioned against these enclosed spaces are the alternative communities of *The Desert Ark, Hamlet of Women*, and even to some extent *Youcef* (the petitioners who congregate around Youcef at the mouth of his cave). If these spaces are not always utopian—the stranded boat on the sands at the end of *The Desert Ark*, for example, is clearly going nowhere—they are important in positing an alternative relationship with space, where the latter is not privatized nor a site of symbolic or literal violence. This is most positively expressed in Chouikh's celebratory representation of infinite spaces. This can be compared to Teshome Gabriel's conception of so-called Third World cinema as concerned with "spatial representation rather than temporal manipulation," manifesting "Nostalgia for the vastness of nature . . . resulting in long takes and long or wide shots" (Gabriel 1989, 33). *The Desert Ark* is emblematic in this respect. When contemplating the vast panorama of land and sky, Amin declares, "How large the earth is!" and compares the desert to a boundless sea. The film begins with a slow pan across the desert dunes, which are first purple, then yellow, then green, and concludes with a similar image as Salim walks into a huge desert vista above which the sky is a series of brilliant colors. In terms of Chouikh's filming of space, it is noticeable that both these sequences (the start and the ending of *The Desert Ark*) are shot with a camera panning from right to left. The direction of movement here evokes progression toward the future in an Arabophone culture, since it is the direction of reading and writing Arabic. As Chouikh says, "I usually start my tracking shots from right to left, as in writing Arabic" (in Taboulay 1997, 72). The same formal choice can be seen in the final scene of *Rachida*, and can be identified as a characteristic of Arab cinema, much as the left-to-right camera movement is prevalent in the cinema of the West. As Gabriel notes, in overly tentative terms, "It is quite possible that the direction of panning toward left or right might be strongly influenced by the direction in which a person writes" (Gabriel 1989, 45).

As regards film style, the documentary *Maqam Echahid* had demonstrated Chouikh's willingness to rely on images rather than on commentary or dialogue to carry the meaning of his work, a choice that also informs his mature fiction films. The reliance on image over language was one means of avoiding the verbosity and ubiquity of the FLN's rhetoric around nationalism and history, hence Chouikh's desire to "articulate a narrative uniquely by means of the image at a time when all around me was empty talk" (cited in Taboulay 1997, 32). And it is imagery rather than dialogue that is the strongest vehicle of meaning—particularly the two levels of meaning in allegory—throughout Chouikh's work. In this he is distinct from the "functionalization of the image by language" that Shafik has identified in mainstream Arab cinema (see Shafik 2007, 55). If Chouikh's use of symbolism places him within an auteur tradition distinct from mainstream cinema and from the rhetoric of the state, his film aesthetic also seems to reflect the legacy of the ornamental in Arab art. According to Shafik, the representation of form as ornamental (rather than realistic or figurative) in Islamic art resulted in an art where "space rests unrestricted, beginning and ending are intertwined, the contradictions between light and shadow, up and down, are indissolubly connected. Rather than the ornament being bound to a finite vanishing point, the transition to the infinite seems open." She continues: "It is because of Islamic art's distance from reality and its refusal of figurative spatial representation that its principles were hardly applied in cinema" (ibid., 55). Yet at times Chouikh seems to present not just an allegorical critique of Algeria but a quasi-ornamental representation of space where "the transition to the infinite seems open." Again, *The Desert Ark* is the best example of this tendency: "beginning and ending are intertwined" in the way that the almost abstract opening and closing shots mirror each other; light and shadow are "indissolubly connected" in the images inside the *marabout*'s tower and also in the desert itself. In the repeated shots of the desert in particular we see no clear vanishing point, no clear lines of Renaissance perspective, no landmarks. Therefore even at the end of such an ostensibly pessimistic film as *The Desert Ark,* the transition to the infinite is still a possibility, as shown in the last shot.

Regarding the aesthetic choices open to Arab filmmakers, Chouikh has asked: "What is expected of us? Certainly not to copy Western style, that would be meaningless. But by asserting our own aesthetic identity, we must be careful not to fall into folklore" (in Taboulay 1997, 40). In effect, over his career Chouikh has developed a film style that attempts to avoid both of these pitfalls, notably via an attention to the possibilities of non-Western form (in the direction of tracking shots for example, or the allusion to the centrality in Arab art of the ornament rather than the figure). In the process he has broken free of the constraints of state-sponsored cinema that informed his earliest roles as an actor and his earliest films as a director. His oeuvre since the late eighties can be said to represent a sustained allegorical critique of the modern-day Algerian state. But more than that, his work also suggests an opening toward other possibilities, be they thematic (the alternative communities of *The Desert Ark* and *Hamlet of Women*) or formal (the place of the infinite and the ornamental in representations of space) that suggest further possibilities for Algerian and Arab cinema.

FILMOGRAPHY OF MOHAMED CHOUIKH

L'embouchure (The River Mouth). 1972. Produced for television by LMF/RTA.

Les paumés (The Wrecks). 1974. Produced for television by LMF/RTA.

Breakdown / Rupture / al-Inquita'. 1982. Distributed in Algeria by ONCIC. 105 minutes.

Maqam Echahid. 1984. Distributed in Algeria by ONCIC. 30 minutes. Documentary.

The Citadel / La citadelle / Al-qal'a. 1988. Distributed in France by K Films. 96 minutes.

Youcef: The Legend of the Seventh Sleeper / Youcef: La légende du septième dormant / Youcef kesat dekra sabera. 1993. Distributed in France by K Films. 105 minutes.

The Desert Ark / L'Arche du désert. 1997. Distributed in the United States by ArtMattan Productions. 90 minutes.

Hamlet of Women / Douar de femmes / Douar al nisaa'. 2005. Distributed by Acima Films. 102 minutes.

L'Andalou / Al' Andalousee. 2014

REFERENCES

Aissaoui, Boualem. 1984. *Images et visages du cinéma algérien*. Algiers: ONCIC.

Austin, Guy. 2012. *Algerian National Cinema*. Manchester: Manchester University Press.

Boughedir, Férid. 2004. "La victime et la matronne: Les deux images de la femme dans le cinéma tunisien." *CinémAction* 111, 103–112.

Bourdieu, Pierre. 1996. *The Rules of Art: Genesis and Structure of the Literary Field*. Translated by Susan Emmanuel. Cambridge: Polity Press.

Bourdieu, Pierre, et al. 1999. *The Weight of the World: Social Suffering in Contemporary Society*. Translated by Priscilla Parkhurst Ferguson. Cambridge: Polity Press.

Brahimi, Denise. 2011. "*Hamlet of Women* (Mohamed Chouikh): Village Chronicles from a Time of Terrorism." In *Film in the Middle East and North Africa: Creative Dissidence,* edited by Josef Gugler, 315–323. Austin: University of Texas Press.

Deleuze, Gilles, and Guattari, Félix. 2004. *A Thousand Plateaus*. Translated by Brian Massumi. London: Continuum.

Djebar, Assia. 1980. *Femmes d'Alger dans leur appartement*. Paris: Des Femmes.

———. 2000. *Algerian White*. Translated by David Kelley and Marjolijn de Jager. New York: Seven Stories.

Fanon, Frantz. 2001. *The Wretched of the Earth*. Translated by Constance Farrington. London: Penguin Classics.

Fletcher, Angus. 1964. *Allegory: Theory of a Symbolic Mode*. Ithaca, NY: Cornell University Press.

Gabriel, Teshome. 1989. "Towards a Critical Theory of Third World films." In *Questions of Third Cinema,* edited by Jim Pines and Paul Willemen, 30–52. London: BFI Publishing.

Khanna, Ranjana. 2008. *Algeria Cuts: Women and Representation from 1830 to the Present*. Stanford: Stanford University Press.

Lazreg, Marnia. 1994. *The Eloquence of Silence: Algerian Women in Question*. New York: Routledge.

Mediene, Benamar. 1992. "Un état déconnecté." In *Le nouvel observateur,* Collection Dossiers, 9: *La Guerre d'Algérie trente ans après:* 72–73.

Sansal, Boualem. 2006. *Poste restante: Alger. Lettre de colère et d'espoir à mes compatriotes*. Paris: Gallimard.

Shafik, Viola. 2007. *Arab Cinema: History and Cultural Identity*. Rev. ed. Cairo: American University in Cairo Press.

Stora, Benjamin. 2001. *La guerre invisible: Algérie, années 90*. Paris: Presses de Sciences Po.

Taboulay, Camille. 1997. *Le cinéma métaphorique de Mohamed Chouikh*. Paris: K Films Editions.

Merzak Allouache with Ali Al Jabri, the director
of the Abu Dhabi Film Festival, 2013.

9

Merzak Allouache

(SELF-)CENSORSHIP, SOCIAL CRITIQUE, AND THE LIMITS OF POLITICAL ENGAGEMENT IN CONTEMPORARY ALGERIAN CINEMA (ALGERIA)

Will Higbee

> I am from a generation that grew up in the years that followed the war of liberation. Like many others, I was patient and idealistic. I attached great hope to the country's independence, tomorrow looked promising, the nation was being rebuilt. Today, we need to reconsider everything, tear it all down, and rebuild from scratch.
>
> —Merzak Allouache in Khatibi, 2011

In a career of almost forty years, comprising fourteen feature films as well as numerous TV films and documentaries, Merzak Allouache has confirmed his reputation as one of the most prolific and critically acclaimed directors in the history of Algerian cinema. From his award-winning directorial debut *Omar Gatlato*, one of the key works of Algerian and indeed Arab cinema of the 1970s, to *The Rooftops*, a film that combines narratives from five different neighborhoods in Algiers as a means of exploring class and religious divides in Algeria, Allouache has repeatedly demonstrated, both on and off-screen, his commitment to engaging with the realities and crises facing Algerian society since decolonization, and, above all, the struggles facing Algerian youth. The director has, moreover, achieved this prominent position among contemporary Algerian filmmakers despite spending almost as much time working in France as he has in Algeria over the past three decades. Such conditions of exile or temporary displacement are not unusual for postcolonial Arab directors, a point acknowledged by Tunisian director and critic Férid Boughedir when writing about the significant contribution of exilic and diasporic filmmakers to New Arab cinema of the 1970s and 1980s (Boughedir 1987, 10). For his part, Allouache defines himself not as an émigré director but as a *cinéaste de passage:* a filmmaker whose movement between France and Algeria is dictated by the political, artistic, and economic conditions associated with each new project. The director's key distinction between émigré filmmaker and cinéaste de passage underlines the complex position occupied not just by Allouache but by many filmmakers of the North African diaspora(s) living and working in France: maintaining a presence that is simultaneously between and *within* the film cultures and industries of France and the Maghreb (Higbee 2007, 62).

Born in 1944 in Algiers, Allouache belongs to a generation of Algerians who grew up toward the end of the colonial period but were too young to fully comprehend or indeed influence the events leading to independence. His films are nonetheless shaped (as the quote that opens this chapter suggests) by this sense of initial optimism and later disillusionment for what a postcolonial Algerian nation might become. An avid cinemagoer since his youth, Allouache began his training as a filmmaker by studying at the Algerian Cinema Institute in the early 1960s. He then spent five years in France, from 1968 to 1973, including a period at the prestigious Institut des hautes études cinématographiques (the IDHEC film school) in Paris. Following his time in France, Allouache returned to work for the Algerian Ministry of Culture, effectively "joining the Algerian production system," organizing projections of short documentary films in the small villages as part of the Agrarian Revolution (Allouache in Khalil 2005, 150). After collaborating on a documentary produced by French television in Algeria in 1974, Allouache went on to direct three features in the space of six years under the control of the Office National pour le Commerce et l'Industrie Cinématographique (ONCIC, the Algerian state controlled film industry).[1] His breakthrough debut *Omar Gatlato* (*'Umar qatlatu alrudjla*, 1976), which won international acclaim and was screened at Cannes in 1977, was at the same time a huge popular success with Arab audiences, attracting over 300,000 spectators in Algeria (Armes 2005, 105). While the film's depiction of Algerian youth as "imprisoned in disastrous working conditions, secluded from the world of women" (Shafik 2007, 102) may have spoken directly to young (male) audiences in Algeria, it was, according to Allouache, criticized by the Algerian authorities for the lack of ideological motivation displayed by the film's eponymous hero (Khalil 2005, 146). However, this perceived lack of political engagement—whereby, more accurately, "engagement" meant endorsing the politics and ideological position of the one-party state in Algeria—was precisely Allouache's intention. As Armes has noted, the film's key formal innovation is its use of voice-over and even direct address to camera to probe Omar's emotions (Armes 2005, 105).

Omar Gatlato was also groundbreaking in the context of a newly emerging postcolonial Algerian cinema due to Allouache's refusal to conform to the dominant mode of an Algerian cinema turned firmly to the past expectation of epic, historical narratives depicting the noble struggle of Algerian nationalists for liberation from the evil (French) colonizer. Instead, Allouache chose to investigate the internal social struggles facing ordinary (young) Algerians in contemporary Algeria (Allouache, cited in Malkmus 1985, 31). Allouache went on to direct two more feature films, produced under the auspices of ONCIC. *The Adventures of a Hero* (*Les aventures d'un héros / Mughamarat batal,* 1978) sees Allouache attempting to copy the narrative structure of *A Thousand And One Nights* but complementing the epic tale with a modern twist that speaks to Algeria's own recent history.[2] He followed this with *The Man Who Was Looking at the Windows* (*L'Homme qui regardait les fenêtres / Al-rajol al-lazi kan yanzor ila al-nawafiz,* 1982), a somber narrative set shortly after independence about the arrest and questioning of a fifty-something patriarch and former colonial civil servant (Mr. Rachid) who is suspected of murdering his former boss.

As Roy Armes notes, Allouache's experience on *Omar Gatlato* had shown the young director that he could be afforded a degree of artistic freedom as a filmmaker in Algeria. However, such liberty of expression was relative given that in the 1970s and 1980s the state, via ONCIC, still controlled all aspects of Algerian cinema, imposing its "chosen subject on the national cinema" to ensure a narrow and uncritical view of Algerian history and society that functioned in relation to an ideologically charged process of national myth-making (Armes 2005, 180). Consequently in the early 1980s, disheartened by the lack of success for *The Man Who Was Looking at the Windows* and disillusioned by the artistic and political constraints upon directors operating under a state-run industry in Algeria, Allouache moved to France. Here he encountered different obstacles to realizing his ambitions as a director, given the paucity of funding opportunities for even established Algerian émigré filmmakers in the French film industry during the 1980s. Nevertheless, in 1986, Allouache directed *Love in Paris* (*Un amour à Paris / Hobb fi Baris*), a love story about the relationship between Ali, a *beur* youth[3] recently released from prison who dreams of becoming an astronaut, and Marie, a Jewish Algerian woman who has arrived in Paris to pursue a modeling career. Despite its romantic premise, the film in fact ends in tragic failure. Ali is shot by the police, while Marie's attempts at modeling come to nothing and she is left stranded at the airport—the suggestion being that she will have to return to Algeria. *Love in Paris* struggled to find an audience in France, attracting a little over 5,000 spectators, while Allouache claims that in Algeria the film drew criticism from conservative critics for the inclusion of an interethnic love affair told from the perspective of a Jewish Algerian woman.

Following the critical and commercial failure of *Love in Paris,* Allouache returned to Algeria in the late 1980s. With ONCIC recently disbanded, Allouache worked independently from the state Office of Cinema on a series of documentaries exploring Algeria's own Arab Spring, which occurred in 1988, from the perspective of rioters, women's groups, and journalists (Allouache in Khalil 2005, 150–151). The optimism surrounding the mass protest movements that led to the disbanding of the one-party authoritarian rule in Algeria and the promise of a "genuinely democratic and transparent multiparty system" was replaced by a return to authoritarianism and eventually terror in the 1990s as Algerian military leaders refused to accept the electoral gains made by the Islamists (Entelis 2013, 652–654).

It was against this background of increasing insecurity and sociopolitical tension that Allouache directed *Bab-el-Oued City* (*Bab El-Wad al-hooma*, 1993). Set in the eponymous working-class neighborhood of the director's childhood, which has featured in a number of his films, *Bab-el-Oued City* explored the growth of intolerance and violence resulting from the rise of Islamic fundamentalism in Algeria in the late 1980s and early 1990s. The film makes reference to the rioting and protests by Algerian youth in October 1988 that led indirectly to the fall of the country's single-party system and failed move to democratic reform, setting in motion the spiral of instability, violence, and political conflict (including the rise of radical Islamism) that led the country to civil war. The events alluded to in *Bab-el-Oued City* that came to be known as Black October form a watershed moment in contemporary Algerian history "when popular trust in the state, eroded for years, finally collapsed" (Austin 2012, 121). While Allouache clearly intends his film to reflect the state of the nation at this time, he also chooses to reflect on the effect of this breakdown of trust between the people and what is commonly called *le pouvoir* (the power, those in power) and the subsequent insecurity and violence on local, working-class, urban communities in Algeria. Referring to comments by the director himself, Spaas notes that this focus on Bab-el-Oued highlights the fact that, since the October riots, "an important social structure of the city has been lost, that of the *quartier*," and how, with this loss, the traditional family structure and the safety of the individual have also come under threat in contemporary Algerian society (2000, 141). Thus in the film we find a working-class urban neighborhood gripped by fear due to the presence of shady figures from within the security forces (who resemble gangsters as much as they do policemen) and Muslim vigilantes from within Bab-el-Oued who seek to control the inhabitants of the neighborhood through violence and intimidation.

The film's central protagonist is Boualem, a young inhabitant of Bab-el-Oued, who works nights in a local bakery. Exasperated by the religious propaganda broadcast from speakers dotted across the neighborhood—it prevents him from sleeping—Boualem defies the growing authority of the local Islamist thugs by stealing the loudspeaker positioned on the roof of his apartment block. *Bab-el-Oued City*'s narrative thus loosely revolves around the search for the loud-speaker and Boualem's confrontation with Saïd, the local Islamist leader, who also happens to be the brother of Boualem's girlfriend, Yamina. As a backdrop to this central narrative strand, Allouache introduces a mosaic of protagonists who inhabit Bab-el-Oued: Mabrouk, Boualem's friend and co-worker, who supplements his income from the bakery by selling goods on the black market; Djamila, a disillusioned revolutionary who confides in Boualem and has turned to drink; Messouad, a French citizen of Algerian origin who finds himself stranded in Algiers; and finally the local imam, whose message of nonviolence and tolerance is ignored by Saïd and his henchmen. Alongside this network of characters representing a cross-section of the neighborhood is the somewhat surreal presence in the narrative of a French tourist and his aunt, a *pied-noir* (European colonial settler in North Africa), who are visiting Algiers. The couple reappears at various points in the film, wandering arm in arm through different locations in the city (the cemetery, the seafront, the rooftops of Bab-el-Oued). The nephew describes the modern-day city to his blind aunt, fabricating an image of Algiers and Bab-el-Oued as prosperous, well-maintained, and peaceful that bears no resemblance to what is shown on screen. The inclusion of these characters—which Austin sees as an homage to the cult film *Alger Insolite* (*Tahia ya didou!* Mohamed Zinet, 1971) (Austin 2012, 130)—evokes a sense of misplaced colonial nostalgia on the part of the pieds-noirs, one that seems absurd given the violence and turmoil unfolding around them. The dutiful nephew's description also suggests a longing on the part of the former colonizer for a (now impossible) return to an idealized moment in Franco-Algerian colonial history that refuses to acknowledge the violence, repression, and exploitation of the system that had produced this colonial "paradise." However, we should not necessarily interpret the inclusion of the pied-noir characters as a simple attack by the director on the continuing influence of French neocolonial attitudes toward Algeria. Indeed, we might even choose to read these characters' presence as allegorical, mimicking the refusal of some Algerians (like the pied-noir tourists) to accept the sociopolitical crisis facing Algerian society in the early 1990s.

Bab-el-Oued City was shot entirely on location and at considerable personal risk to the director, cast, and crew, as political turmoil and violence between the military-backed secular government and the radical Islamic groups escalated in the early 1990s. Aware of the potentially incendiary nature of his film and mistrustful of the response from the ruling authorities in Algeria, Allouache developed *Bab-el-Oued City* as an independent Franco-Algerian co-production, choosing not to circulate his script to potential backers or even potential members of cast and crew in advance of shooting. The director worked with a modest-sized (and mostly French) crew, shooting on Super 16mm with lighter, more portable cameras, using friends' apartments for interior scenes and shooting rapid (often clandestine) takes on the streets of Algiers at a time when even to appear with a camera in public posed a significant risk either of equipment being confiscated by the authorities or of the crew being attacked by local extremists.[4] The shooting of the film under such uncertain, restrictive conditions (at times the crew could shoot only one take at a given exterior location before being forced to leave) meant that parts of the film, such as the scenes where the camera surveys the streets of Algiers from inside a car, or the final scene, where Boualem's departure from the ferry port in Algiers is shot from distance, have a quasi-documentary feel. Nevertheless, in terms of cinematic style and thematic preoccupations, the overall appearance of *Bab-el-Oued City*—such as the insertion of observational views of daily life in Bab-el-Oued and contemplative vistas across the city itself, encouraging the spectator to consider the film's narrative within its wider social context—maintain many similarities with other of Allouache's films, in particular *Omar Gatlato* and *Normal!* (2011).

Although the political climate in Algeria in the mid-1990s made screening of *Bab-el-Oued City* in Algerian cinemas impossible at that time, internationally the film was Allouache's most critically acclaimed work since *Omar Gatlato*. At home in Algeria, Allouache's position as a prominent liberal artist placed him, like many other filmmakers, writers, musicians, and artists, in considerable danger from assassination by Islamic extremists. In a turn of events that mirrors

Boualem's departure at the end of *Bab-el-Oued City,* soon after making the film Allouache was himself forced to escape to France as Algeria entered what was to all intents and purposes a full-blown civil war, in which hundreds of thousands of Algerian civilians, caught up in the violence between government forces and Islamic extremists, lost their lives.

Consequently, during the 1980s and the 1990s, Allouache's career was characterized by his status as a self-declared cinéaste de passage—moving between France and Algeria making films, remaining in France when the economic and political conditions in Algeria made it impossible for him to work there. These periods of self-imposed exile in France have included work in TV—especially in the late 1990s—as well as in feature film production. The most notable work produced by Allouache in France during the 1990s was *Hey Cousin!* (*Salut cousin! / Salam ya ibn al-'amm,* 1997), a socially aware comedy focusing on the status of exile and displacement for a variety of Algerian immigrants in France. As well as the naïve immigrant Alilou and his cousin Mok, who has been raised in France and is for all intents and purposes French, Allouache presents a range of secondary characters, such as Rachid, a former Algerian policeman who now lives illegally in Paris surviving through his dealings on the black market, and Mr. Sentier, a Jewish pied-noir, who, in a similar way to the French tourists in *Bab-el-Oued City,* hankers nostalgically for an impossible return to colonial Algeria. Indeed, by focusing on a range of émigré protagonists beyond the cousins of the film's title, *Hey Cousin!* is able to evoke "both the proximity and the distance between France and Algeria, combining exilic nostalgia for the past with anxiety about the violence and lawlessness of the present" (Tarr 2005, 194). Nevertheless, as Rosello notes, while the cultural and political project that forced the director into exile shapes the film's narrative, it would be a "gross oversimplification to imagine that France was able to offer unproblematic refuge to exiles such as Allouache" (2000, 104–105).

Allouache's position as a diasporic subject in France, an Algerian national observing his own country from the shores of the former colonial *métropole,* has afforded the director the possibility of viewing contemporary sociopolitical events in Algeria simultaneously from an insider and outsider's perspective. Thus in *The Other World* (*L'autre monde / Al-'alam al-akhar,* 2001), Allouache enacts a return to Algeria both on- and off-screen, viewing the violence of the civil war through the eyes of Yasmine, the French daughter of Algerian immigrant parents, whose interstitial positioning between French and Algerian culture in some ways mirrors Allouache's own experience at that time. Yasmine travels to Algeria (a country she barely knows) in search of her Maghrebi-French boyfriend, Rachid, who has disappeared from France to join the Algerian army. Traveling across Algeria, Yasmine sees first hand the devastation that has been wrought on the nation by a decade of violence and political instability.

Finally, the early 2000s also resulted in Allouache's most commercially successful feature to date, *Chouchou* (2003), a French-produced feel-good comedy about an Algerian transvestite residing illegally in Paris, starring Moroccan Jewish comedian Gad Elamleh, which attracted an audience of over three million in France. However, as scholars such as Waldron (2007) and Rees-Roberts (2008) suggest, in order to reach a mainstream audience, Allouache's film retreats from any meaningful engagement with the sociopolitical realities of immigration or queer politics in contemporary France. Reading *Chouchou* through the lens of colonial history and referring to the film's utopian ending, in which Chouchou marries his male French lover, Khalil (2007, 343) takes an even more negative view of the film, arguing that "French sexual conquest of the passive, feminized Algeria has now become the fantasy of the Algerian (Chouchou) who wants to be possessed by the Frenchman." In response to such critiques of the film, Rosello argues that *Chouchou*'s representation of homosexuality and ethnicity is deliberately constructed as politically ambiguous gesture: "In *Chouchou*, narratives of passing and crossing over enable Allouache to set up and trouble several binary systems: the opposition between France and Algeria cannot be reduced to a postcolonial paradigm because the encounter between the member of the former colony and the métropole is primarily articulated via Chouchou's sexual identity. On the other hand, gender issues cannot be examined separately from the discreet, but insistent, references to national foreignness . . ." (Rosello 2011, 15).

After the massive commercial success of *Chouchou*, Allouache turned down a number of lucrative offers from French producers to direct another comedy in a similar vein in order to return to Algeria and direct *Bab el Web* (*Bab al-Weeb*, 2005). The film is essentially a light-hearted romantic comedy with a potential darker twist that involves the criminal underworld of Algiers. A romantic, internet-obsessed Algerian youth from Bab-el-Oued named Bouzid—played by emerging raï star Faudel—is surprised to find that one of the French women he has been corresponding with online agrees to come and visit him in Algiers, with unexpected consequences for all concerned, including his wayward brother Kamel, played by France's first *bona fide* Maghrebi-French star, Samy Naceri.[5] *Bab el Web* was the third of Allouache's films to be set in Bab-el-Oued. The director has claimed that the selection of this location, along with the decision to shoot in CinemaScope to emphasize the inherent beauty of Algiers and the surrounding coastline, were intended to counter the continuing and largely exaggerated perceptions of Algeria found in French and Western media as a nation still paralyzed by the violence and fear of the 1990s civil war (Verdurand 2004). *Bab el Web* thus provides a counterpoint to Allouache's earlier feature films depicting civil war events (*The Other World* and most specifically *Bab-el-Oued City*), which also dealt with the traumatic effects of violence experienced by Algerian society during this period.

However, any reading of *Bab el Web* as an attempt by Allouache to move away definitively from the continuing sociopolitical legacy of the 1990s civil war on Algerian society is misguided. Rather than closure, Allouache's comedy films of the 2000s seem now, with the benefit of hindsight, to represent little more than a brief respite in the Algerian director's urgent concern with the social crises facing his country. Following this foray in the mid-2000s into a pair of more lighthearted (and, in the case of *Chouchou*, utopian) comedies, Allouache marked a return to the more somber tone of *The Other World* as well as to his concern with contemporary sociopolitical issues in Algeria with three films: *Burn* (Harragas, 2009), *Normal!*, and *The Repentant*. All three films were shot on extremely low budgets and largely, if not exclusively, without the support (either financial or political) of the Algerian Ministry of Culture, the ministry to which all proposed Algerian film projects must still be submitted for scrutiny, approval, and the potential allocation of funding. Arguably, a concern with such sociopolitical issues had never entirely left Allouache's comedies of the mid-1990s and early 2000s such as *Hey Cousin!*, *Chouchou*, and *Bab el Web*. Indeed comedy has always been a key element of his filmmaking. However, this considered shift away from using comedy as a means of addressing social issues in a more consensual and less accusatory fashion, toward a more somber, pessimistic, and overtly critical style of filmmaking, was first seen in *Burn*. This film considered the fate of a group of young friends from a coastal town in provincial Algeria who, like many of their peers, decide to embark on a perilous journey across the Mediterranean in a small boat in an attempt to illegally enter Europe and search for a better future.[6] *Burn* was followed in 2011 by *Normal!*, an experimental feature, part documentary, part dramatic fiction, that considers questions of artistic commitment, institutional corruption, and the reasons prohibiting a similar uprising in Algeria to that found in Tunisia and Egypt in the Arab Spring of 2011.

Questions of censorship, artistic freedom, and political expression in contemporary Algerian cinema are brought to the fore in *Normal!*, Allouache's eleventh feature. The project began as a documentary on the 2009 Pan-African festival staged in Algiers. Allouache intended to use his film to explore issues of ministerial corruption and censorship in the control of funding for cultural projects in Algeria, whereby the artistic environment is controlled by "the absence of an intellectual culture, (self-)censorship, and political manipulation" (Allouache in Barlet 2012). The director set about working with a group of young actors and a small crew, shooting on modest DV cameras. Unsatisfied with the edited material and at that time unable to devote any more time or money to the project, Allouache decided to abandon the film. It was not until two years later, when the director was offered additional funding for post-production by the Doha Film Institute (Qatar), that Allouache was able to revive the project, returning to Algeria early in 2011 to screen the existing edit to the actors he had previously worked with. The support of the Doha Institute was of course crucial for Allouache, and a further indication—as with projects he has produced or co-produced in France—of the director's reputation on the international stage, which also allows him to finance his (albeit generally low-budget) projects from a relatively privileged position in comparison to other Algerian filmmakers.

Normal! is set in Algiers in early 2011. As demonstrations in the capital against economic hardship and political corruption take place on the streets, buoyed by the popular campaigns for democratic change in Tunisia and Egypt (the so-called Arab Spring), a young director (Fouzi) meets with a group of actors who worked with him on an aborted film project two years earlier. The young Algerians review the footage from the earlier film (also called *Normal!*). The narrative of this film-within-a-film has three strands: the first concerns the attempts by a young playwright (Rachid) to put on his new play following opposition by government censors. The second explores the blossoming romance between Rachid and Lamia, a young French actress of Algerian origin who is also in Algeria to act in a film and later disappears after spontaneously accepting a lift in the street from a local gangster, who takes her on a trip down the coast. The third and final strand is a documentary of sorts about the Pan-African festival that took place in Algiers in 2009 and forms the backdrop against which the film-within-a-film in *Normal!* takes place.

In many ways, Allouache's attempts in *Normal!* to give agency to the thoughts and opinions of ordinary Algerian youths, who form the clear majority in Algeria's population and are disproportionately affected by issues such as unemployment and lack of social mobility,[7] makes the film a direct descendant, some thirty-five years later, of *Omar Gatlato*. Further intertextual references to *Omar Gatlato* are offered in *Normal!* by the inclusion of establishing shots of the Algiers skyline that look out across (and beyond) the working-class apartment blocks of Bab-el-Oued, as well as Fouzi's recorded confessions, evoking *Omar Gatlato*'s famous and innovative use of direct address to the camera.

In other ways, the film is extremely conscious of the differences for Algerian youth between the 1970s and the 2000s—not least in relation to the ability for the young couples who appear in *Normal!* to realize meaningful and mature connections in a relationship with a member of the opposite sex. Even if the strict divisions between men and women that structure both the mise-en-scène and narrative form of *Omar Gatlato* are less pronounced in *Normal!*, the inhibitions and moral taboos, largely driven by the influence of conservative Muslim attitudes toward relationships between the sexes and especially those outside of marriage, do resurface at various moments in the film. Most obviously this can be found in the sequence from *Normal!* where Fouzi and the cast of his film discuss footage from the scene in which one of the characters (himself playing an actor in a scene) refuses to kiss another female actor on screen, for fear of how this will be perceived by his girlfriend or the rest of his family, were they to see the film. In their critique of the scene, the actors comment that none of them are shocked by the kiss. And yet Allouache's use of editing in the preceding sequence (cutting away to the clearly uncomfortable expression of Mina as she watches her real life partner, Nabil, kissing another woman on screen) suggests that in reality, such moral taboos are so heavily ingrained in Algeria's Arabo-Islamic culture that they cannot help but impact on the reactions of even the most liberal members of society.

In the same way that *Omar Gatlato* is not simply a comedy but also a profound social analysis of contemporary Algerian society (Armes 2005, 113), so *Normal!* is not simply an Algerian reworking of the self-reflexive film about filmmaking that is found in mainstream Hollywood as much as it is in postwar European art cinema. In one particular scene, Fouzi and his wife, Amina, go to inspect a terrace in Bab-el-Oued that could be used as a potential vantage point from which to shoot a demonstration that will take place the following week. The rooftops of Algiers are, in fact, a key element within the landscape of Allouache's filmography. Indeed, they form the cine-spatial structure of his most recent feature film *The Rooftops,* a depiction of contemporary Algerian society viewed from rooftops in five different Algiers neighborhoods. During the rooftop scene from *Normal!,* the owner of the terrace, Mabrouk, speaks at length about how the local neighborhood has fallen into disrepair, of the *harragas* (illegal migrants who cross to Europe by boat), and of local youths who feel betrayed by the government and Islamists, seeing violent demonstration as the only logical outlet for their despair and anger.

Exposing a fragile masculinity: Omar speaks
directly to camera in *Omar Gatlato*.

Yamina and Boualem meet in secret in *Bab-el-Oued City*.

The artist as distanced from the popular struggle against *le pouvoir*:
Fouzi and Amina converse on the rooftops of Algiers in *Normal!*

Rachid negotiates his return from the *moudjahidin*
to Algerian society in *The Repentant.*

In this scene, as elsewhere in the film, direct reference is also made to previous civil protests and key dates in recent Algerian history, such as the demonstrations by Berber nationalists in 2001 that were met with violent repression by the authorities, as well as the anti-government protests of the late 1980s and early 1990s—Algeria's own Arab Spring, which pre-dated that of Tunisia and Egypt by more than two decades, leading to the brief flowering of multiparty democracy before the slide into civil war in the early 1990s. A further reminder of the civil war and the consequences of Islamist violence against the civilian population comes from a scene in *Normal!*'s film-within-a-film, where Lamia walks through the streets of Algiers wearing a headscarf, pausing briefly to contemplate a plaque commemorating the culture journalist Ferhat Cherkit, murdered by Islamic extremists in 1994 (an obvious reference to the events surrounding both the subject matter and the production of *Bab-el-Oued City*). Finally, when Lamia takes off later in the film with a local gangster, he drives her to a location farther down the coast, to show her "the state the country is in." As they survey a beach peppered with small, makeshift huts, the gangster explains that these have been erected by young couples who have nowhere else to go to share moments of emotional and physical intimacy.

The control exerted on the young protagonists in *Normal!* is thus shown to permeate every area of their lives, private and public, social, cultural and political. The film also alludes to this sense of an all-pervasive and repressive authoritarian state in a more elliptical fashion through the near-constant presence of military helicopters circling over the city and above Fouzi's flat. The sound from the helicopters repeatedly intrudes on discussions, at times drowning out what Fouzi and the young actors have to say; it functions in *Normal!* as a metaphor for the way that sociopolitical dissent, already in this context relegated to the private sphere of Fouzi's home, continues to be surveyed and neutralized by the authorities. As such, the sonic intrusion of the helicopters flying overhead—which are heard in the film more often than they are seen—provides a clear allusion to the continued presence and control over Algerian society of le pouvoir: the combined military, intelligence, and (state-controlled) industrial forces that monopolize state power in both the domestic and an international context.[8]

The hostility toward le pouvoir discussed in *Normal!,* and glimpsed on the social media sites of Fouzi and Amina's laptop, is more accurately linked to deeper grievances associated with the apparent contempt of the ruling elite for ordinary Algerians, which has produced decades of "political disillusionment, cultural disaffection and spiritual aridity" among the wider population (Entelis

2011, 655). Fouzi is repeatedly distanced from the protestors and the street itself. Until the very end of *Normal!* he refuses to accompany Amina to the public demonstrations, effectively denying his wife the opportunity to participate in democratic opposition to the state. In fact, other than on the terrace, we never see Fouzi outside of the flat. When he contemplates shooting footage of the demonstrations to include in a new version of his film, he wants to do it from the safety of a balcony high above the street, refusing to take the camera into the crowd—the *modus operandi* of most online footage uploaded by demonstrators on YouTube or Facebook shown in the film.

"There comes a moment when you need to take action," Amina tells Fouzi toward the end of the film. However, for much of the film Fouzi appears incapable of taking on board this advice, of making the transition from abstract discussion (isolation) to direct action (solidarity). Through this inability to act at the crucial moment, Fouzi resembles many of the other flawed male leads who have appeared in Allouache's films across the decades, most obviously the eponymous hero of *Omar Gatlato.* By the end of *Normal!*, Fouzi's film remains in development; much has been discussed about the original footage, but he is no closer to bringing the project to completion. As Fouzi puts it, "We can't change anything, because Algerians have experienced too much violence in their recent past." His sentiment encapsulates the true meaning of the film's title. "*Normal!*," a common expression among the youth of Algeria, articulates a sense of fatalism, reflecting the hopelessness of their current socioeconomic and political exclusion in a society that appears immutable in terms of democratic reform.

What is interesting, however, is that in *Normal!* Allouache refuses to end with the image of the powerless artist and social protest at an impasse. Instead, the final moments of the film show Fouzi and Amina in their flat, watching footage of that week's demonstrations on YouTube. The difference from the start of the film is that this time they are not simply distanced spectators; rather they watch a recording of themselves as participants in the protests that have been posted online. And while we hear Fouzi insisting to his wife that they have "done enough" and won't be going to the demonstrations next week, Amina clearly has other ideas. Echoing Amina's convictions and commitment, the camera pulls up and finally settles on the banner, pinned to the wall, that she had been painting at the start of the film: "ALGERIA: DEMOCRATIC AND FREE."

Despite its extremely limited distribution in Algeria and abroad, *Normal!* is an important statement of artistic intent by Allouache. The film is, moreover, significant in relation to Allouache's oeuvre for a variety of reasons. *Normal!*

addresses a range of themes and issues that have remained constant throughout Allouache's career as a socially aware and politically conscious director: a focus on urban locations in the working-class neighborhoods of Algiers (above all Bab-el-Oued, where the director was raised); an examination of the combined effect of institutional corruption and the dangers of religious fundamentalism to limit personal freedoms; a concern with social inequality (poor housing, high unemployment, a lack of social mobility); the detrimental effects on personal relationships in an Arabo-Islamic society that rigidly segregates and controls relationships between men and women; and finally the frustration and anger felt by a lost generation of Algerian youth. Where *Normal!* departs from Allouache's earlier films, however, is in the space that the director gives for formal experimentation, particularly at the level of narrative structure and the melding of dramatic and documentary styles of filmmaking. Similarly, while *Normal!* shares the more direct confrontation with official versions of Algerian history and sociopolitical realities offered by his other recent films, such as *Burn* and *The Repentant,* it goes much further in terms of form and content, questions of the political and ethical roles and responsibilities of the artist, the struggle for state control and self-censorship over the artist's work and the relationship of the artist's work to direct political action.

Shot in 2011, presented at Cannes in 2012 and eventually released in France in spring 2013, *The Repentant (Le repenti / El taaib,* 2013), deals with yet another legacy of the Algerian civil war of the 1990s: the *concorde civile.*[9] Through a narrative focusing on a young Islamist fighter who takes up the government's offer of exoneration and returns to his home village in an attempt to restart his life, *The Repentant* explores the complex social and psychological consequences of President Bouteflika's granting of a legal amnesty (the concorde civile) in the 2000s for those on both sides of the bloody civil war that claimed more than 200,000 victims in the 1990s. After a brief set of inter-titles explaining the context of the concorde civile, *The Repentant* opens with a visually arresting and enigmatic sequence: a young man runs desperately across the desolate expanse at the foot of a mountain range in rural Algeria. Though we have no idea who he is or what he is running from, the young man, tracked by the camera against the harsh snow-covered landscape, appears fearful and vulnerable. This vulnerability is echoed by the sparse soundtrack which foregrounds the howling wind and the man's steps on the ground, along with his panicked, heavy breathing. Moments later, the young man, who identifies himself as Rachid, arrives at a small village, where he is reunited with his parents, who are overwhelmed by the sudden and unexpected return of their son.

It soon becomes clear that Rachid is the repentant of the film's title. However, the emotional reunion with his family is short-lived. Almost immediately Rachid is confronted by another family from the village, who angrily accuse him of murdering local women and children during the civil war—an act he strenuously denies. Consequently, Rachid is forced to leave the village and move to a nearby town, where he is offered work and lodgings in a local café as part of the armistice between the state and the *moudjahidin*.[10] Rachid's situation is further complicated when he discovers that the local pharmacist, Lakhdar, and his estranged wife, Djamila, are the parents of a young girl killed by the Islamist rebels with whom Rachid fought. Though Rachid is clearly implicated in the child's murder, it is never made entirely clear in the film whether he was responsible for her death or simply witnessed the killing. The film's somber tone and deliberately restrained style (such as a lack of expressive camera movement) echoes that of *Burn;* however, in *The Repentant* this pared-down cinematic style is taken to an even greater degree of detachment in relation to narrative, image, and sound. In narrative terms, Allouache refuses to reveal the true nature of the connection between Lakhdar, Djamila, and Rachid until near the end of the film. Similar strategies are employed in the mise-en-scène to deny the audience any strong emotional identification with the characters. For example, when Rachid's arrives in the town where he is to begin his reinsertion into Algerian society, Allouache eschews a series of close-ups that might indicate the character's emotional state at this pivotal moment in the narrative. Rachid is instead filmed in long-shot, as if being observed by unknown forces tracking his movements. Finally, this sense of the spectator's detachment in *The Repentant* is emphasized by the film's sparse soundtrack, which has no incidental music or non-diegetic elements.

The intention of the concorde civile was to employ a legal amnesty in order to allow Algerian society to overcome the trauma and violence of its recent past and thus promote national unity. However, this highly controversial policy has not been welcomed by all, and has been described by historian Le Seuer as an attempt "to inoculate a population from violence and retribution by giving it a historical lobotomy" (Le Seuer 2010, 206). The impossibility that both the victims and perpetrators of the violence committed during the civil war simply draw a line under the atrocities of the past, as the concorde civile demands, is thrown into sharp relief throughout *The Repentant*. In the final moments of the film, Rachid leads Lakhdar and Djamila to their daughter's unmarked grave. Shots of the three characters by the graveside are intercut with images of advancing moudjahidin. The film ends with a final, extreme long shot of the countryside surrounding the grave (as if viewed from a vantage point high in the mountains) and the sound of gunfire, followed cries of *"Allahu Akbar"* from the moudjahidin as the screen fades to black. The implied murder of Rachid and the two parents at the end of *The Repentant* thus suggests that the concorde civile has utterly failed as an instrument of reconciliation for an Algerian nation so deeply scarred by the events of the civil war, whose violence continues to the present day.

In an interview with French critic Olivier Barlet for *Africultures* following the premiere of *The Repentant* at Cannes in 2012, Allouache spoke of a refusal on the part of the Algerian authorities to finance his more recent, politically controversial films, which offer a harsh critique of the current sociopolitical situation in Algeria and by extension lay the blame on those in power for failing to find solutions to these problems:

> This also happens due to a refusal [by the government] to finance my work, to prevent me filming. They're then surprised to see me with a film. I show them that I can make a film with next to nothing . . . I know how things work in Algeria: we pump billions into useless projects that remain unseen. As long as I'm given permission to shoot, I'll sort out the finances. As long there are possibilities elsewhere, there's a chance. Each time I submit my scripts to the ministry [of culture], if they refuse me funding, I simply get on with it myself. (Allouache in Barlet 2013a)[11]

This more openly critical attitude toward the state authorities in Algeria, in terms of both their funding practices and the way they have responded to the socioeconomic needs of ordinary Algerians, is combined with Allouache's decision, born largely out of necessity (in terms of funding at least) to work outside of the Algerian system. Even though he is to an extent working outside of the system, like many other Algerian filmmakers—and, indeed, many artists across the Arab world—Allouache is still forced to circumvent political and economic censure through elliptical representations of everyday cultural and political realities that Algerian audiences can relate to, rather than always attacking sociopolitical issues head on in his films. Put differently, this response to direct and excessive state control over the filmmaker's work and creative practice involves adopting a strategy of "communicating ideas through what is not said" or what appears to be "left out of the conversation" but is nonetheless evoked or alluded to in the work of art (Khalil 2005, 144).

The decision by the Algerian state authorities to permit these more dissenting films to be made by Allouache in the 2000s, while effectively attempting to censor them economically by denying funding and an outlet for distribution, is also telling. At a recent round table discussion among Algerian filmmakers, distributors, festival organizers and critics (including Allouache) at the 10th African Cinema festival in Le pays d'Apt (Provence, France) in November 2012, the general consensus among participants seemed to be that the greatest problem currently facing Algerian cinema came at the level of distribution and exhibition as much as production (accessing funding and censorship) (Barlet 2013b). For his part, when interviewed in 2013, Allouache lamented the deterioration of the infrastructure for exhibition and the decline in the number of cinemas. He also expressed concern that while they may continue to attract attention at international festivals and certain private screenings in Algeria, his own films have not been screened on Algerian television for twenty years and circulate today in Algeria only by means of pirated (illegal) DVD copies (Allouache in Matias 2013). This situation continues with Allouache's most recent feature film, *The Rooftops* (*Les terrasses / Es-Stouh,* 2013), which, at the time of writing, has not been distributed in Algeria or France, despite being selected for competition in 2013 for the London Film Festival, La Mostra (Venice international film festival), and the Abu Dhabi International Film Festival. The film focuses on five different sets of characters from different social backgrounds, inhabiting five separate terraces across the skyline of modern-day Algiers, with each story starting and ending with the sound of the call to prayer. However, this use of the call to prayer in the film as a linking device between the different locations and protagonists does not suggest that Islam is the unifying force in contemporary Algerian society; rather, as Allouache himself has suggested, the sound of the *Adhan* becomes one more noise emerging from the city (*Les terrasses* 2013). The multi-stranded narrative thus permits Allouache to represent societal divisions that run along class, gender, religious, and generational lines, while also exploring issues of corruption and violence (well-worn themes for this particular director).

With four feature films directed in the last five years, Allouache has moved into one of the most prolific and critically acclaimed stages of a career in cinema spanning five decades. The irony, of course, is that in this most recent phase of his career, his films have gained the least exposure in his native Algeria. We may, in part, be able to attribute this absence of Allouache's films from Algerian screens to the continued decline of the exhibition and distribution infrastructure in Algeria, which, as in many other African and Arab nations, has led filmmakers to seek alternative means of distribution in order to find a local audiences. However, in the case of Allouache, it also results from the director's more recent marginalization in his native film industry, in terms of both state funding and censorship, caused by his openly critical stance toward government corruption, state control, intolerance, and violence, as well as increasing divisions and inequalities in Algerian society. Despite often occupying a space on the periphery of the industry, it must be pointed out that Allouache has also taken advantage of his relatively privileged position as an internationally renowned director to work in France for periods in the 1980s and 1990s when political and economic conditions at home prevented him from directing in Algeria. This position as a self-styled cinéaste de passage has often allowed him a perspective on events in his homeland that combines a critical distance with a sense of despair for the events unfolding in Algeria, at the same time expressing an intense nostalgia for home and the promise of the truly democratic nation that Algeria might have become following independence from French colonial rule. Indeed, many of his most celebrated films—from *Omar Gatlato* to *Bab-el-Oued City* and, more recently, *The Repentant*—make profound statements about the state of Algerian society and the need for democratic change as well as the potential, and indeed necessity, for Algerian filmmakers to speak of (and for) the people if such change is to be achieved.

NOTES

1. Located within the Ministry of Culture and Information, the ONCIC created a state monopoly to oversee the production, distribution, and exhibition of all film-making in Algeria that functioned from the mid-1960s until the late 1980s. For more details see Armes (2005, 179–180).

2. For a more detailed discussion of the film see Shafik 2007, 95–96.

3. The neologism *beur*, derived from *verlan* (French back-slang for *Arabe*), came into common usage in France during the 1980s. It referred to the descendants of North African immigrants who were either French citizens by birth or who had been raised in France from a young age and felt themselves to be as "French" as they were "Arab." For more on the etymology and problematic politics associated with term *beur*, see Durmelat (1998).

4. Allouache speaks at length about the conditions for shooting *Bab-el-Oued City* in an extended interview that appears on the French DVD release of the film.

5. Arguably the first French film stars of North African immigrant origin in the 1980s were Isabelle Adjani (the daughter of an Algerian immigrant father and German immigrant mother) and Smaïn. However, despite two notable successes with the comedy films *L'oeil au beur(re) noir* (Meynard, 1985) and *Les deux papas et la maman* (Longval, 1996) Smaïn was most successful as s standup comedian in the 1980s and

1990s. Adjani, while clearly one of the biggest French film stars of the 1990s, is associated with a star image that has been "recuperated" by French audiences and critics since the 1990s in a way that deemphasises ethnicity, or rather replaces a marked (Arab) ethnicity with a star ethnicity of the "unmarked kind: visible whiteness, stellar luminescence" (Austin 2003: 100–105). Following his leading role in the massively successful series of action comedies—*Taxi, Taxi 2* and *Taxi 3*—in the late 1990s and early 2000s, Naceri thus established himself as France's first film star who was identified overwhelmingly with the cinema and yet whose ethnic origins were not deemphasized in relation to his star image.

6. *Harraga* refers to the practice of illegal immigrants burning their identity papers before leaving Algeria in order to disguise their nationality and demand asylum as stateless refugees upon arrival in Europe. For a detailed analysis of the film see Higbee (2014).

7. Algeria has an extremely youthful population: 40 percent of Algerians are under 15; 70 percent are under 30. Official estimates in 2009 placed unemployment at 21 percent, while unofficial estimates suggest the true figure lies closer to 30 percent (Entelis 2011: 662–663).

8. For more on *le pouvoir* in Algeria see Entelis (2013).

9. The *concorde civile* (civil concord law) was passed by the Algerian government in 1999. The law aimed to secure peace between le pouvoir and the Islamist rebel groups by reintegrating into civil life those who renounced violence and providing an amnesty for those who offered support to terrorist groups during the 1990s. This was followed in 2005 by the Charter for Peace and National Reconciliation, which proposed a definitive amnesty for all Islamist rebel fighters who gave up their arms, provided that they had not been involved in acts of murder, rape, or bomb attacks on civilians. As a result of the 2005 Charter, thousands of Islamist fighters made the decision to give up their arms and return home. *The Repentant* tells the story of one such individual. For more on the concorde civile see Le Seuer (2010, 77, 196–197).

10. The term *moudjahidin* comes from the Arabic for *holy warrior* and was the name used by the FLN to refer to its soldiers who fought against the French in the Algerian War for Independence. In the context of *The Repentant* it refers to guerilla fighters from Islamist rebel groups who opposed the government forces in the civil war between 1991 and 2002.

11. "Cela passe aussi par un refus de me financer, pour m'empêcher de filmer. Ils sont ensuite surpris de me voir avec un film. Je montre que je peux faire un film avec presque rien. . . . Je sais comment c'est en Algérie: on injecte des milliards dans des productions inutiles qui restent dans les boîtes. Tant qu'on me donne l'autorisation de tournage, je me débrouillerai pour le financement. Il y a des possibilités ailleurs, c'est une chance. Je déposerai à chaque fois mes scénarios au ministère et si on me refuse le financement, je me débrouillerai."

FILMOGRAPHY OF MERZAK ALLOUACHE

The Beaches / Les Plages / Al-masabeh. 1968. Documentary.

Nous et la révolution agraire / Nahnu wa al-thawra al-zira'iyya. 1973. Documentary.

Ancient Tipaza / Tipaza l'ancienne / Tipaza al-qadeema. 1975. Documentary.

Omar Gatlato / 'Umar qatlatu alrudjla. 1976. Distributed in the United States by Arab Film Distribution. 90 minutes.

The Adventures of a Hero / Les aventures d'un héros / Mughamarat batal. 1978. Distributed in Algeria by ONCIC. 120 minutes.

The Man Who Was Looking at the Windows / L'homme qui regardait les fenêtres / Al-rajol al-lazi kan yanzor ila al-nawafiz. 1982. Distributed in Algeria by ONCIC. 85 minutes.

Love in Paris / Un amour à Paris / Hobb fi Baris. 1986. Distributed in France by CVC Communications and Visa France. 85 minutes.

After October / L'après Octobre / Ma ba'd October. 1989. Documentary. 50 minutes.

La boîte à chique / Qabsa chemma. 1991. Documentary.

Bab-el-Oued City / Bab El-Wad al-hooma. 1993. Distributed in the United States by Arab Film Distribution. 93 minutes.

Jours tranquilles en Kabylie / Ayyam hadi"a fi mantaqat Al-Kaba'il, 1994. Documentary.

Without Camera / Interdit de caméra / Al-kameera mamnou'a, 1996. Documentary.

Hey Cousin! / Salut cousin! / Salam ya ibn al-'amm, 1997. Distributed in the United States by Leo Films. 97 minutes.

The Other World / L'autre monde / Al-'alam al-akhar. 2001. Distributed in United States by ArtMattan Productions. 95 minutes.

Chouchou. 2003. Distributed in France by Warner Bros. 105 minutes.

Bab el Web / Bab al-Weebb. 2005. Distributed in France by Pyramide Distribution. 99 minutes.

Burn / Harragas. 2009. Distributed in France by Jour2Fête. 95 minutes.

Normal! 2011. Distributed in France by Les Films des Deux Rives. 111 minutes.

The Repentant / Le repenti / El taa'ib. 2012. Distributed in France by Sophie Dulac Distribution. 87 minutes.

The Rooftops / Les terrasses / Es-Stouh. 2013. 94 minutes.

REFERENCES

Armes, Roy. 2005. *Post-colonial Images: Studies in North African Film.* Bloomington: Indiana University Press.

Austin, Guy. 2012. *Algerian National Cinema.* Manchester, UK: Manchester University Press.

———. 2003. *Stars in Modern French Film.* London: Arnold.

Barlet, Olivier. 2012. "*Normal!* de Merzak Allouache." *Africultures,* http://www.afri cultures.com/php/index.php?nav=article&no=10604. Accessed July 20, 2013.

———. 2013a. "'Je déposerai mes scénarios au ministère et si on me refuse le finance-ment, je me débrouillerai": Merzak Allouache, interview with Olivier Barlet. *Le Repenti. Africultures,* http://www.africultures.com/php/?nav=article&no=11449. Accessed April 2, 2013.

———. 2013b. "Le cinéma algérien aujourd'hui. Table ronde au 10e festival des ciné-mas d'Afrique en pays d'Apt." *Africultures,* http://www.africultures.com/php/index.php?nav=article&no=11245. Accessed December 27, 2013.

Boughedir, Férid. 1987. "Malédictions des cinémas arabes." *CinémAction* 43: 10–17.

Durmelat, Sylvie. 1993. "Petite histoire du mot beur: Ou comment prendre la parole quand on vous la prête," *French Cultural Studies* 9 (2), 192–207.

Entelis, John P. 2013. "Algerian Crisis: The Primacy of Le Pouvoir." *Cairo Review of Global Affairs,* January 28, http://www.aucegypt.edu/gapp/cairoreview/pages/articleDetails.aspx?aid=287. Accessed February 7, 2013.

———. 2011. "Algeria: Democracy Denied, and Revived?" *Journal of North African Studies* 16 (4), December: 653–678.

Higbee, Will. 2007. "Locating the Postcolonial in Transnational Cinema: The Place of Algerian Emigré Directors in Contemporary French Film." *Modern and Contem-porary France* 15 (1), February: 51–64.

———. 2014. "Hope and Indignation in Fortress Europe: Immigration and Neoliberal Globalization in Contemporary French Cinema." *Substance* 43 (1): 26–43.

Khalil, Andrea Flores. 2005. "Interview with Merzak Allouache." *Journal of North African Studies* 10 (2), June: 143–156.

———. 2007. "The Myth of Masculinity in the Films of Merzak Allouache." *Journal of North African Studies* 12 (3), September: 329–345.

Khatibi, Saïd. 2011. "Algerian Filmmaker Merzak Allouache Struggles with Censor-ship after Long Career." *Al-Akhbar,* November 23, http://english.al-akhbar.com/content/algerian-filmmaker-merz. Accessed December 12, 2012.

Le Seuer, James D. 2010. *Algeria since 1989: Between Terror and Democracy.* London: Zed Books.

Malkmus, Lizbeth. 1985. "Merzak Allouache: An Interview." *Framework* 29: 30–41.

Matias, Daniel. 2013. "Merzak Allouache: 'La société algérienne n'est pas apaisée'" (interview). *Courrier International,* http://www.courrierinternational.com/article/2013/03/05/merzak-allouache-la-societe-algerienne-n-est-pas-apaisee?page=2#page_2. Accessed March 27, 2014.

Rees-Roberts, Nick. 2008. *French Queer Cinema.* Edinburgh: Edinburgh University Press.

Rosello, Mireille. 2000, "Merzak Allouache's *Salut Cousin!*: Immigrants, Hosts, and Parasites." *South Central Review* 17 (3), autumn: 104–118.

———. 2011. "Dissident or Conformist Passing: Merzak Allouache's *Chouchou.*" *South Central Review* 28 (1), spring: 2–17.

Shafik, Viola. 2007. *Arab Cinema: History and Cultural Identity.* Rev. ed. Cairo: American University in Cairo Press.

Spaas, Lieve. 2000. *The Francophone Film: A Struggle for Identity.* Manchester, UK: Manchester University Press.

Tarr, Carrie. 2005. *Reframing Difference: Beur and Banlieue Filmmaking in France.* Manchester, UK: Manchester University Press.

"*Les terrasses:* l'Algérie vue par Merzak Allouache s'invite sur la lagune." 2013. *Le Nouvel Observateur,* http://cinema.nouvelobs.com/articles/27511-interviews-%20Mostra%20de%20Venise-les-terrasses-l-algerie-vue-par-merzak-allouache-s-invite-sur-la-lagune. Accessed March 27, 2014.

Verdurand, Didier. 2004. "Merzak Allouache: Interview." *EcranLarge.com,* http://www.ecranlarge.com/interview-107.php. Accessed March 27, 2011.

Waldron, Darren. 2007. "From Critique to Compliance: Images of Ethnicity in *Salut cousin!* (1996) and *Chouchou* (2003)." *Studies in European Cinema* 4 (1): 35–47.

Nabil Ayouch (left) with Abdelilah Rachid and Abdelhakim Rachid, the lead actors in *Horses of God,* at Cannes 2012.

10

Nabil Ayouch

TRANSGRESSION, IDENTITY, AND DIFFERENCE (MOROCCO)

Jonathan Smolin

Nabil Ayouch is one of Morocco's most prominent and innovative film directors.[1] Born in 1969 in Paris, he is the son of the well-known Moroccan advertising and micro-credit executive Noureddine Ayouch and a French mother
of Jewish-Tunisian descent.[2] Nabil Ayouch studied theater in Paris during the
late 1980s and worked in advertising in the early 1990s while directing three
short films between 1992 and 1994.[3] Ayouch made his first feature-length film,
Mektoub, in 1997. In 1999, Ayouch moved to Morocco and founded Ali n' Productions in Casablanca, which produced his subsequent films in addition to a
number of successful works for Moroccan television, including the well-known
series *Lalla Fatima.*[4] In 2005, Ayouch and Ali n' Productions were awarded
with unprecedented funding from Radiodiffusion Télévision Marocaine (RTM)
to produce thirty television films that feature Berber-related themes—both in
Berber language and Moroccan colloquial Arabic—as part of a project called
Film Industry, Made in Morocco. Ayouch used this opportunity to train a new
generation of screenwriters, actors, and directors for these films. The project
was completed in 2007.[5] In France, Ayouch founded a new production house,
Les Films du Noveau Monde, in 2006.

Ayouch moved to Morocco to help develop cinema in the country (Ayouch
2013). He sees himself not simply as a filmmaker but also as a producer and

someone who strives to foster young talent in Morocco, creating opportunities for others to express themselves through cinema. In addition to his production and directing work, Ayouch helped create the Mohamed Reggab Prize, which is awarded in Morocco to directors between eighteen and thirty-five years old for their first short work. In Morocco, Ayouch has also led the charge against piracy, which significantly damages the market for local filmmaking.[6] To date, Ayouch has directed five feature-length films and one documentary, *My Land*.[7]

Growing up in France, Ayouch developed his relationship with Morocco through film. According to him: "It's thanks to the camera, thanks to cinema that I discovered Morocco" (Ayouch 2012). Although Ayouch is Moroccan, he felt at times like a foreigner when he visited the country, experiencing a strong sense of split identity between himself and his cultural homeland. This personal history of difference and disconnect with Morocco has served as major theme and inspiration in his work. Ayouch has sought to celebrate difference, to break through pressures in Morocco to reflect singular or dominant concepts of identity. His cinema points to the importance of multiplicity of perspectives, identities, and differences. Through his films, Ayouch has not only worked to provide social and political critique; he has also attempted to launch public debate of issues that have been covered up or hidden in Moroccan society. In the process, Ayouch has broken through a variety of taboos in his films, creating new terrains for representing controversial sociopolitical issues, transgressive identities, and marginalized lives.

MEKTOUB: BREAKING THROUGH PUBLIC SILENCE ON THE TABIT AFFAIR

Mektoub (*Fate*, 1997) is an audacious debut. The film, which was shot in late 1996 and spring 1997, was a commercial and critical success. It sold more than 350,000 box-office tickets in Morocco, won awards at the Cairo and Oslo film festivals, and served as Morocco's official submission for the 1998 Oscars.[8] Among other taboos, the film takes up a real-life scandal that broke in the Moroccan press in early 1993, when a high-ranking police commissioner in Casablanca named Mustapha Tabit was arrested and charged with abducting and raping over five hundred women, crimes that he recorded on over one hundred videotapes. Along with Tabit, several other conspirators were arrested. The country's "trial of the century," as the case became known, began less than three weeks after the initial arrests and created a massive sensation. For the first time in Morocco's history, a police commissioner—a figure symbolizing the country's long decades of authoritarianism known as the Years of Lead—was publicly made accountable for criminal acts.[9] Moreover, the country's mass media had been tightly controlled up to that point, and the police served as a powerful taboo. Before the trial, the press had never reported on the police openly and in such negative terms.

The trial coincided with Ramadan in 1993, and newspaper sales skyrocketed as people of all social backgrounds followed the case. After only a few weeks, the commissioner was found guilty and sentenced to death. The shocking downfall of such a powerful figure, someone who operated above the law for decades, demonstrated to the entire public that the state was moving away from the repression of the Years of Lead and into a new era of openness. As I argue elsewhere, this case—and its sensational coverage in the printed press—represented the launching point for deep changes in state authority and the limits on mass media representation in the country (Smolin 2013).

Nonetheless, once the trial was complete, the case disappeared suddenly from the press, and direct discussion of its implications quickly withered. Ayouch was living in France during the Tabit Affair and was shocked by the way the scandal simply ended, as if it had never happened (Ayouch 2012). For Ayouch, the inability to address the far-reaching ramifications of the scandal for corruption in society, the relationship between state authority and citizens, and the deeply rooted nature of abuse of power in the country pointed to a crisis (Ayouch 2012). According to Ayouch: "In our society, we have problems with public debate so we want to hide everything, we want to bury everything" (Ayouch 2012). Instead of inspiring wide-scale debate and discussion about the place of civil rights in the country, the scandal simply vanished.

When the Tabit Affair took place in early 1993, only the printed press was permitted to cover the trial. Because of the highly sensitive nature of the case, it never appeared in the audiovisual mass media at the time. Cinema therefore provided Ayouch with a new language and medium not only to represent the scandal but also, with the commercial and critical success of his film, to provoke the discussion that never took place after the scandal erupted in 1993.[10] In this respect, Ayouch's first film falls within the tradition of committed social-realist filmmaking, which had become prominent in Morocco during the 1990s.[11]

In *Mektoub*, Taoufik Raoui, a Moroccan doctor who lives in California, and his wife, Sophia, arrive at a Tangier hotel for an ophthalmology conference. Taoufik suddenly falls ill after dinner, and Sophia is abducted as she goes to find a doctor. Sophia awakes with her arms bound; a video camera records as a man slowly approaches to assault her just before the scene cuts. The next morning,

Taoufik discovers what has happened. He goes to his estranged brother, Kemal, a police inspector, and manages to steal his gun. Taoufik finds the house where Sophia was raped, discovers dozens of videotapes that include scenes of sexual assaults, and shoots the ringleader with Kemal's gun. He then flees with the tape containing footage of Sophia's rape.

Kemal soon discovers that the man Taoufik has killed was a well-known police commissioner and independence movement hero named Faysal Darif, an alter ego of the real-life Mustapha Tabit. Realizing that Taoufik and Sophia are powerless before such a figure, Kemal decides to take them to the Rif Mountains, an area known for its independence from state control. The rest of the film depicts how Taoufik and Sophia flee through the Rif and the Sahara as Detective Kebir leads the police hunt to apprehend them and suppress the case. Kebir, who symbolizes the police brutality and corruption of the Years of Lead, discovers Darif's crimes from the outset and wants to arrest the couple and recover the videotape in order to keep them from exposing Darif. After a long chase through the mountains and desert, Kebir manages to recover the tape from an intermediary.[12] This indicates that the police will be able to suppress Darif's crimes and keep the case from becoming a public scandal, unlike the real-life Tabit Affair.

As Taoufik and Sophia flee Kebir through the Rif and the desert, they rediscover aspects of Morocco after being away in California for years, such as beautiful terrain and the strong character of the Rifi people, including a powerful cameo from Malika Oufkir several years before she published her well-known memoir (Oufkir and Fitoussi, 2002).[13] Sequences in the Rif show how Taoufik—despite being Moroccan—encounters the country as a foreigner, much as Ayouch did before moving to Casablanca in the late 1990s. The film ends as Taoufik and Sophia stand together in the desert, a space of freedom and self-discovery in Arabic literature and culture, as the soft voice of a woman singing poetry suggests that despite whatever hardships people might face, they should have faith that God has reserved for them another fate. This final word points to the film's title, *Mektoub,* Arabic for *fate,* suggesting that Taoufik and Sophia's painful and shocking ordeal will lead them unexpectedly to a fulfilling destiny of discovery and self-fulfillment as they bridge the gap between themselves and their birth country.

Despite a small budget, which was the equivalent of €500,000, Ayouch strove to give the film high production value.[14] In *Mektoub,* Ayouch uses the medium of cinema to transform the Tabit Affair, one of the most significant events in modern Moroccan history, for the Moroccan public. The real-life scandal served

as a watershed moment for revealing abuses of power within the police estab-
lishment to the widest possible public and expanding freedom of expression
in the mass media. In the film, however, the scandal is suppressed after Kebir
manages to recover the videotape of Sophia's rape, pointing to the way the Tabit
Affair quickly disappeared from the press and the public turned away from the
scandal after the trial was complete. The end of the film therefore alludes to the
inability to have public debate about deep-rooted issues in society. However,
while the case within the film does not reach the public, it radically transforms
Taoufik and Sophia. The crisis of rape and vigilante justice ultimately redefines
the couple's identity and sense of place with their country, a fate utterly unfore-
seen when they arrived in Morocco at the beginning of the film.

ALI ZAOUA: PRINCE OF THE STREETS: TRANSCENDING THE LIVES OF STREET CHILDREN

During the mid- to late 1990s, Moroccan film and literature began taking up
subjects that were considered taboo in previous decades, such as human rights
violations, illegal immigration, and sexual themes. This paralleled a larger
opening taking place in society during the final years of Hassan II and the initial years of Mohammed VI, as the mass media enjoyed expanding freedom of
expression, the political opposition led the government, and a variety of NGOs
became more active in supporting groups and causes that had been largely neglected in the past, such as battered women and abused housemaids.[15] Among
these NGOs, Bayti, which means "my house," was founded in 1995 to provide aid
and work for homeless children.[16] Nabil Ayouch worked directly with Bayti to
identify and cast the child actors for *Ali Zaoua: Prince of the Streets* (*Ali Zaoua:
Prince de la rue*, 2000), his second film.[17] The film, which boldly depicts four
children living on the streets of Casablanca, is to date his best-known work.[18] *Ali
Zaoua* continued the social-realist genre of *Mektoub* and also built on the commercial success of his first film, selling approximately 500,000 box-office tickets
in Morocco and winning some forty-four prizes at international film festivals.[19]

The film begins with brightly colored painted images and a dialogue between
a female interviewer and Ali about his life on the streets. The scene then cuts to
a cropped image of Ali, standing with a number of other homeless children and
people, as the interviewer stands off camera holding a microphone toward Ali.
The exchange takes place in Moroccan Arabic, but the woman orders the cam-
eraman in French to focus in on Ali's face and then to cut. With this beginning,
Ayouch points to the role that street children typically play in the Moroccan

and French mass media—as an object for pity and surprise, something kept at a distance and safely cropped from the lives of the public. Ayouch, however, immediately transitions from this documentary exchange to the four children running and playing together in an empty building lot, delving directly into their world and bridging the distanced and guarded exchange that began the film.

Ali and his three friends, Kwita, Boubker, and Omar, have broken free from a large group of street children led by the mute and sexually abusive Dib, played by the French-Moroccan star Saïd Taghmaoui. After the opening scenes, Ali tells Kwita that he will leave them to become a sailor so that he can reach his island, a fantasy land with two suns. Dib suddenly arrives with a large number of followers and demands that the four return to his group. When Ali refuses, one of Dib's children throws a rock at his head and kills him. This forces Ali's three companions to confront the challenge of providing Ali with a proper burial. Much of the remainder of the film traces how the children—despite living in neglect on the margins of civil society—navigate the process of trying to bring dignity and recognition to Ali in his death.

Kwita insists to the others that they will bury Ali like "a prince." However, the children quickly discover that burying Ali will not be simple. Kwita steals one hundred dirhams from a schoolgirl and then goes to a cemetery hoping to use the money to pay for the burial. A child his own age chastises him, saying that the cemetery only buries the "pure." This exchange emphasizes not only religious hypocrisy but also how children are just as capable as adults of looking down on and discriminating against people like Kwita and his friends. In the following scenes, the film depicts how the children squander Kwita's money, endangering any possibility for a burial, and how Kwita struggles to find a sailor uniform in which to bury Ali.

Ali had befriended an older boat captain before he died. The captain, played by the Moroccan actor Mohamed Majd, finds the group, asks for Ali, and soon learns that Ali has died. The captain helps Kwita provide the burial by building a small boat for Ali's body that they will set adrift at sea. Just as he heads to the port with Ali's mother, Kwita finds a sailor's uniform for sale at a small store. The film ends as the three children, Ali's mother, and the captain head out into the Atlantic. Ali receives the dignity in death that he never found in life. Dib and his group watch speechless as the boat sets out and, as the animation in the final moments suggests, Ali will achieve his dream of becoming a sailor and reaching the island with two suns.

One of the most powerful aspects of the film is the way it depicts the harsh daily life of Moroccan children on the streets. Abandoned by civil society, the children are left to fend for themselves, not only for sustenance but also for establishing power relations among each other. No one is there to intervene when Dib rapes Boubker, Omar nearly slits Kwita's throat, or Ali is killed. The boys easily obtain sniffing glue and use it in order to escape the misery of their daily life. Ayouch uses his widescreen shots and rich colors to present audiences with the marginal and neglected city spaces that the children navigate daily. The children also speak in a colloquial Moroccan that matches the harshness and brutality of their world. This kind of graphic and vulgar language had not appeared in Moroccan cinema before.

A striking element in the film is the way it takes the perspective of the children as they attempt to cope with the world around them. The film juxtaposes harsh realism with the use of animation within the narrative, as seen from Kwita's perspective. In this, the film emphasizes how Kwita's brutal surroundings have pushed him inward, encouraging him to build his own fantasy world into which he can escape. Kwita's declarations to the schoolgirl of a life together further underscore this point. In this, perception becomes fantasy as a strategy to transcend the present. The painful naïveté of the children is further stressed—for example, when Kwita thinks Ali is still alive after he discovers that Ali's body released a bowel movement, or when Omar and Boubker make fun of the way Ali's mother, who is a prostitute, has sex with a customer. Moreover, the scenes of the children playing at the port show how the concept of home in the film is highly flexible. They demarcate the concrete space with chalk, calling one square the living room, a second the kitchen, and a third the bathroom. Boubker, for example, scolds Kwita when he cooks sardines in the "bathroom" instead of the "kitchen." Later in the film, Omar finds Ali's mother and hesitatingly seeks out affection from her as a kind of surrogate mother. In this, the film offers a hint of optimism in displaying how the children seek ways to cope with the reality of their daily life. By providing Ali with the funeral he deserves, the film presents a wrenching yet hopeful message that street children can transcend their dire circumstances to achieve a sense of agency and fulfillment.

A MINUTE OF SUN LESS: NARRATIVE EXPERIMENTATION AND TRANSGRESSIVE SEXUAL IDENTITIES

Ayouch's third film, *A Minute of Sun Less* (*Une minute de soleil en moins*, 2002), is a police procedural that was made for ARTE's masculine/feminine series.[20] In this work, Ayouch turns away from the social realism of *Mektoub* and *Ali*

Zaoua in order to explore new forms of cinematographic language and experiment with types of editing and shooting. The film, which uses the police procedural format to explore the concepts of identity and sexuality, was shot in 2002 in Tangier and screened on ARTE in 2003. It caused a scandal in Morocco for its graphic depiction of sex, homosexuality, and a transgendered character. Parliamentary representatives of the Islamic Parti de la Justice et du Développement (PJD) attacked the film, demanding that Ayouch return the funds that he received from the state-sponsored Centre Cinématographique Marocain (CCM) to produce it.[21]

When he began the project, Ayouch did not concern himself with whether the film would be authorized for screening in the country or how politicians would react to it; for Ayouch, these concerns would only encourage self-censorship, something that he rejects in his work (Ayouch 2012). While he was not surprised by the scandal, he was shocked by the way members of the parliament reacted, especially when PJD politicians called for banning the film even though they had never viewed it and were unwilling to discuss it (ibid.). For Ayouch, this reaction points to one of the main problems in Moroccan society—the inability to discuss issues publicly and conduct open debate over charged political, social, and cultural topics. Because Ayouch has steadfastly refused to cut the explicit sex scenes in the film—mostly because they serve as the vehicle for the film's exploration of transgressive identities—*A Minute of Sun Less* has yet to screen in Moroccan cinema houses or national television.[22] Nonetheless, many saw the film when it aired on ARTE, and pirated copies of the work circulate openly in DVD markets across the country. Ten years after making the film, Ayouch is still optimistic that it will eventually appear in Moroccan cinemas; he plans to resubmit the film for approval for public screening (Ayouch 2013).

A Minute of Sun Less is a prequel to *Mektoub*. Ayouch links the two films through the Tangier setting and the character Kemal Raoui, even though a different actor plays the role in each film.[23] *A Minute of Sun Less* opens in Kemal's spare apartment as he is called down to the scene of a murder. The victim, Hakim Tahiri, owned a yacht-building and wood business and was known in Tangier for hosting wild sex parties. The commissioner tells Kemal that they suspect Tahiri and his family of controlling a large drug-smuggling operation to Europe. Touria, Hakim's mysterious employee, played by Lubna Azabal, discovered the body of Tahiri floating in a large bathtub with a phallic object penetrating him anally after he was shot in the heart.

Kemal begins investigating the case and soon finds the manager of Hakim's wood business, a taciturn man named Bougemza, who explains that they make a new kind of material at the factory named Strati-décor. Kemal learns that the Tahiri family sent Bougemza to Tangier to watch Hakim after he had been found sexually assaulting a fourteen-year-old boy. Kemal takes in Touria's adolescent brother, Pipo, played by Hicham Moussoun (who appeared in *Ali Zaoua* as Boubker), and Touria joins them after she is released from police custody. Even though they are never shown speaking to each other throughout the film, the attraction between Kemal and Touria boils over and the two begin having sex, despite the fact that she is the prime suspect in the murder case.

The investigation proceeds, and after several false leads Kemal follows up on Strati-décor, which he learns is made from sawdust fused together by specialized machines. Kemal rushes to the wood factory, suspecting that the Tahiris smuggle drugs out of the country by mixing them in Strati-décor, but finds that the factory has suspiciously burned down. He takes some of the remaining wood for analysis and the crime lab determines that it is mixed with cocaine. Fearing for Touria's safety, Kemal returns to his apartment looking for her, but she has already left with Pipo. In the final moments of the film, the scene shifts between Kemal, who is driving along the Atlantic shore, and Touria, who rides in a taxi with Pipo. Bougemza also follows Touria and Pipo in his car. Kemal now realizes that Bougemza killed Hakim, not Touria. Pipo convinces Touria to stop the taxi and go for a swim in the ocean. As Touria stands on the beach watching Pipo in the water, Bougemza appears, takes out a long-range rifle, and shoots them both, presumably to silence them after they had grown too close to Kemal. Driving on the highway, Kemal notices police cars and gets out of his car. After discovering the murders, he rushes frantically into the water, screaming in grief.

A Minute of Sun Less marks a significant development in Ayouch's work. The film boasts highly stylized camera work, including quick transitions between images, pauses and skips between shots, and delays between images and audio elements, with images appearing first. Sounds are exaggerated at times, such as when the ticking of Kemal's alarm clock turns into an elongated pounding. From the outset, the film also features many quick images and rapid scenes spliced into the narrative, including shots of Touria holding the phallic object found in Hakim's dead body, Hakim assaulting Pipo, or Bougemza shooting Hakim. These various elements serve to construct Kemal's identity through his perceptions and internal deliberations on the case as he investigates the murder. The washed-out colors, bare sets, and varied music soundtrack—from Indian music to 1970s style bass—give the film a retro-cool feeling, quite distinct from Ayouch's previous work. These simple and, at times, highly artificial visual and audio elements point to the film as a prequel to *Mektoub,* establishing the setting as during the 1970s or '80s.

The most daring aspect of the film is the way it problematizes the concept of identity, gender, and sexuality. Kemal is involved with a transgendered dancer named Yasmine, played by the actor Noor.[24] Yasmine talks provocatively about her sex change operation and jokes with Pipo that he can call her mister or ma'am, since "it's all the same." The physical encounters between Kemal and Touria also complicate the film's depiction of sexuality and undermine traditional sexual roles in the Arab world. When they have sex for the first time, she pulls down his pants to reveal his erect penis, demonstrating his attraction for her. Nonetheless, Kemal submissively turns over and raises his backside to Touria, inviting her to straddle him from behind. She dominates him in this initial encounter as she fingers his anus. A similar sequence takes place in their second sex scene. During their third scene, however, instead of remaining passive, Kemal becomes dominant, overpowering her and roughly penetrating her from on top. This sequence leaves Touria grief-stricken at the transformation of aggression and virility that has taken place in him since their first two encounters. These scenes are central to the film's exploration of sexuality, showing the audience how sexual identity is a performative act depending on individual encounters, moving along a spectrum rather than remaining stable. Ayouch has pointed to the thematic importance of these scenes in a variety of interviews about the film, defending his decision not to cut them for any screenings in Morocco (Laghzawi 2003b).

These scenes point to the importance of transgression in the film. According to Ayouch: "I am doing cinema in a country where, for me, there is not enough space for difference" (Ayouch 2012). The depiction of sexuality in *A Minute of Sun Less* indicates the way Ayouch seeks to transgress categories of sameness and the pressure to be alike in society, to provoke public recognition and respect for difference. In the film, singular categories, such as homosexual, heterosexual, or even bisexual, have broken down. Moreover, the depiction of sexuality is anchored in the film's exploration of identity. Kemal takes on different identities depending on context and environment. Even within the space of the bedroom and with the same people, Kemal performs different sexual identities. This points to the importance of the multiplicity and instability of roles in the film. With *A Minute of Sun Less,* Ayouch hoped to provoke a public debate and acceptance of sexuality and fluid identities in Moroccan society.

Despite the significant developments in style, content, and theme, there are important continuities between *A Minute of Sun Less* and Ayouch's earlier work. The first is the use of fantasy. In *Ali Zaoua,* animation appears as a way to display the children's perspective as they cope with their environment, to show their ability to find momentary happiness and escape the challenges of their daily existence. Fantasy reappears in *A Minute of Sun Less* when Kemal, Touria, and Pipo go to Fez in order to meet with Driss, Hakim's uncle. As they drive on the highway, the car begins to ascend and soar through the sky as the film mixes images of the three with animation. The use of fantasy in the film points to the Kemal's newly discovered joy and happiness with Touria and Pipo. Just as the children in *Ali Zaoua* create a new concept of home by delineating squares on the ground with chalk, the scene suggests that Kemal feels a deep sense of contentment as Touria and Pipo become a new kind of family for him.

At the beginning of the film, there are shots of Kemal looking into his bathroom mirror, depressed and barely able to smile. As the film progresses, however, he becomes increasingly content and happy through his relationship with Touria and Pipo, despite the fact that she is the main suspect in his murder investigation. Just as in *Ali Zaoua,* the film points to the ability of human beings to find fulfillment in personal interactions, even if those interactions are not based on standard concepts of family, home, sexuality, or gender. And this explains Kemal's grief at the end of the film as he rushes into the ocean—with the murder of Touria and Pipo, he has lost his only chance to transcend his daily existence. This is further emphasized by the film's final images, which show Kemal at an outdoor café. Sitting in the same chair and location, he morphs into a much older man, showing that his circumstances will not change even after several decades. His life without Touria and Pipo has come to a stop.

While the form of a police procedural seems like a radical break for Moroccan cinema, it represents another connection with *Mektoub,* which included elements of the genre as well. *A Minute of Sun Less* also bears important links with Moroccan television production at the time. During 2001 and 2002, the local stations RTM and 2M produced and screened a number of police television films for the first time.[25] The most popular of these films, *The Blind Whale* and *The Black Butterfly,* also depict the local police investigating a large drug smuggling operation from Morocco to Europe (Rhanja 2001 and Rhanja 2002). In these two works—as in *A Minute of Sun Less*—the Moroccan police fail to bring the main suspect to justice or crack the drug smuggling operation at the heart of the investigation. By incorporating aspects of local Moroccan television at the time—yet premiering on ARTE—*A Minute of Sun Less* is not simply an audacious film, experimenting with audiovisual techniques and transgressing concepts of identity. It is also a powerful work of transnational filmmaking, connecting Morocco to Europe through the medium of television and cinema.

WHATEVER LOLA WANTS: BRIDGING DIFFERENCES BETWEEN THE ARAB WORLD AND THE WEST

In his fourth film, *Whatever Lola Wants* (2007), Ayouch continued building bridges between the Arab world and the West. The film was a commercial and critical success, winning the top prize at the Tangier International Film Festival and selling over 100,000 box office tickets, a considerable number considering the decline in moviegoers in Morocco during the past decade.[26] The film is a major departure from Ayouch's previous work, and not only because of its commercial melodramatic style. His first English-language film, it stars an American actress, Laura Ramsey, in the lead role of Lola. Moreover, it is his first work shot partly outside of Morocco, as Ayouch used both New York City and Cairo, in addition to Rabat and Casablanca, as filming locations. He also enjoyed a comparatively larger budget of approximately €10 million to make the film, finding much of the funding from French sources.[27] Finally, the lighthearted theme of the film—a New York City postal worker travels to Cairo to learn belly dancing from a former star—differs significantly from the social and political engagement of his first three works.[28]

Whatever Lola Wants opens in New York City as Lola struggles to balance her part-time work as a mail carrier for the United States Postal Service with her ambitions to become a successful dancer. While delivering mail on her route one day, Lola meets a preppy Egyptian man named Zack, played by the Moroccan actor Assaad Bouab. The two soon become intimate, but they argue when Lola tells him that she will not accept her boss's offer of full-time work since she is afraid that it will crush her dreams of becoming a dancer. Zack thinks Lola is being childish, and the two fight before he suddenly returns to Cairo. At a crossroads in her life, Lola impulsively decides to raise money for a ticket to Cairo so that she can reconcile with Zack.

After arriving at the crowded Cairo airport, Lola goes to Zack's house, which is in an affluent part of the city. Zack is shocked to see Lola, as he is accustomed to keeping his life in the United States separate from his family and personal life in Egypt. Zack takes Lola to a cheap hotel, has sex with her, and then gives her a large amount of cash to buy a plane ticket home. Crushed by the rejection, Lola

Sophia and Taoufik at the end of *Mektoub*.

Ali Zaoua (in the skull-and-swords shirt) and his friends in *Ali Zaoua*.

Lola performing in *Whatever Lola Wants*.

Hamid, Nabil, Yachine, and Fouad after turning to
radical Islam in *Horses of God*.

is desperate. She remembers how her Egyptian neighbor in New York played her videos of a legendary former belly dancer named Ismahan and decides to seek her out in the hope that Ismahan will teach her Oriental dance.

Lola finds Ismahan's house and quickly discovers that she is a pariah. Nonetheless, after much persistence, Lola convinces Ismahan to train her. At first Lola is stiff and nervous; but Ismahan pushes Lola to use her body as a medium for articulating her emotions, to use Oriental dance as a form of self-expression. Their relationship blossoms as Lola's joy and enthusiasm transforms Ismahan, breaking down her harsh exterior and livening up her somber life. Ismahan eventually confesses to Lola that the reason that she is a pariah is because she was photographed by the local paparazzi with a man who was not her husband. Ismahan explains that she loved the man but that they could not be together.

While studying with Ismahan, Lola begins dancing at a nightclub in the city and is discovered by a dance promoter named Nasser Radi. Nasser eventually books her at a theater named the Nile Tower, where Lola becomes a star combining American stage sensibilities with Oriental dance. She performs for packed houses night after night and eventually announces to the crowd that she will return home to share Oriental dance with New Yorkers, a nod to cross-cultural understanding and fusion between the Unites States and the Arab world. She also declares that Ismahan was her teacher. Stunned silence turns to applauds, showing that Lola has managed to bring Ismahan out of her seclusion and reconcile the public with her.

Now that Lola has found herself through dance, she can return home. Ismahan's reconciliation with the public opens the possibility for her to find herself as well. It turns out that the man Ismahan loved was none other than the dance promoter, Nasser Radi, who helped Lola achieve fame as a ploy to reinsert himself into Ismahan's life. For years he had been sending her letters, but she never replied. Now that Lola has left for New York and success in her own Broadway show, Ismahan finally opens her door to Nasser, accepting his love, bridging the difference between the two, and presumably finding the same fulfillment through him that Lola found through dance. In these ending scenes the film presents a striking display of cross-cultural understanding, as it is the relationship between the American Lola and the Egyptian Ismahan that has cut across national and cultural boundaries, ended the public's intolerance toward Ismahan, and led both to deep personal fulfillment.

Despite the stark differences in subject matter, language, style, and social critique, *Whatever Lola Wants* shares important links with Ayouch's previous work. Most prominently, the film explores the concept of difference and identity. Just as Ayouch showed in *A Minute of Sun Less,* human beings operate on multiple levels and environments, and the concept of identity can morph depending on circumstances and environment. According to Ayouch, "I don't think that one should have only one identity. I think we are all dealing with many identities" (Ayouch 2012). This multiplicity in *Whatever Lola Wants* leads to bridging cultural divides and provides a highly optimistic perspective on difference.

Moreover, as in Ayouch's previous films, *Lola* focuses on a personal struggle that, in the end, fundamentally transforms the individual. In *Mektoub,* Taoufik and Sophia's tragic encounter with Darif leads them to an unexpected and radically new fate that bridges the gap between them and their homeland. In *Ali Zaoua,* Ali's death pushes the three children to bring respect and dignity not just to Ali but also to their lives for the first time. Kemal, in *A Minute of Sun Less,* temporarily transcends his deep depression through the self-discovery he experiences in his physical and emotional relationship with Touria. Lola too has been struggling with her identity and sense of place in the world when she turns down the full-time position at the post office and when she faces the end of her relationship with Zack. It is through overcoming her differences with Ismahan—as well as her persistence at Oriental dance—that she is able to find herself, bridge misunderstanding, and achieve the success in life that she so desperately craves. Through this common theme—the ability of the individual to transcend difference and their environment—Ayouch manages to connect his work to the social life and aspirations of the Moroccan and Middle Eastern public as well as to give his work a human and universal dimension.

HORSES OF GOD: MICROTRAUMAS AND
THE CONSTRUCTION OF TERRORISTS

On May 16, 2003, fourteen suicide bombers from the Sidi Moumen shantytown of Casablanca attacked five separate locations in the center of the city. Forty-four people in total died during the attacks, which were a deeply traumatic event for the country because the attackers were young Moroccans, not members of an international terrorism network. Moreover, Islamic terrorism had never struck the country before. Much like the September 11 attacks in the United States, May 16 ushered in wide-ranging legal, security, and social changes aimed at stopping another attack (Smolin 2013). Because of the taboo nature of the attacks, however, there was little public debate in Morocco in the initial years after the event about the causes of the bombings or their social, political, and cultural implications. As with the Tabit Affair, Ayouch believed that this silence pointed to the inability of the Moroccan public to face painful realities. For Ayouch, the young men who carried out the attacks were victims of the bombings as well: "Above all, the bombers were human beings. I wanted to humanize them and humanize their doubts" (Ayouch 2013). As he did in his first film, *Mektoub,* Ayouch looked to cinema as a means to reopen public debate about a traumatic national event that was being suppressed. Ayouch has remarked, "The denial of identity gives birth to violence" (Ayouch 2013).

In his fifth feature film, *Horses of God (Les cheveaux de dieu / Ya khayl Allah,* 2012), adapted from Mahi Binebine's novel (Binebine 2013), Nabil Ayouch examines the social genealogy of the May 16 bombings in order to explore the origins of the Islamic terrorism in the country.[29] The film weaves the lives of several young men, as they come of age in Sidi Moumen during the decade before 2003, together with historic events, such as the death of Hassan II in 1999 and the September 11 attacks.[30] The film, which was an official selection at the 2012 Cannes Film Festival, unfolds over ten years, beginning in 1994 as the boys in the shantytown play soccer.[31] The game quickly breaks down into insults and violence as these initial sequences establish the harsh environment in which the children live. Immediately after the soccer match, the two brothers Hamid, played by Abdelilah Rachid, and Yachine, played by Abdelhakim Rachid, return home and their mother yells at them that they "stink like garbage," showing how the verbal abuse among the children is rooted in the family as the boys find little love and affection at home. Moreover, Hamid and Yachine's family is a site of socioeconomic crisis. Their mother can barely find work as a cleaning lady while one older brother is a soldier in the Western Sahara and the other is autistic, unable to leave the home. Most importantly, their father is overwhelmed by depression, creating a lack of authority in their lives. With the absence of a father figure, the two brothers are left to the vicious world of the slum, with no one to protect or guide them.

This implosion of the traditional Arab family in the shantytown is also seen in the characters' inability to develop warm and loving human relationships outside of the home. In the scenes that take place during the 1990s, the children treat each other brutally. In one of the most disturbing sequences in the film, the boys go to the house of one of their friends, Nabil, as the adults are celebrating a wedding. Left alone, they drink a bottle of wine and Hamid rapes Nabil in front of the others.[32] This sequence points not only to the violence and abuse surrounding the lives of the boys as they grow up without authority figures but also to the lack of outlets to develop intimate relationships in the shantytown environment. The children learn about sex through violence, not affection. In another sequence, Nabil, who is left alone once Islamists force his mother out of Sidi Moumen for working as a prostitute, carefully puts lipstick on himself while watching in a mirror. This scene suggests that the violent homoerotic environment of the shantytown has left Nabil with no outlet to explore his sexuality and forced him to hide elements of his identity. These scenes of sexual abuse and suppression serve as a precursor for the violence of radical Islam later in the film.

The theme of suppressed identity is further emphasized in the way the film develops the relationship between Yachine and Ghislaine. Even as a young boy at the beginning of the film, Yachine smiles at Ghislaine, hoping to attract her attention. As they get older, the two continue to flirt with each other. Nonetheless, the social environment and geographical space of the shantytown make it impossible for the two to be alone together as Yachine is repeatedly blocked when he attempts to speak with Ghislaine alone. Yachine's love for Ghislaine continues to develop throughout the film. Even in the days before the suicide bombings at the end of the film, Yachine asks Nabil what Ghislaine will think when she learns that he has died as a martyr, as if committing his act of terrorism will impress her. These words can also be heard in the initial moments of the film, suggesting that the lack of space for intimacy links the inability to develop loving human relationships with the emergence of Islamic terrorism in the country.

Competition for love and affection also lies at the heart of the relationship between Hamid and Yachine in the film. When they are children, Yachine looks up to Hamid and is eager to please him even though Hamid repeatedly belittles him. Without the guidance of older brothers or the authority of a father figure, the children are left to compete among themselves for their mother's rare moments of affection. When Hamid brings her a gift of perfume, she kisses him and tells him how pleased she is with him. When Hamid is arrested, however, he still looms large over Yachine's relationship with their mother. The mother tells him how much she misses Hamid and how he, unlike Yachine, was able to bring money home for her. Yachine brings perfume home for his mother but she is too busy watching television to open the box, a clear rejection of his gesture.

In the initial sequences of the film, Ayouch uses a long and wide crane shot to establish a global view of the shantytown in 1994. The second crane shot depicts

Sidi Moumen in 1999, after the death of Hassan II, showing the significant expansion of the slum and the explosion of garbage surrounding it. With no state services such as education, running water, or urban planning, the shantytown is a world abandoned by and cut off from civil society. The state intervenes in Sidi Moumen only through the police, who are depicted as brutal and corrupt. One police detective, known as Pitbull, takes kickbacks from Hamid, who deals drugs under police protection in the shantytown to make money. Once Pitbull is transferred out of the area, this last vestige of the state disappears from the shantytown and the residents are left to fend for themselves in the face of the growing presence of radical Islam.

The abandonment of civil society works both ways in the film. Only weeks before the suicide attacks, the group of young men drives in a van from the shantytown into the city center and, with a wide smile of anticipation, one says: "It's the first time I'm going to visit the city." Only several miles separate the city center from Sidi Moumen, but the characters in the film have never left the shantytown. This points to the way they have lived fully cut apart from civil society, with no crossing between the two. Sidi Moumen and Casablanca therefore appear as two separate worlds that are developing not only at different speeds but also in radically different directions.

It is this void of dignity, belonging, and affection that radical Islam fills in the film. Islamists make their first appearance while harassing Tamou, Nabil's mother, for working as a prostitute, eventually forcing her to leave the shantytown. Hamid soon returns home from two years in prison wearing a beard and traditional religious clothing, visibly reborn in his relationship with Islam. While jail provided the forum for Hamid to embrace radical Islam, trauma soon brings Yachine and Nabil into the fold. Ba Mousa, the coarse mechanic who verbally abuses the boys, gets drunk and begins kissing Nabil in front of Yachine. When Nabil refuses him, Ba Mousa becomes enraged and attacks Nabil. Yachine intervenes and hits Ba Mousa over the head with a crowbar and then kills him. Hamid soon arrives with his new Islamist friends and disposes of the body. This disturbing event quickly pushes Yachine and Nabil into closer contact with the Islamists of the shantytown. Fearful that they might be arrested and with nowhere else to turn, Yachine and Nabil visit the Islamists' compound and meet the emir, or leader, of the group, Abou Zoubier. The emir tells Yachine that he is not at fault for the murder and that he now has the chance to atone for his sins and restart his life. In this, Islam and the group offer Yachine and Nabil their sole path for redemption.

The Islamist group also presents opportunities for attaining self-respect and dignity. It is during these scenes that the language in the film changes. Unlike the harsh form of Moroccan Arabic at the beginning of the film, the Islamists speak in an educated mix of standard and Moroccan Arabic, showing how the group also serves as a means of education in the absence of the state. In addition, the film shows how the Islamists play the role of the state in offering social services such as providing medical care and basic food for the shantytown's residents.[33] The increasing entrenchment of radical Islam in the shantytown is also reflected in the colors and shots in the film. The bright sun-drenched colors and wide pan shots in the first half of the film turn to shots in dark enclosed spaces with flat gray and black colors in the second half.

Yachine struggles at first to accept his new place within the group but eventually submits. This only accentuates the rivalry between the brothers as they now compete for the affection and approval of the emir instead of their mother. Hamid, for example, feels threatened when he thinks that Yachine is becoming too close with the emir. As the group moves increasingly toward the suicide bombings, Yachine appears more committed and confident while Hamid becomes increasingly uncertain about the operation. The police arrive in the shantytown and viciously beat some of the Islamists, including Yachine. Nonetheless, Yachine hides his pain and appears strong before the emir, leading the emir to praise Yachine. This sparks Hamid's jealousy even further. The rivalry pushes the two brothers to accept participating in the suicide bombings as the emir explains that Yachine, Hamid, Nabil, and Fouad have been chosen for the operation, inciting them with the expression "Fly, horses of God, and the gates of paradise will open for you."[34] Despite the fact that Hamid is older, Yachine is chosen as the leader of the operation. Hamid's growing skepticism stands in stark contrast with Yachine's unwavering determination for carrying out the attack. In this, Ayouch suggests that, in addition to the implosion of the family and the abandonment of the state, the rivalry between the brothers—an example of what he calls the "microtraumas" of their lives—is more important than religion in motivating their actions (Ayouch 2013).

In the closing sequences of the film, the four young men trim their beards, cut their hair, and cross over into the city center with backpacks full of explosives. The group then approaches their target, the Casa de España, but before they enter, Hamid attempts to convince Yachine to change his mind at the last moment. Driven by his rivalry with his brother, however, Yachine pushes Hamid away and enters the restaurant. This space points to Morocco's heritage of religious tolerance and multiculturalism in Andalusia, a past that the bombers are attempting to destroy with their act. The explosion is then seen in the distance from the shantytown as a number of children, presumably the next group of Yachines and Hamids, with their own personal rivalries and experiences of abuse and abandonment, play soccer.[35]

Horses of God daringly depicts how ten-year-old boys can be transformed into Islamic terrorists as a result of their environment and personal relationships. The film shows the human face of terrorism, presenting it as a social construct, one resulting from the implosion of the traditional Arab family, the complete absence of the state in the shantytowns, and the lack of dignity and future prospects for young Moroccans. The film blends these socioeconomic factors with the microhistories of characters like Hamid and Yachine, whose personal traumas, desires for belonging, and rivalries, more than religious fervor, fuel the violence of the shantytown and, eventually, radical Islam. With *Horses of God*, Ayouch sets in full display the horrific results of abandoning young Moroccans in areas like Sidi Moumen and demonstrates the enormous consequences for the country of suppressing trauma on both the national and the individual level.

From *Ali Zaoua* to *Horses of God*, Nabil Ayouch has attempted to bridge disconnected worlds in order to break through taboos and call for the integration of marginalized figures into Moroccan society and public consciousness. He has sought to provoke public debate around painful national traumas, developing a new cinematic language in Morocco in the process. By embracing difference and celebrating multiplicity of identities, Ayouch has used cinema as a vehicle not only for self-expression but also as a means to bring exposure and dignity to those abandoned and rejected by traditional elements in order to foster a more inclusive society. Bridging difference in his work, not only within Morocco but also between Israel and Palestine, as in *My Land*, as well as between the Arab world and the West, leads to the embrace of suppressed forms of identity and a fostering of cross-cultural understanding.

Ayouch is at the forefront of a new generation of filmmakers attempting to raise the art of Moroccan cinema to global standards. For Ayouch, "We should be capable in the current generation of talking to the rest of world. We are not doing films for our own audiences only" (Ayouch 2012). In his effort to accomplish this, Ayouch has developed a cinematic language that transgresses boundaries within Morocco as well as national borders. His films reflect both local and universal content and form, standing at the frontline of a new terrain for Moroccan cinema both in the country and abroad.

NOTES

1. I would like to thank Nabil Ayouch for discussing his work with me. I would also like to thank Ayouch's assistant, Jawad Lahlou, for providing me with photographs of Ayouch and the funding information for Ayouch's films. Many thanks too to Josef Gugler for generously commenting on earlier drafts of this chapter and making valuable suggestions for improvement.

2. Noureddine Ayouch is also well known for publishing the Moroccan magazine *Kalima* during the 1980s. *Kalima* focused on women's issues in Morocco and broke numerous sexual taboos, leading to state authorities shutting it down several times. Noureddine Ayouch was also the founding president of Daba 2007, an association that aimed to increase public participation in the legislative elections of 2007.

3. For more on Ayouch's early short work, see Carter (2009). Ayouch also lived in Morocco when he was between three and five years old. According to Ayouch, advertising was a training ground for learning how to direct works, tell stories, and learn the technical aspects of filmmaking (Ayouch 2013).

4. For more on Ali n' Productions, see the Ali n' Productions web site, http://www.alinprod.com (accessed September 12, 2014).

5. For more on these films, see www.alinprod.com/doc/brochure_film_industry_1.pdf (accessed September 12, 2014).

6. At the time of writing, there are only forty-six screens in Morocco. Ayouch is also working to locate funding to open more cinemas in marginalized areas such as the Sidi Moumen shantytown in Casablanca. Except for film festivals and university screenings, there is little distribution of Moroccan films outside of the country. Coupled with the problem of piracy, this helps explain why Moroccan films rarely reach a mass audience.

7. Ayouch's documentary, *My Land* (2011), screened at film festivals during 2011 and opened in France in February 2012. In it Ayouch interviews a number of Palestinian refugees in Lebanese camps, as well as Israelis, about the 1948 war and the possibility of peace between the two peoples, attempting to create a dialogue between them. As Ayouch explains in a voice-over at the beginning of the documentary, the project was inspired by his experience of growing up half Muslim and half Jewish. Ali n' Productions (Morocco) and Les Films du Noveau Monde and French Connection (France) produced the film with a budget of approximately five hundred euros. Private sponsorship provided major funding.

8. See www.alinprod/mektoub.html (accessed September 12, 2014).

9. The Years of Lead, which lasted from the early 1970s until the early 1990s, were a period of brutal repression, severely restricted freedom of expression, and human rights abuses committed against political activists, among others. For more on this era, see Slyomovics (2005).

10. The film was so sensitive that, according to the Ayouch, it was almost censored. When he refused to cut any scenes from the film, however, the film was eventually accepted without any changes (Ayouch 2013).

11. For more on this style of cinema in Morocco, see Orlando (2011).

12. During the filming, Ayouch and his team of assistants and actors were held hostage in the desert town of Kalaat M'Gouna for seven days (Ayouch 2013). They were eventually released without any harm.

13. At the time of filming, Oufkir was working for Ayouch's father. She also helped Nabil Ayouch on the production of *Mektoub* (Ayouch 2013).

14. The film's major source of funding was from the Centre Cinematographique Marocain (ccm) and rtm. It was produced by Maroc n' Production (Morocco) and Playtime (France).

15. For a survey on this period, see Vermeren (2006). See also Smolin (2013).

16. For more on Bayti, see Bayti: L'enfance en situation difficile, www.bayti.ma (accessed September 12, 2014).

17. For more on the way Ayouch cast and worked with the children, see Gugler (2007).

18. The budget for the film was approximately €1.5 million. Major sources of funding were from Canal+, rtm, Fonds Sud, Belgium Coproduction, and Agency for Francophony. It was produced by Ali n' Production (Morocco), Playtime (France), and Alexis Films (Belgium).

19. For more on the film, see Gugler (2011). See also Armes (2005), Khayati (2005), Shafik (2007), and Carter (2009).

20. The series included ten films, broadcast between March 14 and April 15, 2003. For more on the series, see http://download.pro.arte.tv/archives/fichiers/01622162.pdf. Accessed September 12, 2014. *A Minute of Sun Less* was produced by Ali n' Productions and B.C. Films, arte, and gmt (France) with an approximate budget of €1 million. Major sources of funding were arte and ccm.

21. The Minister of Communication at the time, Nabil Benabdallah, told the press that the government gave Ayouch a filming permit based on a script that did not include the sex scenes. See Laghzawi (2003a).

22. Prominent Moroccan filmmakers such as Jilali Ferhati, Hassan Benjelloun, and Mohamed Ismail publically defended Ayouch against calls to censor the film. See, for example, "al-Yawm al-sinima" 2003.

23. Ayouch wanted Faouzi Bensaïdi to return to the role of Kemal Raoui in *A Minute of Sun Less* but was unable to cast him for a variety of reasons (Ayouch 2012). Nouraddin Orahhou instead plays Kemal in the film.

24. For more on Noor, who is a transgendered dancer in Morocco, see Ziraoui and Alaoui (2008).

25. For more on Moroccan police téléfilms, see Smolin (2013).

26. For more on the film, see Whatever Lola Wants, www.alinprod.com/lola.html. For more on dwindling ticket sales in Morocco, see Dwyer (2011, 325–338).

27. *Whatever Lola Wants* was produced by Pathé Renn Production. Major sources of funding were Pathé, French Center of Cinematography, and Canal+.

28. For a further discussion of the film's focus on East-West relations, see Orlando (2011).

29. Ayouch went to great lengths to ensure the credibility of the film. He spent two years in Sidi Moumen, studying the area and getting to know its residents and the local NGOs (Ayouch 2013). According to Ayouch, his experience of growing up in Sarcelles, a suburb outside of Paris but disconnected from the city center, made him feel comfortable in the area and allowed him to connect with the people there (Ayouch 2013). Ayouch also spent a month working with Mohamed Fizazi, an Islamist preacher who had been released from jail in 2011. Ayouch attempted to cast Fizazi in the role of the emir, but Fizazi refused (Ayouch 2013). Ayouch also worked with sociologists and political scientists while making the film and brought ex-Islamists to oversee the shooting. Casting non-professional actors from Sidi Moumen in the film's major roles was another element of trying to make the film as realistic and credible as possible.

30. While the film includes documentary television footage and is based on the events of May 16, Ayouch did not attempt to include biographical details from the lives of the real-world bombers in his depiction of the characters in the film (Ayouch 2013).

31. *Horses of God* received the François Chalais Prize at the 2012 Cannes Film Festival.

32. According to Ayouch, this scene was particularly difficult to shoot (Ayouch 2013). Ayouch spoke at length with the child actors and their parents and focused on the editing process to make the scene as realistic as possible.

33. Sidi Moumen has changed significantly since the May 16 bombings. Much of the shantytown has been destroyed and the area has been connected with the center of Casablanca city thanks to the new tramway that winds through the city.

34. The Arabic expression "Ya khayl Allah irkabi," "Fly, horses of God," which was used during the early Islamic expansion to incite Muslims to Jihad, has reappeared in speeches and statements by members of al-Qaeda for similar purposes during the past decade.

35. This final sequence was the only one that Ayouch shot in Sidi Moumen. Because of the vast changes in Sidi Moumen since 2003, Ayouch selected as a shooting location a different shantytown on the outskirts of the city that resembled what Sidi Moumen looked like before 2003.

FILMOGRAPHY OF NABIL AYOUCH

The Blue Rocks of the Desert / Les pierres bleues du désert. 1992. 21 minutes. Short film.
Herzienne Connection / Herzienne connexion. 1993. 4 minutes. Short film.
The Silent Seller / Vendeur de silence. 1994. 26 minutes. Short film.

Mektoub / Fate. 1997. Distributed by Ali N' Production. 88 minutes.

Ali Zaoua: Prince of the Streets / Ali Zaoua: Prince des rues. 2000. DVD distributed in the United States by Film Movement. 98 minutes.

A Minute of Sun Less / Une minute de soleil en moins. 2002. 98 minutes.

Whatever Lola Wants. 2007. Distributed by Pathé Distributions. 115 minutes.

My Land. 2011. Distributed by Les Films d'Atlante. 80 minutes. Documentary.

Horses of God / Les cheveaux de Dieu / Ya khayl Allah. 2012. Distributed in United States by Kino Lorber. 115 minutes.

REFERENCES

Armes, Roy. 2005. *Postcolonial Images: Studies in North African Film.* Bloomington: Indiana University Press.

Ayouch, N. 2012. Personal Communication, June 28. J. Smolin.

——— 2013. Personal Communication, March 5–8. J. Smolin.

Binebine, Mahi. 2013. *Horses of God.* Translated by Lulu Norman. Portland, Tin House Books. Originally published as *Les étoiles de Sidi Moumen.* Paris: Flammarion, 2010.

Carter, Sandra Gayle. 2009. *What Moroccan Cinema? A Historical and Critical Study, 1956–2006.* Lanham: Lexington Books.

Dwyer, Kevin. 2011. "Morocco: A National Cinema with Large Ambitions." In *Film in the Middle East and North Africa: Creative Dissidence,* edited by Josef Gugler, 325–338. Austin: University of Texas Press.

Gugler, Josef. 2007. "Ali Zaoua: The Harsh Life of Street Children and the Poetics of Childhood." *Journal of North African Studies* 12 (3): 369–379.

———. 2011. "Ali Zaoua, Prince of the Streets (Nabil Ayouch): The Harsh Life of Street Children and the Poetics of Childhood." In *Film in the Middle East and North Africa: Creative Dissidence,* edited by Josef Gugler, 339–348. Austin, University of Texas Press.

Khayati, Abdellatif. 2005. "Picturing the Homeless in Casablanca." *Moving Worlds* 5 (1): 21–32.

Laghzawi, al-Mukhtar. 2003a. "'Amal jadid li-Nabil 'Ayush yuthir hafidhat islamiyi al-barlaman!" [Nabil Ayouch's new work stirs up rancor of parliament Islamists!]. *al-Ahdath al-Maghribiya,* January 12, 16.

———. 2003b. "Nabil 'Ayush: 'Lan ahdhif laqta wahida'" [Nabil Ayouch: "I won't cut a single frame"]. *al-Ahdath al-Maghribiya,* January 17, 18.

Orlando, Valérie K. 2011. *Screening Morocco: Contemporary Film in a Changing Society.* Athens: Ohio University Press.

Oufkir, Malika and Michèle Fitoussi. 2002. *Stolen Lives.* New York: Miramax. Originally published as *La prisonnière.* Paris: Grasset & Fasquelle, 1999.

Rhanja, Hassan. 2001. *al-Hut al-a'ma* [The Blind Whale]. Morocco: 2M.

———. 2002. *al-Farasha al-sawda* [The Black Butterfly]. Morocco: 2M.

Shafik, Viola. 2007. *Arab Cinema: History and Cultural Identity.* Cairo: American University in Cairo Press.

Slyomovics, Susan. 2005. *The Performance of Human Rights in Morocco.* Philadelphia: University of Pennsylvania Press.

Smolin, Jonathan. 2013. *Moroccan Noir: Police, Crime, and Politics in Popular Culture.* Bloomington: Indiana University Press.

Vermeren, Pierre. 2006. *Histoire du Maroc depuis l'indépendence.* Paris: La Découverte.

"al-Yawm al-sinima wa-ghaddan madha?" [Today cinema and tomorrow what?]. 2003. *al-Ahdath al-Maghribiya,* January 18.

Ziraoui, Youssef and Mehdi Sekkouri Alaoui. 2008. "Noor: Pourquoi et comment je suis femme." *Tel Quel,* October 25. Casablanca.

ILLUSTRATION CREDITS

CHAPTER 7

Photo of Yousry Nasrallah. Courtesy Dubai International Film Festival.
Screenshots from *Summer Thefts* and *Scheherazade Tell Me a Story*.
Still from *The Gate of the Sun*. Courtesy Pyramide Films.

CHAPTER 8

Photo of Mohamed Chouikh. Courtesy Olivier Barlet, © Olivier Barlet.
Screenshots from the films of Mohamed Chouikh.

CHAPER 9

Photo of Merzak Allouache and Ali Al Jabri. Courtesy Abu Dhabi Film Festival.
Still from *Bab-el-Oued City*. Courtesy Trigon-Film, © www.trigon-film.org.
Screenshots from *Omar Gatlato, Normal! and The Repentant.*

CHAPTER 10

Photo of Nabil Ayouch. Courtesy Ali n' Productions.
Stills of *Mektoub, Whatever Lola Wants,* and *Horses of God*. Courtesy Ali n'
    Productions.
Still of *Ali Zaoua*. Courtesy Samir Farid.

CONTRIBUTORS

Refqa Abu-Remaileh is an Alexander von Humboldt Postdoctoral Fellow at the Forum Transregionale Studien Berlin and Philipps Universität Marburg. Her research focuses on Arabic literature and cinema, particularly Palestinian writers and filmmakers. She co-edited a volume titled *The Meeting Place of British Middle East Studies: Emerging Scholars, Emergent Research and Approaches.*

Guy Austin is Professor of French Studies at Newcastle University. His books include *Algerian National Cinema; Contemporary French Cinema; Claude Chabrol;* and *Stars in Modern French Film.*

Benjamin Geer has taught at the National University of Singapore, the American University in Cairo, and the University of Tübingen. He obtained his doctorate at the School of Oriental and African Studies, University of London.

Josef Gugler is Professor of Sociology Emeritus at the University of Connecticut. He is the author of *African Film: Re-Imagining a Continent* and has edited, and contributed to, *Film in the Middle East and North Africa: Creative Dissent.* In 2010 he served as a member of the jury at PanAfrica International, Montreal.

Will Higbee is Associate Professor of French Film and Deputy Director of the Humanities Graduate School at Exeter University. His books include *Post-Beur Cinema: Maghrebi-French and North African Emigré Filmmaking in France since 2000* and *De-westernizing Film Studies.*

Tim Kennedy obtained his doctorate from the University of Reading in 2007 with a thesis titled "Cinema Regarding Nations: Re-imagining Armenian, Kurdish, and Palestinian National Identity in Film." He has published articles on Michel Khleifi in *Film Quarterly* and Palestinian Cinema in *Senses of Cinema,* Yilmaz Guney in *Kurdish Cinema,* Armenian cinema in the *Armenological Review,* and on Andrzej Wajda in *Jump Cut.*

Dalia Said Mostafa is Lecturer in Arabic and Comparative Literature at the Department of Middle Eastern Studies, University of Manchester. She has published in both English and Arabic on the contemporary Arabic novel, Arab cinema, and popular culture in Egypt.

Christa Salamandra is Associate Professor of Anthropology at Lehman College and the Graduate Center, City University of New York. She is the author of *A New Old Damascus: Authenticity and Distinction in Urban Syria* and numerous articles on Arab culture and media. She is working on an ethnography of Syrian television drama production.

Viola Shafik is the author of *Arab Cinema: History and Cultural Identity* and *Popular Egyptian Cinema: Gender, Class and Nation*. She has lectured at the American University in Cairo and elsewhere, has worked as a film curator, supervises a training program for Arab documentary, and cooperates as a creative consultant with the Rawi Screenwriters Lab (Jordan) and the Berlinale World Cinema Fund. She has directed a number of documentaries, most notably *My Name is not Ali* (2011).

Jonathan Smolin is Associate Professor of Arabic at Dartmouth College and author of *Moroccan Noir: Police, Crime, and Politics in Popular Culture*, which was awarded the 2014 L. Carl Brown AIMS Book Prize for North African Studies. In addition to his research, he has translated the first Arabic police novel to appear in English, Abdelilah Hamdouchi's *The Final Bet*.

FILM INDEX

NAME INDEX

Italicized page numbers refer to illustrations.

CPSIA information can be obtained
at www.ICGtesting.com
Printed in the USA
LVOW01*0317240316

480493LV00007B/10/P